FISCAL
MANAGEMENT

Introduction to the Public Sector Governance and Accountability Series

Anwar Shah, Series Editor

A well-functioning public sector that delivers quality public services consistent with citizen preferences and that fosters private market-led growth while managing fiscal resources prudently is considered critical to the World Bank's mission of poverty alleviation and the achievement of Millennium Development Goals. This important new series aims to advance those objectives by disseminating conceptual guidance and lessons from practices and by facilitating learning from each others' experiences on ideas and practices that promote *responsive* (by matching public services with citizens' preferences), *responsible* (through efficiency and equity in service provision without undue fiscal and social risk), and *accountable* (to citizens for all actions) public governance in developing countries.

This series represents a response to several independent evaluations in recent years that have argued that development practitioners and policy makers dealing with public sector reforms in developing countries and, indeed, anyone with a concern for effective public governance could benefit from a synthesis of newer perspectives on public sector reforms. This series distills current wisdom and presents tools of analysis for improving the efficiency, equity, and efficacy of the public sector. Leading public policy experts and practitioners have contributed to the series.

The first seven volumes in the series (*Fiscal Management, Public Services Delivery, Public Expenditure Analysis, Tools for Public Sector Evaluations, Macrofederalism and Local Finances, International Practices in Local Governance, and Citizen-Centered Governance*) are concerned with public sector accountability for prudent fiscal management; efficiency and equity in public service provision; safeguards for the protection of the poor, women, minorities, and other disadvantaged groups; ways of strengthening institutional arrangements for voice and exit; methods of evaluating public sector programs, fiscal federalism, and local finances; international practices in local governance; and a framework for responsive and accountable governance.

Public Services Delivery

Edited by Anwar Shah

Tools for Public Sector Evaluations

Edited by Anwar Shah

Macrofederalism and Local Finances

Edited by Anwar Shah

Public Expenditure Analysis

Edited by Anwar Shah

International Practices in Local Governance

Edited by Anwar Shah

Citizen-Centered Governance

Matthew Andrews and Anwar Shah

PUBLIC SECTOR
GOVERNANCE AND
ACCOUNTABILITY SERIES

FISCAL
MANAGEMENT

Edited by ANWAR SHAH

THE WORLD BANK
Washington, D.C.

The findings, interpretations, and conclusions expressed herein are those of the author(s) and do not necessarily reflect the views of the Executive Directors of the International Bank for Reconstruction and Development / The World Bank or the governments they represent.

The World Bank does not guarantee the accuracy of the data included in this work. The boundaries, colors, denominations, and other information shown on any map in this work do not imply any judgement on the part of The World Bank concerning the legal status of any territory or the endorsement or acceptance of such boundaries.

Rights and Permissions

ISBN-13: 978-0-8213-6142-9
ISBN-10: 0-8213-6142-2
eISBN: 978-0-8213-6143-6
DOI: 10.1596/978-0-8213-6142-9

Library of Congress Cataloging-in-Publication Data

Fiscal management / edited by Anwar Shah.
    p. cm. — (Public sector, governance, and accountability series)
  Includes bibliographical references and index.
  ISBN 0-8213-6142-2 (pbk.)
    1. Government productivity—Evaluation. 2. Country services—Evaluation.
  3. Municipal services—Evaluation. 4. Budget. 5. Finance, Public. 6. Expenditures, Public.
I. Shah, Anwar. II. World Bank. III. Series.

JF1525.P67F57 2005
352.4—dc22

2005043245

Contents

CHAPTER

CHAPTER

A Framework for Evaluating Institutions of Accountability   229

by Mark Schacter

Foreword

In Western democracies, systems of checks and balances built into government structures have formed the core of good governance and have helped empower citizens for more than two hundred years. The incentives that motivate public servants and policymakers—the rewards and sanctions linked to results that help shape public sector performance—are rooted in a country's accountability frameworks. Sound public sector management and government spending help determine the course of economic development and social equity, especially for the poor and other disadvantaged groups such as women and the elderly.

Many developing countries, however, continue to suffer from unsatisfactory and often dysfunctional governance systems, including inappropriate allocation of resources, inefficient revenue systems, and weak delivery of vital public services. In recent years there has been renewed interest in understanding the political economy of public finance, and in particular, a desire to gain insights into the precise institutional arrangements that guide public policies and processes with respect to budgets, expenditures, revenues, and policies on the delivery of public services.

This book addresses these issues by providing tools to help assess a government's fiscal health from the perspective of public accountability, including the political economy of the budget, performance-based budgeting, revenue performance, debt management, measuring a government's net worth, assessing fiscal risks, reforming civil service, and strengthening institutions of accountability.

Fiscal Management will be of interest to public officials, development practitioners, students of development, and those interested in fiscal policy and governance in developing countries.

Frannie A. Léautier
Vice President
World Bank Institute

Preface

Strengthening responsive and accountable public governance in developing countries is critical to the World Bank's mission of poverty alleviation. This series attempts to facilitate the knowledge on institutional practices that foster incentive environments compatible with prudent fiscal management and efficient and equitable delivery of public services. The first volume in this series, *Fiscal Management,* provides tools of analysis to address issues of fiscal prudence, fiscal stress, bureaucratic inefficiency, citizen empowerment and public integrity. These tools are intended to enable a policy maker/practitioner to carry out the following diagnostic tests of the institutional arrangements for fiscal management and accountable governance:

Fiscal Prudence Test: Are institutional arrangements appropriate to ensure that the government decision making on fiscal management is constrained to ensure affordability and sustainability of program?

Fiscal Stress Test: Is the government maintaining a positive net worth?

Citizen Accountability Test: How does the government know it is delivering what the citizens have mandated? What happens when it does not conform to these mandates?

Public Integrity Test: How is the executive branch held accountable for any abuses of public office for private gains?

Application of the above tests is expected to enable policy makers and practitioners to develop a diagnosis of the institutional weaknesses as well as possible options to overcome these constraining factors for a well functioning public sector for their countries.

I am grateful to the Swiss Development Cooperation Agency for their support and to the leading experts who contributed to this series.

Roumeen Islam
Manager, Poverty Reduction and Economic Management
World Bank Institute

Acknowledgments

The completion of this book has been made possible through assistance from the Swiss Development Cooperation Agency and Swedish International Development Agency. The editor is grateful to their staff for guidance on the contents of the book. In particular, he owes a great deal of intellectual debt to Walter Hofer, Hanspeter Wyss, Werner Thut, Gerolf Weigel, and Alexandre Widmer. The editor is also grateful to senior management of the Operations Evaluation Department, World Bank, World Bank Institute, and CEPAL (the UN's Economic Commission for Latin America and the Caribbean) for their support. Thanks are due to Juan Carlos Lerda, Frannie Léautier, Ziad Alahdad, Ruben Lamdany, and Roumeen Islam for their guidance and support.

The book has also benefited from comments received by senior policy makers at the CEPAL–World Bank joint workshop held in Santiago, Chile, in January 2001 and PREM (Poverty Reduction and Economic Management) seminars held at the World Bank. In addition, senior finance and budget officials from a large number of countries offered advice on the contents of the book. The editor is also grateful to the leading academics who contributed chapters and to Bank and external peer reviewers for their comments. Matthew Andrews, Azam Chaudhry, Neil Hepburn, and Theresa M. Thompson helped during various stages of preparation of this book and provided comments and contributed summaries of various chapters. Agnes Santos formatted and prepared the book for publication. Finally, Theresa M. Thompson deserves special thanks for steering this book through various stages of review and final publication.

Contributors

MATTHEW ANDREWS, public sector management specialist at the World Bank, is a South African with a doctorate in public administration from the Maxwell School, Syracuse University. He has worked at all levels of government in South Africa and has published on topics such as public budgeting and management, evaluation, and institutional economics.

RICHARD M. BIRD is professor emeritus, Department of Economics, and adjunct professor and codirector of the International Tax Program, Joseph L. Rotman School of Management, University of Toronto. He has also taught at Harvard University; served with the Fiscal Affairs Department of the International Monetary Fund; been a visiting professor in the Netherlands, Australia, and elsewhere; and has been a frequent consultant to the World Bank and other national and international organizations. He has published extensively on the fiscal problems of developing and transitional countries.

HANA POLACKOVA BRIXI is senior economist in charge of World Bank country economic work in China. Since 1998, Dr. Brixi has been leading the World Bank's research on government fiscal risks and heading the World Bank Quality of Fiscal Adjustment Thematic Group. Previously, Dr. Brixi worked as a senior economist and public sector management specialist in the East Asia and Europe & Central Asia Regions of the World Bank in Washington, D.C. and led projects and technical assistance programs in a number of countries. Recently, she was a visiting fellow at the Sloan Business School of the Massachusetts Institute of Technology in Boston, and at the New Zealand Treasury Department in Wellington, New Zealand. Before joining the World Bank, Dr. Brixi was a special advisor to the president of then Czechoslovakia Vaclav Havel.

HOMI KHARAS is the chief economist of the East Asia and Pacific Region of the World Bank and director of the region's Poverty Reduction and Economic Management (PREM) Financial and Private Sector Unit. In this capacity, he is responsible for the World Bank's policy advice, and for lending in support of that advice, to countries in the region on matters of poverty reduction strategies, trade and competitiveness, public sector debt and fiscal policy, public expenditure management, governance, anticorruption, and financial and private sector development.

DEEPAK MISHRA, an Indian national, is an economist in the World Bank's South Asia region. He has a Ph.D. in economics from the University of Maryland and an M.A. from the Delhi School of Economics. Before joining the World Bank, Dr. Mishra had worked in various capacities in a number of private and public sector institutions, including the Federal Reserve Board, University of Maryland, and Tata Engineering and Locomotive Company, India. His research interests include the real impacts of macroeconomic crisis, debt and liquidity management, fiscal policy and contingent liabilities, and determinants of growth and capital flows. Some of his recent works have appeared in the *Journal of Development Economics*, the World Bank's *Economist Forum*, *Finance and Development*, and *Global Development Finance*.

MAHESH PUROHIT is a professor at the National Institute of Public Finance and Policy, New Delhi. He has worked as member-secretary of the Empowered Committee of State Finance Ministers to Monitor Sales Tax Reforms and Introduction of Value Added Tax (VAT) for the government of India. He has also worked as secretary to the Committee of State Finance Ministers and to the Committee of State Chief Ministers for Introduction of VAT in the Indian States. Dr. Purohit has been actively involved in the preparation of the Model VAT Law for the states. He is on the advisory committees of various state governments of India for the implementation of VAT. He has been to Cambodia as a fiscal expert of the International Monetary Fund and to Somalia for the United Nations Development Programme as an adviser in tax policy and chief technical advisor. He has been a visiting professor at Maison des Sciences de l'Homme, Paris, and the Institute for Monetary and Fiscal Policy, Ministry of Finance, Tokyo. He has also been a senior research fellow in the Department of Economics, University of California, Berkeley, and a Shastri Fellow at the University of Toronto.

MARK SCHACTER is President of Mark Schacter Consulting; formerly he was a director of the Institute on Governance, a public policy think tank based in Ottawa, Canada. Before joining the Institute on Governance in early 1998, he served on the staff of the World Bank, where he worked on public sector reform and institutional development. Mr. Schacter has written extensively on matters related to accountability, public sector performance management, and development assistance.

ANWAR SHAH is the lead economist and the team leader for Public Sector Governance with the World Bank Institute and a fellow of the Institute for Public Economics, Edmonton, Canada. He has previously served in the Ministry of Finance, Government of Canada and Government of Alberta, Canada, responsible for federal-provincial and provincial-local fiscal relations, respectively. He has advised the governments of Argentina, Brazil, Canada, China, Indonesia, Malaysia, Mexico, Pakistan, the Philippines, Poland, South Africa, and Turkey on fiscal federalism issues. He has lectured at the University of Ottawa, Canada; Peking University; Wuhan University; Quaid-i-Azam University, Islamabad, Pakistan; Harvard University; Duke University; the Massachusetts Institute of Technology; and the University of Southern California. His current research interests are in the areas of governance, fiscal federalism, fiscal reform, and global environment. He has published several books and monographs on these subjects, including *The Reform of Intergovernmental Fiscal Relations in Developing and Transition Economies* (World Bank 1994) and a 1995 Oxford University Press book on *Fiscal Incentives for Investment and Innovation*. His articles have appeared in leading economic and policy journals. He also serves as a referee and on editorial advisory boards for leading economic journals.

JÜRGEN VON HAGEN (Ph.D. in economics, University of Bonn, 1985) has taught at Indiana University, the University of Mannheim, and the University of Bonn, where he is a director of the Center for European Integration Studies. Dr. von Hagen's research is in macroeconomics and public finance. He has been a consultant to the International Monetary Fund, the World Bank, the Inter-American Development Bank, the European Commission, and the European Central Bank, among others. He has published numerous articles in academic journals and books. He is a research fellow of the Centre for Economic Policy Research (London) and a member of the Advisory Council to the German Ministry of Economics, and was the first winner of the Gossen Prize of the German Economic Association.

Abbreviations and Acronyms

ALM	asset and liability management
CAC	collective action clause
EMU	European Monetary Union
ESA	European System of Integrated Accounts
EU	European Union
GASB	Governmental Accounting Standards Board
GDP	gross domestic product
GDR	German Democratic Republic
IA	institution of accountability
IMF	International Monetary Fund
INTOSAI	International Organization of Supreme Audit Institutions
MCF	marginal cost of funds
MTEF	medium-term expenditure framework
NGO	nongovernmental organization
OECD	Organisation for Economic Co-operation and Development
PREM	Poverty Reduction and Economic Management
ROME	results-oriented management and evaluation
SAI	supreme audit institution

Booktitle:

Overview

ANWAR SHAH

H60
H70

This book is concerned with incentives that ensure the accountability of the public sector. It provides tools to address issues of fiscal prudence, fiscal stress, citizen accountability, and public integrity.

Fiscal Prudence

Fiscal Prudence Test: Are institutional arrangements appropriate to ensure that the government is constrained to raising taxes, expenditures, deficits, debts, and other liabilities only within affordable and sustainable limits?

This question is the focus of several chapters.

Jürgen von Hagen in chapter 1 is concerned with the political economy of the budgeting processes and discusses the implications of incomplete contracts of voters with politicians. In view of these incomplete contracts, politicians can use targeted public policies to ensure their confirmation in office. Because there is a disconnect between those who bear the burden of financing and those who benefit from such policies, such an environment generates the potential for excessive levels of spending, taxation, and borrowing—as is commonly observed in developing countries. Societies can react to these problems by creating institutions that mitigate their adverse effects. There are three basic institutional approaches to doing so.

The first is to impose ex ante controls on the scope of the choices elected politicians can make regarding public finances. Examples are balanced-budget constraints that force policy makers to limit the amount of debt they can incur, or referendum requirements for raising tax rates. Ex ante controls such as balanced-budget amendments or limits on borrowing are attractive for their simplicity. However, they are generally regarded as ineffective or possibly counterproductive to the ability of voters to monitor policy makers' behavior, because such quantitative limits often have substitution effects where spending or borrowing is shifted to levels of government not covered by the rule. Outside authorities that monitor adherence to rules, such as the International Monetary Fund (IMF) or European Union (EU), are not seen as effective either.

The second institutional approach is to strengthen accountability and competition among elected politicians, increasing their incentives to deliver the policies voters prefer and so lengthening their tenure in public office. This is the main function of electoral systems. Under the two commonly practiced forms of voting there are trade-offs between accountability and competition. Under the plurality rule, accountability to citizens is enhanced but political competition is weakened, since the rule acts as a barrier to entry for small parties. The proportional representation rule has the opposite effect, since it weakens accountability but promotes more intense competition.

The third approach is to structure the processes of making decisions about public finances in ways that force policy makers to recognize more fully the marginal social benefits and costs of their policies. This is the principal task of the budgeting process. A centrally coordinated budgeting process may help reduce the common pool problem through coordinating the spending decisions of individual politicians, by forcing them to take a comprehensive view of the budget. Competing claims must be resolved within the budgeting process, but this limit may be undermined by use of off-budget funds, spreading of *nondecisions* (such as indexation), mandatory spending laws, and contingent liabilities (for example, promised bailouts).

Chapter 1 provides perspectives on institutional reform to strengthen the budgetary institutions, as a safeguard against the perverse incentives faced by politicians and bureaucrats. In this context, it discusses two approaches to the centralization of the budgeting process: delegation and contracts. With delegation, the budgeting process lends special authority to the finance minister, whose function it is to set the broad parameters of the budget and to ensure conformity with these constraints by all participants. Under this approach, the finance ministry coordinates departmental submissions. Any unresolved issues are referred to the prime minister for final decision. The finance ministry also assumes a central role in budget implementation. This approach lends large agenda-setting powers to the executive branch over the legislative branch.

The contracts approach emphasizes the negotiation of binding agreements among all participants. It starts with negotiations among cabinet members, fixing spending limits for each department. At the legislative stage, the contracts approach places less weight on the executive's role as an agenda setter and more weight on the legislature's role as a monitor of the implementation of the fiscal targets. The key to the institutional choice between the two approaches (delegation or contracts) lies in the type of constitutional government in effect. Delegation is the preferred approach under single-party parliamentary governments, while the contracts approach is more appropriate for multiparty coalition governments. This is because under a single-party government the finance minister represents the views of the ruling party, and under a coalition government a budgetary compromise must be struck among coalition partners. Under the presidential form of government, delegation will be considered appropriate when the president's party controls the legislature. A contracts approach would be more appropriate when the president faces an opposition-controlled legislature or when the two institutions are on an equal footing.

In chapter 2, Matthew Andrews is concerned with introducing incentives for fiscal prudence in developing countries through the budgeting process. He reviews South African experience with such reforms and draws some general lessons for other developing countries from this experience.

Andrews observes that, in the past decade, some governments have shown interest in reforms aimed at establishing a results-oriented (or performance-based) budgeting approach. The emphasis on results or performance in the budgeting process reflects a belief that public sector accountability should focus on what government does with the money it spends, rather than simply how it controls such expenditures. In the parlance of new institutionalism, these reforms introduce rules and norms that make it culturally appropriate for or induce (through positive and negative incentives) public representatives and managers to concentrate on outcomes and outputs rather than inputs and procedures. Andrews asks how well reforms have worked in introducing a results orientation into budgeting processes (with representatives and managers being accountable for results) and where reformers should be concentrating to improve such efforts.

Andrews examines this question with regard to recent experience with budget reform around the globe, in particular taking a critical look at reform adoption in a setting considered one of "better practice" in the developing world, the South African national government. The Department of Health's budget is used as a representative example of the general path of reform progression in this setting. In looking at the budget's structure, it is apparent that the government has gradually moved from a purely line-itemized budget to a medium-term program budget and finally to a performance-based budget—a progression that mirrors developments in other national and subnational governments around the world.

On the basis of the South African analysis and comparisons with experience in other settings, Andrews suggests that there are three reasons why reforms still have a way to go in establishing performance-based accountability systems in governments. First, even though performance targets are now being developed, they are generally kept separate from the actual budget. This is the case in South Africa and Singapore, as well as in most U.S. states. This separation minimizes the legitimacy of performance targets and entrenches a "specialization" and "separation" culture common in governments, in which planners, development experts, and performance-minded evaluators do certain tasks and accountants and budgeters do other tasks, without much communication between the two groups. Second, performance information in the South African case suffers weaknesses commonly alluded to in literature related to other settings: Outputs are confused with inputs, and outcomes remain unconsidered. Targets appear to have been technocratically identified and thus lack real-world value. Targets are poorly detailed, making actual measurement unlikely. And it is unclear exactly how the targets will be reached, with no connection between outputs and activities in some cases and arguments as to why poor service could lead to target achievement in others. This information fails to create results-oriented bottom lines, leaving political representatives and managers no reason or incentive to meet them.

The third, and possibly most important problem faced by reformers is the lack of a relational construct in the budget itself. Even where effective performance-based targets are provided, the budgets in South Africa and many other nations moving toward this kind of system commonly fail to specify who should be accountable for results, who should hold them accountable, and how. Very little thought appears to have been given to the process of institutionalizing political or managerial accountability for the targets identified in budgets, hampering the move toward a norm-based culture of results achievement and incentives that facilitate a results focus. Building on the progress made in countries such as South Africa and responding to these three problems, Andrews provides some pointers for reform progress in the future. The discussion centers on a proposed budget structure that links fiscal allocations to clearly defined and measurable performance targets at the project level and identifies those accountable for outputs (managers) and for outcomes (political representatives)—all in one document. The proposed approach is seen as a progression beyond the current reform position, one that should effectively entrench a results-oriented accountability in governments through a series of bottom lines that have meaning, that can be evaluated, and that can be enforced.

Mahesh Purohit (in chapter 3) reflects on fiscal prudence from a revenue performance perspective. For this purpose, he considers the revenue performance of a government as satisfactory if yields from available revenue sources are increasing over time, are income elastic, and enable the government to raise spending enough to provide adequate levels of public services. Revenue yields are affected by the composition of revenue bases, tax rates, and tax effort. The composition of revenue bases tends to vary between developing and developed country groupings—developing countries place a greater reliance on taxes on commodities and services, while developed countries make a greater effort to tax corporate and individual income directly.

Purohit presents a guide to developing simple measures of revenue performance. In ascending order of complexity, they include the growth rate of revenue, the buoyancy or income elasticity of revenue, the relative revenue effort, the performance index, and the principal components method.

The growth rate of revenue is an absolute measure of the compound growth rate of revenues. This measure's merit is its simplicity, but it fails to take into account the causes of revenue growth (or decline). The buoyancy of revenue provides a simpler measure of relative growth. It shows the percentage change in revenue with respect to percentage change in the revenue base. The measure of relative revenue effort tries to judge a government's revenue performance against its estimated revenue capacity. Variables used to measure the revenue capacity include changes in personal and corporate incomes, composition of taxes, type of public services, public investments, GDP, population, urbanization, openness of the economy, and the size of manufacturing and commercial sectors in GDP. Revenue performance variables include tax revenues, changes in tax revenues, and effective tax rates on income from wages, capital, and real estate. The performance index is an average of several indicators of revenue performance aggregated by using subjective weights. The principal components method uses statistical analysis to identify sets of variables that have the largest impact on revenue performance.

Although revenues and expenditures are inextricably linked, most formal economic analysis of tax or expenditure changes traditionally has been conducted under the assumption that there is no connection between what happens on one side of the budget and what happens on the other. Richard M. Bird (in chapter 4) explores the issues that arise when both sides of the budget are analyzed simultaneously. He argues that issues on the financing side are too critical to be ignored and that an explicit consideration of these issues will improve analysis and provide incentives for fiscal prudence. The key to good results in public expenditures lies not in any particular budgetary or financing procedure, but rather in implementing a public finance system that, to the extent possible, links specific expenditure and revenue decisions as transparently as possible. The combined effect of tax and expenditure changes is, however, very difficult to measure; therefore, simplifying assumptions have been made that separate the two sides.

Bird presents a survey of the historical or orthodox approaches to evaluating public expenditures. A significant portion of this literature was dedicated to estimating a "shadow price of public finance" or the "marginal cost of public funds." Most of these estimates focused on the excess burden imposed by taxation. The chapter then examines some of the questions that have been raised about both the conceptual and the empirical applications of this approach. Of these, Bird attempts to answer three questions: Should the shadow price of public finance be explicitly taken into account in expenditure evaluation? If so, how should this shadow price be estimated? How much attention should be paid to the institutional links between expenditures and revenues?

The answers to the first two questions do not lead to simple rules. For example, when the financing of a project can be firmly linked to a properly designed benefit charge (such as a user charge, an earmarked benefit levy, or loan finance) or to some other form of "burdenless" or budget-neutral fiscal change (such as a land tax, a Pigouvian tax, or the reduction of a distortionary tax), the application of a shadow price of fiscal resources (marginal cost of funds) seems inappropriate because there is no distortion that needs to be corrected for in these cases. But even when the source of budgetary finance is a distorting tax system, the level of the correction will be sensitive to the nature of that system, the nature of the anticipated tax changes, and the nature of the expenditure being financed. And finally, to at least some extent, distortions associated with tax finance may reflect the distributional (or redistributional) goals of society and should not be used as a discount factor that limits the extent of the public sector. However, some authors may be correct in suggesting that at least a minimal marginal cost of funds correction could be called for, unless there is a good reason for not making such a correction.

In response to the third question, more attention should be paid to links between expenditures and revenues than has been given so far. Some of these links include user charges for public services, earmarked benefit taxes, local taxes to finance local services, income taxes to finance general public goods, and loan finance for investment projects.

Bird's conclusion is that financing matters. Taking into account the financing side of public expenditures is an essential component of the process by which good budgetary decisions—decisions that should reflect people's real preferences—can be obtained in any society. Much of the rationale for accountability-building decentralization lies in such arguments.

The staffs of the IMF and the World Bank (in chapter 5) have prepared a set of guidelines for debt management. These guidelines cover both domestic and external public debt and are designed to assist policy makers in considering reforms to strengthen the quality of their public debt management and to reduce their country's vulnerability to international financial shocks. Vulnerability to such shocks is greater for small and emerging-market countries because their economies may be less diversified, may have a smaller base of domestic financial savings and less developed financial systems, and may be more susceptible to financial contagion through the relative magnitudes of capital flows. Governments should ensure that both the level and rate of growth in the public debt are sustainable and can be serviced under a wide range of circumstances while meeting cost or risk objectives. There may be a trade-off between cost of debt and risk or sustainability that must be taken into account. For example, crises have often arisen because of an excessive focus by governments on possible cost savings associated with large volumes of short-term debt, which has left government budgets seriously exposed to changing financial market conditions—including changes in the country's creditworthiness—when this short-term debt has to be rolled over.

Each country's capacity-building needs in sovereign debt management will be shaped by the capital market constraints it faces, its exchange rate regime, the quality of its macroeconomic and regulatory policies, the institutional capacity to design and implement reforms, the country's credit standing, and its objectives for public debt management.

The chapter gives a detailed description of each reform; the guidelines for prudent debt management are summarized below:

■ *Sharing debt management objectives and coordination:* Debt management should encompass the main financial obligations over which the central government exercises control. Debt managers, fiscal policy advisers, and central bankers should share an understanding of the objectives of and information about debt management, fiscal, and monetary policies, given the interdependencies among their different policy instruments. However, there should be a separation of debt management and monetary policy objectives and accountabilities.

■ *Building transparency and accountability:* There should be clarity as to the roles, responsibilities, and objectives of debt managers. The ways in which the responsible agencies—the finance ministry, the central bank, and others—formulate debt management policy should be open and visible. The agencies should publish regular information on the size and the composition of the debt, including its term structure and obligations that are denominated in foreign currencies. The accountability framework for debt management should be public, as should details of any arrangement for an external, independent audit of the debt management function.

■ *Strengthening the institutional framework:* Countries should develop a governance framework (legal and organizational frameworks for undertaking debt transactions and debt management) and management of internal operations (operational controls, including well-articulated responsibilities for staff, monitoring and control policies, reporting arrangements, and code of conduct and conflict of interest guidelines).

■ *Developing a debt management strategy:* The risks of the government debt structure, including currency risk and the risks of short-term debt, should be monitored.

■ *Developing a risk management framework:* The trade-offs of risk and cost in the government's debt portfolio must be identified and managed. Debt managers should consider the impact of contingent liabilities on the government's financial position.

■ *Developing and maintaining an efficient market for government securities:* To minimize cost and risk over the medium to long run, debt managers should ensure that their policies and operations are consistent with the development of an efficient government securities market. This includes portfolio diversification and instruments to achieve a broad investor base and treat all investors equally. In the primary market, debt management operations should be transparent and, to the extent possible, debt issuance should use market-based mechanisms, including competitive auctions and syndications. Governments should promote secondary markets, and the systems used to settle and clear transactions should reflect sound practices.

Fiscal Stress

Fiscal Stress Test: Is the government maintaining a positive net worth?

The next set of chapters is concerned with determining the extent to which a government is under fiscal stress.

Homi Kharas and Deepak Mishra (in chapter 6) attempt to shed light on the puzzling empirical observation that the realized growth of debt in developing countries has been much greater than the accumulated sum of conventional budget deficits. This is the phenomenon of *hidden deficits.* Hidden deficits occur when budgetary accounting practices and guidelines leave room for discretion and encourage financial engineering.

The computation of the budget deficit in practice can be a complicated exercise, given the alternative methodologies, measurement issues, and valuation techniques that exist, among other complexities. Researchers have discovered various sources of discrepancies in budget calculations and items that have not been included in the recorded budget deficit. These items include noncash operations (such as drawing down assets and shifting expenses to the outside bounds of the budget) and off-budget expenses (such as debt stock adjustments and contingent liabilities). Some specific examples of problems in deficit calculation are exclusion or only partial inclusion of corporate and bank restructuring expenses, the treatment of present and expected costs of entitlements and contingent liabilities (bailouts), exclusion of capital gains and losses from the budget, the use of different valuation methods, and the use of grants and aid to finance the budget deficit.

Kharas and Mishra show that conventional deficit is only one of six components that contribute to the realized, if unpredicted, accumulation of government debt. The other five factors are the contribution of growth, the movement of the real exchange rate, domestic inflation, seignorage revenue, and expenditures outside the purview of the budget.

The authors then estimate the size of the hidden deficit for several developed and developing countries using a hypothetical level of debt that the government would have accumulated had there been no capital gains and losses in the government's liabilities (due to, for example, inflation or depreciation of the currency) and had it not incurred any expense outside the purview of the budget. In other words, the hypothetical debt-GDP ratio is the one that the government would have had if past budget deficits and seignorage were the only two sources financing it. Calculations for 7 developed and 14 developing countries found that the hidden deficit was on average much smaller in the developed countries (0.3 percent compared with 2.6 percent of GDP). The two major reasons for this difference are that the problem of bailing out failed financial institutions and corporations is more serious in developing and transition countries and that developing countries incur more losses due to exchange rate movements and cross-currency movements.

Hana Polackova Brixi (in chapter 7) is also concerned with hidden deficits or liabilities that governments face but that are not recorded as part of the measured fiscal deficit. For example, in many countries, governments reduce their expenditures (and therefore the measured deficit) by providing loan or outcome (such as minimum pension) guarantees. Brixi examines closely the various categories of fiscal risks and proposes ways that governments can manage these risks. Transition and emerging-market economies face particularly large fiscal risks. Weak institutions elevate failures in the financial and corporate sectors, which in turn generate political pressures on governments to provide bailouts.

There are four categories of fiscal risks: direct explicit (debt payments, budget expenditures, civil service pay), direct implicit (public investment completion and maintenance, future pensions, health care), contingent explicit (state guarantees of debt and state insurance), and contingent implicit (defaults of subnational government- and state-owned enterprises, failures of private pensions, natural disasters, private capital flows, balance of payments, the financial system).

The acceptance of contingent liabilities (whether implicit or explicit) by a government is a commitment to take on obligations contingent on future events. It amounts to a hidden subsidy that can become a major unexpected drain on government finances. A government's acceptance of contingent liabilities can also create serious moral hazard problems—there is a serious risk of default (and exercise of the contingent liability), especially when risks are not shared. Many governments have yet to consolidate all these obligations and their total magnitude in a single balance sheet and to include them in their overall fiscal analysis and expenditure planning. Contingent implicit risks create the greatest risk for governments.

Accrual-based accounting, while it encourages governments to prepare a statement of contingent liabilities, requires neither that they be included on the balance sheet nor that the risks be evaluated. However, accrual-based budgeting does require that contingent liabilities enter budget documents and therefore the fiscal analysis.

In dealing with fiscal risks, the first necessary condition is that policy makers identify, classify, and understand the fiscal risks facing the government. Internal groups such as the principal audit institution or external groups (like the IMF, World Bank, or sovereign credit rating agencies) can assess these risks.

Brixi suggests the following systemic measures to reduce fiscal risks: (a) conduct fiscal analysis that factors in the cost of the implicit subsidies in the government's contingent support program; (b) identify, classify, and analyze all fiscal risks in a single portfolio (take stock of liabilities, conduct qualitative analysis of risk, and evaluate correlations and sensitivity to different macro and policy scenarios); (c) determine government's optimal risk exposure and reserve policy (reserve funds can provide liquidity but there is a trade-off between the opportunity cost of withholding resources and the benefits of having the reserve in case of emergency); (d) internalize and disclose the full fiscal picture (public disclosure is more important than accounting systems to address the problem of government accountability because it allows the public and markets to monitor the government's full fiscal performance); (e) monitor, regulate, and disclose fiscal risks to the public and private sectors; and (f) undertake measures to reduce the fiscal risk of individual government programs and promises.

Concrete advice is given for dealing with the risks of individual government programs: (a) before the obligation is taken on, assess how the obligation fits the announced role of the state, consider the policy choices with respect to the risks, design the program against risk (including risk sharing), and define and communicate standards for and limits of government intervention to reduce moral hazard; (b) when the obligation is held, stick to the set limits of government responsibility, disclose the obligation, and monitor risk factors and reserve funds; and (c) after the obligation falls due, execute it within the set limits, and if implicit, determine whether fulfilling it coincides with the state's announced role and responsibilities.

Finally, the author offers as an example the case of the Czech Republic as a country whose hidden deficit is quite large due to off-budget spending and implied subsidies extended through state guarantees.

Matthew Andrews and Anwar Shah (in chapter 8) argue that citizens increasingly ask of their governments questions that they ask about their own household matters: "Is the government maintaining a good cash balance?" "Apart from its short-term position, how is it faring over the long run—do government assets exceed liabilities, especially those that could be called contingent liabilities?" "How valuable are the government's long-term assets, are they holding their value, and is government using them efficiently?" "How much value does government add on an annual basis—what kind of performance does government achieve through its operations?"

These questions relate to the multiple dimensions of a household or organization's worth or value: short-term value, long-term worth, and value added (or performance). Andrews and Shah argue, however, that common financial management practices in the developing world—often influenced by reforms focused on deficit reduction—tend to concentrate on short-term value alone and encourage the entrenchment of incentives associated with it. They ask three important questions of such one-dimensional fiscal management: Do good short-term evaluations in terms of deficit figures outweigh bad evaluations in terms of service performance and long-term financial condition? Will the neglect of two dimensions of government value—long-run financial position and service performance—hurt countries in the long run, or will the achievement of short-run value facilitate a multidimensional perspective in the future? How can government finances be managed (and reported) to facilitate a multidimensional reflection of government value?

The first two questions are addressed in a section exploring the incentives created by the short-term control bias in fiscal management practices in developing countries. It is suggested that all evaluation methods have an impact on incentives. The old performance adage is "what gets measured gets done." The argument is that focusing on one aspect of government value (the short-run fiscal discipline), when in fact government value consists of three aspects, leads to incentives that make a more comprehensive valuation perspective difficult to establish in the future. These incentives become entrenched in public sector budgeting, leading to a focus on inputs instead of results, capital neglect, and intergenerational money shifting.

An obvious response to this argument is to look for ways in which governments can move beyond an emphasis on short-run fiscal discipline to measure all aspects of public sector value or worth and thus create incentives for managers to develop all three dimensions of worth as well. In this light Andrews and Shah look at the experiences of countries such as New Zealand, the United Kingdom, and Malaysia, all of which have built on traditional accounting approaches to provide more complete measures of the three dimensions of government value. The main accountability dimension emphasized in the new financial management practices in these countries is the performance focus. The particular tools that have been adopted to improve internal and external evaluation in these governments include accrual accounting, explicit valuation of contingent liabilities, intergenerational accounting, capital charging, activity-based costing, and the publication of performance statements. The importance of each tool is briefly discussed and it is shown how their combined use yields a fuller picture of the fiscal health of the government.

Bottom-Up Accountability

Citizen Accountability Test: How does the government know it is delivering what the citizens have mandated? What happens when it does not conform to these mandates?

Chapter 9 by Anwar Shah is concerned with creating a new culture of public governance that is responsive and accountable to citizens. The chapter argues that results-oriented management and evaluation (ROME) holds significant promise for overcoming the ills of a dysfunctional command-and-control economy and an overbearing and rent-seeking public sector in many developing countries. ROME de-emphasizes traditional input controls and instead is concerned with creating an authorizing environment in which public officials are given the flexibility to manage for results but are held accountable for delivering public services consistent with citizen preferences. Further, under ROME, incentive mechanisms induce public and nonpublic (private and nongovernment) sectors to compete in the delivery of public services and to match public services with citizen preferences at a lower tax cost per unit of output to society.

Public Integrity

Public Integrity Test: How is the executive branch held accountable for any abuses of public office for private gains?

Mark Schacter (in chapter 10) describes mechanisms through which elected leaders can be held accountable to the public. Since the ballot box is often not sufficient to ensure accountability, other institutional mechanisms have been developed to enhance it. More specifically, there are two types of accountability: vertical accountability (to citizens directly through the ballot box) and horizontal accountability (to public institutions of accountability—IAs). The institutions of horizontal accountability include the legislature, the judiciary, electoral commissions, auditing agencies, anticorruption bodies, ombudsmen, human rights commissions, and central banks. Institutions of horizontal and vertical accountability are fundamentally interconnected, in that horizontal accountability is not likely to exist in the absence of vertical accountability: Governments will bind themselves with institutions of horizontal accountability only when they will be punished by citizens for failing to do so. Civil society is believed to be another influential factor in the development of institutions of horizontal accountability.

The analytical model presented concentrates on the interaction between IAs and the executive branch of government. At the core of the model is the idea of an *accountability cycle,* which is an idealized model of the relationship between an IA and a unit of the executive branch and describes the internal logic of the IA-executive relationship. This cycle consists of three stages: information (or input), action (or output), and response (or outcome). Timely and accurate information about the activities of the executive is the critical input for the accountability cycle. Based on the information inputs, the IA should be able to take action by making demands on the executive to justify the manner in which it is carrying out its responsibilities. Finally, the IA's outputs are intended to incite a response from the executive to the demands that the IA has made on it.

The IA's effectiveness depends critically on the ability of the IA to understand and analyze information about the executive, transform the analysis into coherent demands, communicate those demands, and have sufficient power to elicit a meaningful response from the executive. When an IA is not functioning, a rule of thumb is to focus on the lowest rung of the hierarchy that is not working properly. In addition, contextual information about social, economic, and political factors are important to understanding the accountability cycle more fully. Examples of such contextual factors include the history of relations between citizens and the state; social tensions based on ethnic, regional, or class distinctions; the structure of the economy; and the nature of civil society.

In applying IAs to the study of corruption reduction, two things must be kept in mind: IAs alone will not cure corruption, and broader environmental factors beyond the inner working of the IA must be considered. Klitgaard's formula for corruption is useful in clarifying this link. According to him, Corruption = Monopoly + Discretion − Accountability. As one can see, accountability is only one variable contributing to corruption. Therefore, the policies that contribute to monopoly and discretion must also be addressed in the context of an anticorruption initiative.

The absence of political or administrative commitment to accountability and the insufficient availability of information about the activities of the executive are the two primary constraints on the effective operation of IAs. In cases in which the political elite is unlikely to act, civil society may have an important role in initiating such reforms.

Finally, the author proposes a list of performance indicators, while fully recognizing their limitations.

1

Budgeting Institutions and Public Spending

JÜRGEN VON HAGEN

H61 H50

D72 H70

E62

Public spending is a story of some people spending other people's money. To exploit economies of scale in government, voters in modern democracies elect politicians—individuals who specialize in policy making—to make decisions about public spending for them, and they provide the funds spent by paying taxes. Thus public spending involves delegation and, hence, principal-agent relationships. As in other such relationships, the elected politicians can extract rents from being in office. That is, they can use some of the funds provided by the voters (taxpayers) to pursue other interests, including the use of public funds for outright corrupt purposes or for goods benefiting only their individual interests (perks), or they may simply waste funds out of negligence.

In principle, voters could eliminate the opportunity to extract rents by subjecting the elected politicians to ex ante rules specifying precisely what they can and must do under given conditions. However, the need to be able to react to unforeseen developments and the complexity of such situations makes the writing of such contracts impossible. For the same reason, it seems unrealistic to assume that politicians can commit themselves fully to the promises they make during election campaigns. Hence, like principal-agent relations in many other settings, the voter-politician relationship resembles

1

an "incomplete contract" (Seabright 1996; Persson, Roland, and Tabellini 1997, 2000; Tabellini 2000).

The distinction between general public goods, such as defense or home justice, which benefit all citizens (taxpayers) alike, and targeted public policies, such as local public goods, sectoral policies, or transfers targeted to subgroups of citizens (taxpayers) in society, is another fundamental aspect of public finance. Targeted public policies, when paid for from the general tax fund, involve redistribution of resources among citizens (taxpayers); we therefore refer to them as *distributive policies*. Because citizens living in different circumstances demand different targeted public policies from their government, the voter-politician relationship is best characterized as a principal-agent relationship with multiple, heterogeneous principals that compete for public monies. Voters belonging to a group that benefits from targeted public policies can reward politicians by reelecting them. This implies that politicians can use distributive policies strategically to ensure their confirmation in office (Persson and Tabellini 2004).

A second important implication of distributive policies is that those who benefit from a specific, targeted public policy are generally not those who pay for it. Instead, those who benefit typically pay a small share of the total cost. As a result, politicians who represent the interests of individual groups tend to overestimate the net social benefit from targeted public policies. They perceive the full social benefit from policies targeting their constituencies but only that part of the social cost that the latter bear through their taxes. This is the *common pool property* of public budgeting (von Hagen and Harden 1996).

Both the multiple principal-agent relationship and the common pool property generate potentials for excessive levels of spending, taxation, and public borrowing. The more severe the principal-agent problem, the greater will be the divergence between voter preferences and the level and composition of public spending. A comparison of jurisdictions in which public finances are determined by direct democracy with jurisdictions in which representative democracy prevails illustrates the point. Empirical studies show that, all else being equal, direct democracy leads to lower levels of government expenditures and taxes, lower levels of government debt, an increase in local versus state spending, and a tendency to finance government expenditures with charges rather than broad-based taxes (Pommerehne 1978, 1990; Matsusaka 1995; Feld and Kirchgässner 1999; Kirchgässner, Feld, and Savioz 1999). Other empirical studies suggest that government spending and debt increase with the intensity of conflict among the principals, measured by the severity of ideological or ethnic divisions within a society (Roubini and Sachs 1989; Alesina and Perotti 1995; Alesina, Baqir, and Easterly 1997) or by ethnolinguistic and religious fractionalization (Annett 2000). Annett (2000) argues that the impact of ethnic and other divisions among voters on public spending works through political instability: The more fractionalized a society is, the more unstable is its government, and instability leads to higher levels of public spending.

Similarly, the more severe the common pool property is, the greater will be the divergence between the marginal social utility and the marginal social cost of targeted public policies. Empirical studies show that this leads to excessive levels of spending, deficits, and debt (von Hagen 1992; von Hagen and Harden 1994a; Strauch 1998; Kontopoulos and Perotti 1999). As Annett (2000) points out, empirical evidence showing that ethnic and other types of social fractionalization induce higher public spending is also consistent with the common pool argument of excessive public spending, as fractionalization leads the representatives of one group in society to disregard the costs of public spending borne by other groups.

Societies can react to these problems by creating institutions that mitigate their adverse effects. One approach is to impose ex ante controls on the scope of the choices that elected politicians can make regarding public finances. Examples are balanced-budget constraints to limit the amount of debt policy makers can raise or referendum requirements for raising tax rates. A second approach is to strengthen accountability and competition among elected politicians, increasing their incentives to deliver the policies that voters prefer so as to ensure tenure in office. This is the main function of electoral systems in our context. A third approach is to structure the decision-making processes about public finances among policy makers in ways that force them to recognize more fully the marginal social benefits and costs of their policies. This is the principal task of the budgeting process. In this paper, we subsume all three approaches under the term *budgeting institutions*. We thus take a rather broad perspective.

The remainder of this paper proceeds as follows. The next section discusses ex ante controls as instruments to limit the principal-agent problem and the common pool problem. The third section discusses the role of electoral institutions in shaping and limiting the principal-agent problem. The fourth section considers the institutional aspects of the budgeting process. The last section concludes with some remarks on institutional reform.

Ex Ante Controls

The most straightforward approach to controlling the performance of policy makers is to subject them to ex ante—controls, constitutional constraints on budgetary aggregates. In practice, such constraints impose quantitative limits either on deficits or on spending. Balanced budget constraints mandated by the constitution are often used as a mechanism to limit the borrowing of subnational governments (von Hagen and Eichengreen 1996; Stein, Grisanti, and Talvi 1999). Most state governments in the United States are subject to a balanced-budget requirement of some sort, and many state constitutions require public referenda on increases in tax rates. Such constraints seem attractive because they are simple, easily understood, and very visible. The historical events leading to the imposition of such constraints in the United States and in Canada suggest that they are often the result of the desire of disgruntled taxpayers to impose constraints on the spending profligacy of their elected representatives (Eichengreen and von Hagen 1996; Millar 1997).

It is interesting, therefore, to see how successful such constraints are. The experience of U.S. state governments is very instructive in this regard. Almost all state governments have some constraints on either the size of the deficits they can run or the size of the public debt they can issue. These constraints come in varying degrees of strictness, ranging from requirements that the governor's budget proposal be balanced to outright bans on realized revenues falling short of realized expenditures. The Advisory Council for Interstate Relations (ACIR 1987) and Strauch (1998) provide overviews and characterizations of these constraints.

Strauch (1998) reports empirical results indicating that strict balanced-budget constraints effectively limit the size of the annual balance on the government's current account (total less investment spending). Eichengreen (1990) shows that the stringency of balanced-budget constraints has a significant and negative effect on a state's debt ratio. However, Eichengreen considers only the level of *full faith and credit debt*—that is, debt that is fully and explicitly guaranteed by the state government. Von Hagen (1991) takes a broader perspective and includes other types of public debt in the empirical analysis, such as debt issued by public authorities. He finds that the stringency of numerical constraints has no effect on the total debt.

The two results are easy to reconcile: They suggest that states subject to stringent numerical deficit constraints tend to substitute debt instruments not covered by the legal rule (resulting from off-budget activities) for full faith and credit debt. Kiewiet and Szakaly (1996) find a similar effect by showing that where more restrictive borrowing constraints are imposed on the state government, municipal governments tend to incur larger debts. Von Hagen and Eichengreen (1996) show in a cross-country comparison that in countries where subnational governments are subject to stringent statutory borrowing constraints, the central government tends to have a higher debt ratio. This indicates a third substitution effect: Where subnational governments are not allowed to borrow on their own authority, they tend to pressure the central government to borrow on their behalf.

Furthermore, Poterba (1994) shows that state governments subject to stricter balanced-budget constraints tend to cope less efficiently with fiscal shocks, as they tend to cut spending in response to negative revenue shocks, which results in pro-cyclical policies. Strauch (1998) shows that constitutional expenditure limits, which are found in many U.S. state constitutions, do not constrain spending effectively. Instead, they induce a shift from the current to the investment budget.

The important insight from these studies is that ex ante controls on fiscal choices constrain politicians more effectively in the short run than in the long run. In the long run, policy makers find ways around such controls. Since it is impossible, in practice, to impose rules that cannot be circumvented, and since the individual citizen's incentive to monitor policy makers' behavior and turn to the courts to enforce the rules is weak, the effectiveness of ex ante controls seems limited. To the extent that creative practices to circumvent them reduce the transparency of public finances and of the relevant decision-making processes, such controls may actually reduce the voter's ability to monitor the performance of the elected politicians and, therefore, aggravate rather than mitigate the principal-agent problem.

As in other principal-agent relationships, a solution to this problem is to rely on an outside authority that enforces ex ante rules effectively. One alternative would be an international financial organization. Specifically, International Monetary Fund (IMF) assistance programs typically come with fiscal constraints on the recipient country. The IMF's enforcement power derives from the threat that the financial assistance will not be disbursed if the fiscal constraints are violated. But the IMF approach has at least two severe limitations. First, assistance programs are based on agreements between the IMF and the executive, and the legislature may not feel bound by the agreement. It is, therefore, doubtful that outside enforcement works in political settings where the executive has weak control over the legislature. Second, IMF assistance programs come in times of crisis, when public finances are already in disarray. In more normal times, the IMF has little enforcement power, since it has no penalties to impose.

The European Monetary Union (EMU) furnishes another example of enforcing budgetary rules through an international organization. In the Maastricht Treaty first, and the Stability and Growth Pact later, the EMU states signed agreements committing them to a set of fixed targets. These countries have to submit annual Stability and Growth Programs explaining their governments' strategies to meet these targets. After reviewing these reports and the relevant data, the European Commission issues judgments of the countries' fiscal stance, which become the basis for the European Council's assessment and possible recommendations. Before the start of EMU on January 1, 1999, external enforcement power was based on the threat of exclusion from the monetary union. Today, it is based on the threat of public reprimand for fiscal profligacy and the possibility of financial fines.

But the success of the European approach has been limited so far (von Hagen 1998). When the Maastricht process started in 1992, the average debt ratio of the European Union (EU) states stood at 60 percent of gross domestic product (GDP); in 1998, it was over 75 percent. A closer look reveals that this increase was driven entirely by fiscal developments in Germany, France, Spain, Italy, and the United Kingdom, which did not commit itself to EMU. It is probably no coincidence that the first four countries are the largest among the 12 EMU states, given that the role of external political pressures, such as admonitions brought by the European Commission, is not strong enough to coerce internal politics in large countries. Note also that the European Commission, in its assessment of the fiscal criteria for EMU membership, treated the large countries with considerable lenience. The threat of excluding Germany or France from EMU was hardly credible, since the union would not have made much sense without these countries. All this suggests that the effectiveness of outside actors in enforcing ex ante fiscal rules depends critically on the importance of international organizations in domestic politics, which is plausibly a function of the size of the country.[1]

Political Systems: Competition and Accountability

The essence of the interpretation of the voter-politician relationship as an incomplete contract is that voters vest policy makers with discretionary powers to execute their offices and, at the same time, introduce procedures for holding them responsible for their actions (Persson, Roland, and Tabellini 1997, 2000). The election process is the most important procedure for doing so. Here, we focus on two aspects of electoral institutions. They allow voters to hold policy makers personally accountable for past policies, and they create competition among politicians.

If politicians cannot make binding commitments during election campaigns, voters have little reason to elect them on the basis of their campaign promises. But if politicians are also opportunistic in the sense that they care about their rents and wish to remain in office, elections give voters the opportunity to hold them accountable for their performance. This is the basic idea of the retrospective-voting paradigm. According to this paradigm, voters assess the performance of policy makers on the basis of the information available. If they regard the incumbents' behavior as satisfactory, they reappoint them. If not, they vote for alternative contestants. This mechanism suggests that rents can be contained if accountability is strong and competition is fierce.

In this section, we compare two electoral rules and two principles of organizing the executive branch of government from this perspective. The two electoral rules are plurality and proportional representation. The two organizational principles are parliamentarian government and presidential government.

Electoral Rules

Electoral rules can be compared according to district magnitude—the number of representatives in parliament elected from each electoral district. At one extreme, exactly one representative is chosen from each district, so the candidate with the largest number of votes in a district wins the seat. This is plurality rule, which prevails, for example, in the United States and in the United Kingdom. At the other extreme, the entire country is essentially one large electoral district, and candidates for all seats are drawn from national party lists according to the share of votes cast for that list in the entire country. This is proportional representation, which prevails, for example, in the Netherlands. Less extreme forms of proportional representation divide a country into several large electoral districts, with party lists presented for each of them.

Plurality rule focuses elections on the personal performance of the individual candidates and, hence, maximize personal accountability. Voters have reason to monitor the performance of the individual in office and to reelect that individual if he or she delivers the kind of policies that please them. Proportional representation, in contrast, weakens personal accountability. Voters can judge politicians only on the basis of the average performance of all candidates elected from the party list. This gives politicians more freedom to work for their own interests. At the same time, proportional representation gives voters less opportunity to reward politicians for channeling general tax funds to the specific region where they live. Thus, proportional representation reduces politicians' incentives for using distributive policies to secure reelection.

This reasoning has three public finance implications. First, as personal accountability puts a check on the politician's ability to extract rents, we should expect less waste and smaller levels of public spending under plurality rule than under proportional representation.

Second, as voters reward politicians for attracting money from the general (national) tax fund to their districts through distributive policies, we should expect a higher share of money to be spent on such policies and a lower share of money to be spent on general public goods in total government spending under plurality rule (Tabellini 2000). Note, however, that this argument assumes that geography is the dominant dimension for targeting public policy programs. Although this is true for items such as public infrastructure, many subsidies and transfer programs are targeted to individual groups in society such as professional groups, business sectors, or minorities. If political parties under proportional representation are organized around such particular interests and the number of parties is large, each party faces strong incentives to spend money from the general tax fund on programs benefiting its constituency. As a result, the share of money spent on local public policies would be small, but the share of money spent on policies targeting specific groups could be as large as the share of money spent on policies targeting individual districts under plurality rule. Thus, with regard to the mix of public spending, the distinction is sharpest between plurality rule and proportional representation when the latter is combined with a small number of large parties, each representing a large spectrum of interests in society.

Third, representatives from different districts have strong incentives to engage in logrolling and games of reciprocity to find majorities for policies that favor individual districts. Thus, plurality rule also contributes positively to the common pool problem. From this perspective, we should expect larger levels of spending and larger deficits and debts in countries with plurality rule. However, following the logic of the previous argument, this distinction should again be sharpest between plurality rule and proportional representation when combined with a small number of large parties.

This leads us to the other aspect of political systems—namely, competition. The need to gain a large share of votes in a district under plurality rule is an important barrier to entry for small parties. Political newcomers find it difficult to challenge incumbent politicians, because they need a majority to succeed from the start. In contrast, newcomers can win at least a small number of seats under proportional representation. Political competition is, therefore, more intense under that system. If contestants use the election campaign to identify waste and point to instances of rent extraction, one can expect more intense competition to lead to less waste and smaller rents. Thus, the consequences of weaker accountability under proportional representation may be compensated for by more intense competition. At the same time, proportional representation allows interest groups that are too small to win any individual districts under plurality rule to form political parties for countrywide platforms and to win some seats.

In practice, systems of proportional representation often include minimum vote thresholds to keep very small, particularistic parties out of parliament. Such thresholds mitigate the political pressures for more spending on targeted public policies. At the same time, however, they act as barriers to entry into the political market and, therefore, reduce competition. Consequently, minimum vote thresholds increase the likelihood of having a small number of large parties under a system of proportional representation.

Presidential versus Parliamentary Government

Presidential governments are characterized by the fact that the leader of the executive, the president, is appointed in direct elections, whereas in parliamentary governments the leader of the executive is typically chosen from among a stable majority coalition. For our purposes, two differences are most important. First is the greater separation of powers between the executive and the legislative branches and, often in practice, within the legislative branch. Second, in parliamentary systems the greater reliance of the executive on stable majorities, based on party allegiance or coalition contracts, to pass legislative proposals restricts competition more than in presidential systems.[2]

In presidential systems, new legislation is typically proposed either by the president or by legislative committees with well-defined jurisdictions. Individual legislators are not bound strongly by party membership. Instead, they vote for or against legislative proposals depending on what they perceive to be best for their constituencies. To pass, proposals must attract minimal winning coalitions within the legislature, and these coalitions can change across legislative fields and over time. This instability creates fierce competition among the legislators for rents and distributive policies that benefit their constituencies—competition that can be exploited by the committee that is making proposals.

As Persson and Tabellini (2004) show, separation of powers in this setting can be used to create checks and balances on the power of politicians. Specifically, giving the right to propose the level of taxation to the president (or the tax committee in the legislature) and the right to propose the level and composition of spending to parliament (or to a different spending committee) implies that voters hold the president (the members of the tax committee) accountable for the level of taxation and the legislators (the members of the spending committee) accountable for delivering the desired amount and composition of public services. Thus, the president (the members of the tax committee) and the legislators (the members of the spending committee) face different and partially conflicting incentives in making their proposals.

If taxes are determined before expenditures, the president (or the tax committee) will propose the lowest possible level of taxation.[3] Members of the spending committee will then submit proposals that use the smallest possible amount of distributive policies targeting other groups of voters to finance policies benefiting their own constituencies. Competition for distributive policies among the legislators who are not members of the spending committee drives the amounts spent in favor of their constituencies to zero in equilibrium. At the same time, the members of the spending committee will favor public policies targeted to their constituencies over general public goods, since they can make other voters pay for them. Anticipating this, the president (or the tax committee) sets the level of taxes low enough to minimize rents and distributive policies that favor the members of the spending committee. As a result, the separation of powers combined with unstable winning coalitions in the legislature leads to underprovision of general public goods, small rents, small levels of distributive policies, and relatively low levels of government spending and taxation.[4]

Parliamentary governments, in contrast, are characterized by a smaller degree of separation of powers and more cohesion among legislators. Even if the formal right to initiate legislation in parliament exists, legislative proposals are typically made by the executive, which counts on its stable majority to pass them. As a result, voters cannot hold different politicians accountable for setting taxes and expenditures. Instead, taxes and spending are negotiated among the members of the executive, and voters can hold policy makers accountable only for the entire package of tax and spending decisions. With less accountability, the scope for rent extraction increases. Furthermore, legislators do not compete in the same, intensive way for distributive policies because party allegiance and coalition agreements generate more cohesion among them. Negotiations among party leaders for taxes and the level and composition of public spending, therefore, internalize the interests of a broader range of constituencies. This implies a stronger representation of the voters' interest in general public goods. Furthermore, in this less competitive environment, the participants in these negotiations can secure higher levels of distributive policies that favor their constituencies than they could in a presidential system. Compared with presidential systems, parliamentarian systems, therefore, lead not only to higher rents and targeted public policies, but also to a more efficient provision of general public goods.

Empirical Evidence

Empirical research into the public finance implications of electoral systems has only recently begun. Persson and Tabellini (1999) find that countries with presidential governments tend to have smaller governments (measured in terms of government spending in GDP) than countries with parliamentary governments. They also find that countries with plurality rule have smaller governments, although this result is not statistically robust. Persson, Tabellini, and Trebbi (2003) find that countries with proportional representation are characterized by higher levels of corruption than countries where plurality rule prevails. Taking corruption as a proxy measure for rents confirms the hypothesis that the lower degree of electoral competition and accountability to voters under proportional representation entails larger rents. Persson and Tabellini (1999) also report evidence showing that plurality rule elections and presidential government lead to lower supply of general public goods than do proportional representation and parliamentary government.

Hallerberg (2000) presents a case study of the Italian electoral reforms and their public finance consequences. In 1994, Italy replaced its former system of proportional representation by one that has three-quarters of all seats in parliament elected by plurality rule and the remaining seats elected on the basis of proportional representation. The reform was introduced with the hope that plurality rule would generate more stable governments and a two-party system. This did not happen immediately. But when elections were called again in 1996, the tendency toward a two-party system became stronger. Hallerberg argues that this was an important step in preparing for Italy's accession to EMU.

Empirical research in this area is difficult not least because political systems, in practice, do not conform neatly to the stylized characterizations used above. For example, in some countries with proportional representation, voters can influence which rank individual politicians have on the party list. This strengthens accountability. Presidential systems offer the possibility for separation of powers, but this possibility is not necessarily used in practice. Thus, more detailed characterizations are necessary.

Nevertheless, the existing evidence, scant as it is, supports the view that electoral institutions have important consequences for public spending. The policy inference one can draw is that accountability of and competition among politicians are effective controls of rents and affect the provision of general and public goods and distributive policies. In practice, accountability and competition can be strengthened by institutional design even without the sweeping reforms that a move from a parliamentary to a presidential system or from proportional representation to plurality rule would entail.

Limiting the Common Pool Problem: The Budgeting Process

The core of the common pool problem of public budgeting is that the budget involves an externality—money from a general tax fund is used to finance distributive policies that benefit particular groups in society. At the heart of the problem is a misperception about the true budget constraint. Individual politicians each assume that an increase in public spending on targeted policies will provide their constituencies with more of the public services they desire at only a fraction of the total cost, since the rest is paid by other taxpayers. As a result all politicians ask for more public services than they would if they realized the true budget constraint—that is, if each benefiting group were charged the full cost of the services delivered. The larger the number of politicians drawing on the same general tax fund is, the lower seems the marginal cost of distributive policies for each of them and the greater is the overspending bias. Putting this argument into a dynamic context, we find that where money can be borrowed to finance current spending, one can show that the common pool problem leads to excessive deficits and government debts in addition to excessive spending levels (von Hagen and Harden 1996; Velasco 1999).

The analogy with a common pool problem suggests that excess spending and deficit bias can be reduced if politicians can be made to realize the true budget constraint. This is the main role of the budgeting process for our purposes. Broadly speaking, the budgeting process consists of the formal and informal rules governing the decisions regarding public spending within the executive and the legislative branches of government. It includes the rules relating to the formulation of a budget by the executive, to its passage through the legislature, and to its implementation by the executive. These rules divide this process into different steps, they determine who does what and when, and they regulate the flow of information among the participants. The budgeting process thus distributes strategic influence and creates or destroys opportunities for collusion. As discussed in more detail below, appropriate rules in the budgeting process can induce politicians to take a comprehensive view of the costs and benefits of all public policies financed through the budget, while inappropriate rules fail to do that and encourage politicians to care only about the rents and distributive policies they can attract for themselves. In the latter case, we call a budgeting process fragmented. The opposite of fragmentation is centralization. A centralized budgeting process thus coordinates the spending decisions of individual politicians by inducing them to take a comprehensive view of the budget.[5]

Institutional design of the budgeting process can serve this purpose effectively only if all conflicts between competing claims on public finances are indeed resolved within the budget process. Four deviations from this principle undermine the functioning of the budget process.

The first deviation is the use of off-budget funds to finance government activities. This allows policy makers to circumvent the constraints of the budgeting process and prevent their decisions from being challenged by conflicting distributional interests. The second deviation is the spreading of *nondecisions*, which occur when expenditures included in the budget are determined by developments exogenous to the budgeting process. Prime examples are (a) the indexation of spending programs to price levels or aggregate nominal income and (b) "open-ended" spending appropriations, such as the government wage bill and welfare payments based on entitlements with legally fixed parameters.[6] Nondecisions conveniently allow policy makers to avoid tough decisions (Weaver 1986), but they degrade the budgeting process to a mere forecast of exogenous developments.[7] The third deviation is the existence of *mandatory spending laws*—nonfinancial laws that make certain government expenditures compulsory. The budget then becomes a mere summary of existing spending mandates created by simple legislation. An effective budgeting process requires a clear distinction between nonfinancial laws, which create the authorization for certain government undertakings, and the budget, which makes specific funds available for a specific time period. The fourth deviation occurs when the government enters into contingent liabilities such as guarantees for the liabilities of other public or nonpublic entities. Promises, implicit or explicit, to bail out subnational governments (as in Germany in the late 1980s), regional development banks (as frequently in Brazil), or financial institutions (as in the savings and loans debacle in the United States) can suddenly turn into large government expenditures outside the ordinary budget. One must recognize that contingent liabilities cannot be fully avoided and that a proper accounting of them is a difficult task. However, their existence and importance for the government's financial stance can be brought to the attention of decision makers in the budgeting process by requiring the government to submit a report on the financial guarantees it has entered into as part of the budget documentation.

Institutional Elements of Centralization

Budgeting processes can be divided into an executive planning stage, a legislative approval stage, an executive implementation stage, and an ex post control stage. Each involves different actors with different roles. The executive planning stage usually begins about a year before the relevant fiscal year and ends with the submission of a draft budget to the legislature. It involves the setting of budget guidelines, the bidding for budget appropriations from the various spending departments, the resolution of conflicts between the spending interests in the executive, and the drafting of the revenue budget. The legislative approval stage includes the process of making parliamentary amendments to the budget proposal, which may involve more than one house. This stage ends with the passing of the budget law. The executive implementation stage covers the fiscal year to which the budget law applies. During this stage deviations from the budget law can occur, either formally by adopting supplementary budget laws in parliament, or informally by shifting funds between chapters of the budget law and by overrunning the spending limits provided by the law.

Institutional elements of centralization primarily concern the first three stages, with different elements applying to different stages.[8] At the executive planning stage, the purpose of such elements is to promote agreement on budget guidelines (spending and deficit targets) among all actors involved, ensuring fiscal discipline. Elements of centralization at this stage must foster consistent setting of such guidelines and ensure that they constrain executive decisions effectively. A key element concerns the way conflicts are resolved. Uncoordinated and ad hoc conflict resolution involving many actors simultaneously promotes logrolling and reciprocity and, hence, fragmentation. Centralization is increased if conflict resolution is the role of senior cabinet committees or the prime minister.

At the legislative approval stage, elements of centralization control the debate and voting procedures in the legislature. Because of the much larger number of decision makers involved, the common pool problem is even larger in the legislature than in the executive. Fragmentation is rampant when there are no limits to the changes that parliament can make to the executive's budget proposal, when spending decisions are made in legislative committees with narrow and dispersed authorities (the "Balkanization of committees"—see Crain and Miller 1990), and when there is little guidance of the parliamentary process either by the executive or by the speaker of the legislature. Centralization comes with strengthening the executive's agenda-setting power by placing limits on the scope of amendments, controlling the voting procedure, and raising the political stakes of a rejection of the executive's budget, such as by making it equivalent to a vote of no confidence. Centralization can also come with strengthening the roles of the speaker and the financial committee in the legislature.

At the implementation stage, elements of centralization ensure that the budget law effectively constrains the spending decisions of the executive. One important element is strengthening the finance minister's ability to monitor and control spending flows during the fiscal year. Other important elements are strict limitations on changes to the budget law during the year.

Reviewing elements of centralization in Organisation for Economic Co-operation and Development (OECD), Latin American, and Asian countries reveals that centralization follows two basic approaches. The first is based on delegation. Under this approach, participants in the budgeting process who are assumed to have a more comprehensive view of the budget are vested with special strategic powers. The second approach is based on contracts. Under this approach, binding agreements are negotiated among all participants, without giving special authority to any one.

Delegation

In the delegation approach, the budgeting process vests special authority in a "fiscal entrepreneur" whose function it is to set the broad parameters of the budget and to ensure that all other participants in the process observe these constraints. To be effective, this entrepreneur must have the ability to monitor the other members of the executive and to use selective punishments against possible defectors. Among cabinet members, the entrepreneur is typically the finance minister. Since the finance minister is not bound by individual spending interests as much as the spending ministers are, and since the finance minister typically is charged with drafting the revenue budget, it is plausible to assume that the finance minister takes the most comprehensive view of the budget among the members of the executive.

In practice, delegation can take a variety of forms. In the French model, the finance minister and the prime minister together determine the overall allocations of the spending departments. These targets are considered binding for the rest of the process. Here, the finance minister has a strong role as agenda setter in the budgeting process. The U.K. model, in contrast, evolves as a series of bilateral negotiations between the spending departments and the finance minister in which the latter bases bargaining power on superior information, seniority, and political backup from the prime minister.

Under the delegation approach, drafting the budget proposal is mainly the responsibility of the finance ministry, which monitors the individual bids, negotiates directly with the spending departments, and approves the bids submitted to the final cabinet meeting. Unresolved conflicts between spending ministers and the finance minister are typically arbitrated by the prime minister.

At the legislative stage, the delegation approach lends large agenda-setting powers to the executive over the parliament. One important instrument here is to limit the scope of amendments that parliamentarians can make to the executive's budget proposal. In France, for example, amendments cannot be proposed unless they reduce expenditures or create a new source of public revenues. In the United Kingdom, amendments that propose new charges on public revenues require the consent of the executive. Such restrictions make the budget constraint felt more powerfully.

A second element concerns the voting procedure. The French government, for example, can force the legislature to vote on large parts of or the entire budget in a block vote, with only those amendments considered that the executive is willing to accept. In the United Kingdom, the executive can make the vote on the budget a vote of confidence, considerably raising the stakes for a rejection.

A final element concerns the budgetary authority of the upper house. Where both houses have equal budgetary authority, as in Italy or Belgium, finding a compromise is a necessary part of the budgeting process. This tends to weaken the position of the executive because it now faces two opponent bodies. The executive may be strengthened by limiting the budgetary authority of the upper house, as in France and Germany, where the lower house prevails if an agreement between the two chambers cannot be reached. In the United Kingdom, the upper house has no budgetary authority at all, leaving the executive with only one chamber to deal with. The position of the executive can also be strengthened by giving the finance minister veto power over the budget passed by the legislature, as in Germany and Spain.

At the implementation stage, finally, centralization requires that the finance minister be able to monitor and control the flow of expenditures during the year. This may take the form of requiring that the spending departments obtain the finance minister's authorization to disburse funds during the year. The finance minister's authority to impose cash limits during the year is another control mechanism. Monitoring spending flows during the year requires a unified system of financial accounts that enables the finance minister to watch the inflow and outflow of resources. Effective monitoring and control are also important to prevent spending departments from behaving strategically—that is, from spending their appropriations early in the year and demanding additional funds later under the threat of closing down important public services.

Furthermore, centralization requires tight limits on any changes in the original budget law through the modification of appropriations once the fiscal year has begun. One example is the requirement that transfers of funds between different chapters of the budget be authorized by the finance minister or parliament. The same applies to transfers of funds between different fiscal years. Although carryover provisions have obvious efficiency gains, their use should be limited and strictly monitored to ensure that the finance minister can keep track of a spending department's financial position. Another example is to restrict the use of supplementary budgets. Where supplementary budgets during the fiscal year become the norm, as in Italy and Belgium in the 1980s and in Germany in the 1990s, one cannot expect that policy makers will take the constraints embedded in the original budget law seriously.

Contracts

Under a contract approach, the budgeting process starts with an agreement on a set of binding fiscal targets negotiated among the members of the executive. Emphasis here is on the bargaining process as a mechanism to reveal the externalities involved in budget decisions and on the binding nature of the targets. In contrast to the hierarchical structure created by delegation, the contract approach relies on a more equal distribution of strategic powers in the executive. A prime example is the Danish budgeting process, which, since 1982, has started with negotiations among the cabinet members to fix spending limits for each spending department. Often, these spending limits are derived from medium-term fiscal programs or the coalition agreement among the ruling parties. In Ireland, for example, coalition agreements since 1989 have included medium-term fiscal strategies to reduce the public debt, which have provided the background to the annual negotiations over budget targets.

The finance ministry's role under this approach is to evaluate the consistency of the individual departments' spending plans with these targets. In the Netherlands, for example, the finance minister usually has an information advantage over the spending ministers in the budget negotiations but no extra strategic powers. Conflict resolution involves senior cabinet committees and often the leaders of the coalition parties in the legislature.

At the legislative stage, the contract approach places less weight on the executive's role as an agenda setter and more weight on the role of the legislature as a monitor of the faithful implementation of the fiscal targets. Institutionally, this means that the contract approach relies less on the executive branch of government controlling parliamentary amendments and more on the legislature's ability to monitor the fiscal performance of the executive. One important element is the legislature's right to request information from the executive. This element can be strengthened by setting up committees whose authorities reflect the authorities of the spending departments and by giving committees a formal right to request information from the executive and to call witnesses from the executive to testify. The Danish parliament, for example, has all three of these rights, while the German parliament has only the first and the U.K. parliament has none of the three.

At the implementation stage, the contract approach resembles the delegation approach in emphasizing the monitoring and control powers of the finance minister.

Empirical Evidence

A fast-growing literature starting with von Hagen (1992) has presented empirical evidence supporting the hypothesis that centralization of the budgeting process leads to smaller government deficits and debts. Von Hagen (1992) provides evidence from 12 EU countries showing a significant negative association between the centralization of the budgeting process and general government deficits and debts relative to GDP. Von Hagen and Harden (1994b) extend and broaden the analysis and confirm the hypothesis that centralization is associated with smaller deficits and debts. De Haan and Sturm (1994) again work with EU data and show that the hypothesis holds up empirically, even when a number of political factors such as the composition and stability of governments is controlled for. Hallerberg and von Hagen (1998, 1999) use panel data analysis for 15 EU countries to show that centralization goes along with smaller annual budget deficits, even when one controls for a number of economic determinants of the budget deficit and other political variables.

Turning to other geographical areas, Stein, Grisanti, and Talvi (1999) use panel data analysis from Latin American countries to show that centralization goes along with lower central government deficits. Jones, Sanguinetti, and Tommasi (1999) analyze a panel of annual budget deficits of Argentine provinces and confirm the same hypothesis. Lao-Araya (1997) provides similar results for 11 Asian countries. Strauch (1998) uses data from the 50 U.S. state governments to show that centralization significantly reduces annual budget deficits. Taking a different methodological approach, the country studies of Strauch and von Hagen (1999), Molander (2000), and Stienlet (2000) point to the importance of centralization in achieving (or in the case of Germany losing) fiscal discipline.

In summary, the hypothesis that centralization of the budgeting process leads to lower government deficits and debts can be considered as empirically well established today. It has been confirmed in very different geographical and political settings. Evidence showing that centralization reduces the size of government—as it should in theory—is still very scant, however, because of the difficulties of constructing the appropriate data sets and of empirically modeling the fiscal preferences of voters in cross-country studies. Only Strauch (1998) shows that this holds among U.S. state governments. Nevertheless, one can conclude that centralization of the budgeting process is an important and effective way to mitigate the common pool problem of public budgeting.

Institutional Design of the Budgeting Process

While the delegation approach relies on hierarchical structures within the executive and between the executive and the legislature, the contracts approach builds on a more even distribution of authorities in government. In democratic settings, hierarchical structures typically prevail within political parties, while relations between parties are more even. This suggests that the key to the institutional choice between the two approaches lies in the number of parties in government.

Parliamentary Systems

In parliamentary systems, delegation is the proper approach to centralization for single-party governments, while contracts is the proper approach for multiparty coalition governments (Hallerberg and von Hagen 1998). There are two reasons for this statement.

First, members of the same political party are more likely to have similar political views regarding the basic spending priorities than are members of different political parties. Spending ministers in a one-party government can, therefore, be fairly sure that the finance minister holds more or less the same spending preferences as they do. Disagreement will be mainly a result of the common pool problem—that is, the perceived cost of distributive policies. In a coalition government, in contrast, cabinet members are likely to have more diverging views regarding the distribution of government spending over different groups of recipients. Agreement on a budget, therefore, involves a compromise among the coalition partners. For a coalition government, delegation of strategic powers to the finance minister would create a new principal-agent problem. A strong finance minister might abuse his or her powers and unduly promote the political interests of his or her own party.

The same principal-agent problem does not arise in the contracts approach, because the contracts are negotiated by all cabinet members. Thus, governments formed by two or more parties are more likely to opt for the contracts approach.

Second, delegation and contracts rely on different enforcement mechanisms for the budget agreement. In one-party governments, the ultimate punishment for a spending minister reneging on the budget agreement is dismissal from office. Such punishment is heavy for the individual minister who overspends but generally light for the government as a whole. It can be used because the prime minister is typically the strongest cabinet member in one-party governments and has the authority to select and replace cabinet members. In coalition governments, in contrast, punishments cannot be applied easily to defecting ministers. The distribution of portfolios is set by the coalition agreement. Therefore, the prime minister cannot easily dismiss intransigent spending ministers from parties other than his or her own, since that would be regarded as an intrusion into the internal party affairs of coalition partners.

The most important punishment mechanism in coalition governments is the threat of breaking up the coalition, if a spending minister reneges on the budget agreement. This punishment is heavy for the entire coalition, as it leads potentially to the death of the government rather than the dismissal of a single individual. The point is illustrated by the fact that fiscal targets are often part of the coalition agreement. The credibility of this enforcement mechanism hinges on two important factors. The first is the existence of alternative coalition partners. If other potential partners exist with whom the aggrieved party can form a coalition, the threat to leave the coalition is clearly more credible than if no alternative coalition partner is available. The second factor is the expected response of the voters, as a coalition may be broken up with the anticipation of new elections.

The different enforcement mechanisms also explain the different relations between the executive and the legislature in the legislative phase of the budgeting process. Single-party governments typically arise in two-party settings such as pre-1994 New Zealand, the United Kingdom, or the United States, where each party is large and party discipline is low. Although the ruling party enjoys a majority, the main concern in the legislative stage of the budgeting process is to limit the scope of defections from the budget proposals by individual members who wish to divert government funds to their electoral districts. Multiparty coalitions, in contrast, typically arise in settings where parties are small and relatively homogeneous and party discipline is strong. In that situation, defections from the budget agreement are a weaker concern, but each party involved in the coalition will want to watch carefully to be sure that the executive sticks to the coalition agreement. The delegation approach, therefore, typically makes the executive a much stronger agenda setter in parliament than the contracts approach, while the contracts approach gives more monitoring powers to the legislature.

Finally, the commitment to fiscal targets embedded in the contracts approach is not credible for one-party governments. Consider a single-party government with a weak prime minister and a weak finance minister. Assume that this government announced a set of fiscal targets at the outset of the budgeting process and that some spending ministers renege on the agreement during the implementation phase. Other cabinet members cannot credibly threaten the defectors with dissolving the government, since they would punish themselves. Absent a credible threat, the entire cabinet would just walk away from the initial agreement.

To summarize, the contracts approach is more likely to be found in countries where coalition governments are the norm, while the delegation approach is more likely to be found in countries where the government is typically formed by a single party.[9]

Electoral institutions strongly influence the number of parties in government. Intuitively, if there are fewer parties, there is a higher chance that one party can win an absolute majority, and an absolute majority is a virtual certainty in two-party systems. Several studies indicate that the number of parties in a given system is strongly and positively correlated with district magnitude (Duverger 1954; Taagepera and Shugart 1989, 1993). Plurality rule encourages the emergence of two-party systems, and they are consequently most likely to have one-party majority governments. Proportional representation allows for more variation in district magnitude but is consistently characterized by multiparty coalition governments (Lijphart 1984, 1994; Taagepera and Shugart 1989, 1993).

The correlation between electoral institutions and the number of parties in government suggests that countries with proportional representation should be more likely to adopt a contracts approach, while countries with plurality rule should opt for the delegation approach, if they adopt centralizing institutions at all. Hallerberg and von Hagen (1998) show that this hypothesis is confirmed among the EU states.

Presidential Systems

Presidential systems of government differ from parliamentary systems in that presidents do not rely directly on the legislature for their position as leader of the executive. Voters can, and often do, support a president from one party while denying that party a majority in the legislature. In the United States, for example, presidents faced an opposition-controlled legislature in 24 of the 30 years between 1969 and 1998. In Latin American and Caribbean countries during the period 1990–95, half of the 20 countries with presidential systems had presidents facing opposition-controlled lower houses (Stein, Grisanti, and Talvi 1999). Coordination of budgetary decisions between the executive and the legislative branches becomes obviously more difficult when the president and the majority come from two different parties. Inman and Fitts (1990) show that, historically, U.S. federal government deficits have been significantly lower in times when the president faced a majority from his own party in the legislature.

The role of the executive in the budgeting process is not much different in presidential systems than in parliamentary ones. The president typically appoints the members of the administration, with confirmation by the legislature where applicable. The structure of the administration thus lends itself more to a delegation approach than to a contracts approach in centralizing the budgeting process. The relationship between the executive and the legislature, however, is often more difficult, since the two are conceived to be more equal than in parliamentary governments.

Centralization in presidential systems then must emphasize two institutional dimensions. One is the internal organization of the legislature. Here, centralization can be achieved by creating strong leadership through an elevated position of the speaker and through a hierarchical committee structure. For example, the Budget Enforcement Act passed under the George H.W. Bush administration in the 1990s reformed congressional procedures to protect decisions about budgetary parameters reached at the budget summit between the president and the legislature against later modifications.[10]

The other dimension regards the relationship between the executive and the legislature. The more the constitution puts the two institutions on an equal footing, the more budget agreements between the two must rely on the contracts approach. Inman (1993) emphasizes the importance of the president's command over sufficient resources to build congressional coalitions and the president's veto power to discipline the legislature.

Centralization and Flexibility of Budgetary Policies

Centralization of the budgeting process mitigates excessive spending and deficits that result from the common pool problem of public budgeting.

Because centralization emphasizes strict adherence to fiscal targets, one might suspect that it implies rigidity of budgetary policies—that is, it reduces the scope for reaction to unforeseen events during a fiscal year. If so, there could be a trade-off between achieving a higher degree of fiscal discipline and achieving a desirable degree of macroeconomic stabilization.

However, flexibility to react to unforeseen events can be achieved at the implementation stage in a number of different ways without working against centralization. For example, the Swedish government adopted a budgeting process in the early 1990s that allows spending departments to charge expenditures against future budgets or to transfer unused appropriations to the next year. Both transfers are possible, however, for only a limited number of years. Because the charges and the transfers must be budgeted in the following year, the provision combines flexibility with transparency and gives both the legislature and the finance minister the ability to control the flow of expenditures.

An alternative way to achieve flexibility is the creation of a "rainy day fund"—an unspecified appropriation that can be used for emergencies. An example is the (Contingency) Reserve included annually in the U.K. budget (von Hagen and Harden 1994b). The purpose of the Reserve, which amounts to 2 to 4 percent of the budget total, is to deal with unanticipated expenditures without overrunning the aggregate targets imposed on the spending departments. According to a rule introduced in 1976, a refusal by the finance minister to charge an expenditure against the Reserve can be overruled only by the entire cabinet. An allocation made from the Reserve does not increase a spending department's baseline allocation for the subsequent budget planning processes. Again, the critical point is to budget the fund annually and to submit spending out of this fund to the same rules of expenditure management as ordinary spending.

To see whether delegation and contracts tend to reduce a government's capacity to react appropriately, Hallerberg and von Hagen (1999) estimate the cyclical elasticity of government deficits in 15 EU states. On the basis of panel data, they find that centralization in itself does not change the cyclical elasticity. In fact, countries with a strong finance minister are characterized by a larger cyclical elasticity than both countries with centralization achieved through contracts and countries with rather fragmented budgeting processes. An intuitive interpretation is that a strong finance minister can react more quickly to economic downturns and upswings than the spending ministers. Also important, there is no indication of a trade-off between macroeconomic stabilization and mitigation of excessive spending in the design of a budgeting process.

Institutional Reform

This chapter has argued that the political economy of public finances can be interpreted in terms of a principal-agent relationship between voters (the political principals) and policy makers (the agents) and the common pool problem of public budgeting. The theory and empirical research reviewed here shows that the institutional designs of the principal-agent relationship and of the budgeting process have important consequences for the spending performance of governments in terms of the level of spending, the composition of spending, and the levels of deficits and debts. This suggests that appropriate institutional design can help mitigate problems of waste, divergence between public preferences and public sector deliveries, and fiscal profligacy.

This claim rests on the basic conjecture that institutions frame the decisions made within them—that is, that a given group of individuals facing a given problem makes predictably different decisions under different institutional arrangements. This requires that institutions effectively constrain the choices of these individuals. The obvious objection is that these individuals—and policy makers in particular—would rid themselves of the institutions and ignore or change the rules if they feel constrained by them. After all, institutions are constructed and subject to change. Without a satisfactory answer to this objection, the power of institutions and the promises of institutional reform must remain in doubt.

Such an answer has three points. First, the individuals involved in decisions about public finances do not always have the authority to change the rules. The relevant institutions may be cast in constitutional law or historical traditions that are hard to modify. Second, the claim that institutions impose constraints on individual decisions does not imply that these individuals will want to change the institutions. They will want to do that only if they can be reasonably sure that they can reach more desirable outcomes in a modified environment. Since complex political and economic decisions made by groups of people are prone to instability and irrationality, an environment with fewer rules is often much less desirable than an environment with more rules, even if the constraints of those rules are being felt. Third, institutional rules in the budget context serve to coordinate individual choices. Specifically, they give individual participants assurance that excessive budget demands by other participants will not be successful and thus make it easier for each participant to agree to demand less. Again, the implication is that abolishing institutional constraints is not necessarily desirable.

Nevertheless, one should not interpret the theory and evidence outlined here as saying that a change in the letter of the law is an effective means to reduce rents, excessive spending, and deficits. Precisely because changing institutions takes some extraordinary effort, policy makers are unlikely to do so unless they are aware of an acute fiscal problem. But if that is the case, how can we prove that the institutional change contributed to the fiscal correction, if the correction was what policy makers wanted anyway?

We can make two points. First, institutional changes are very visible to the public and the markets and, therefore, provide an important signaling function. Governments showing their resolve for more disciplined fiscal policy by reforming pertinent institutions will find it easier to convince the public and financial markets of their good intentions. To the extent that this reduces opposition to fiscal reforms and cutbacks, the necessary policy changes are made easier.

Second, awareness of a fiscal problem may not be permanent. As other problems arise and deficits return to normal levels, attention to the problems of waste, excessive spending, and deficits is reduced and the tendency for over-spending and excessive deficits rises again. At that point, having better institutions in place can be an important mechanism to preserve the collective memory of the previous difficulties.

Notes

1. This is consistent with Katzenstein's (1984) conjecture that governments in small open economies are typically more responsive to pressures from outside than governments in large countries are.
2. This is obviously a rough characterization only. The following discussion is based largely on Persson and Tabellini (1999) and Tabellini (2000).
3. As Persson and Tabellini (1999) show, there is a lower bound on taxes resulting from the incentive constraint that public expenditures must be large enough to keep the incumbent members of the spending committee interested in remaining in office—that is, to keep them from appropriating all public revenues for themselves and being voted out of office in the next elections.
4. Unsurprisingly, this result depends on the sequence of votes in parliament and the strict separation of committee jurisdictions.
5. Centralization of the budgeting process should not be confused with the regional centralization of government.
6. Note that there is nothing natural about determining wage, social security, and welfare expenditures outside the annual budgeting process. Indeed, setting the relevant parameters is a part of the annual budget process in some countries. Another way to limit the open-endedness of entitlements, as used in Denmark, is to set cash limits on welfare appropriations and require the relevant minister to propose spending adjustments and changes in the relevant nonfinancial laws if these limits are overrun (von Hagen and Harden 1994a).
7. Where nondecisions prevail strongly, the government budget becomes heavily dependent on institutions outside the annual budgeting process, such as wage-setting

institutions in the public sector, the social security system, the welfare system, and labor market regulations. Under such circumstances, fiscal discipline becomes heavily dependent on the quality of a country's institutions outside the budgeting process as well. Germany's experience with unification illustrates the point. There, weaknesses in the labor market legislation that was extended immediately to the territory of the German Democratic Republic (GDR) allowed unions and employers' associations to raise the fiscal cost of unification by reaching wage agreements that kept former GDR laborers from competing for jobs in the territory of the Federal Republic of Germany and implied generous unemployment payments to former GDR workers instead. (See von Hagen 1997 for details.)

8. At the last stage of the process, the legality of the budget is checked by the appropriate accounting body. Obviously, the design of the budgeting process becomes ineffective if policy makers operate outside the law. Thus, the last stage provides an important, necessary condition for the effectiveness of institutional design.

9. This conclusion is qualified by the observation, made above, that the effectiveness of the contracts approach depends on the availability of alternative coalition partners. German governments of the past 30 years have been coalitions between a large party and a small party with no alternative partner available for either. Germany's budget process, which build on delegation, therefore, fits this environment. When the German government was formed by the two large parties Christlich Demokratische Union and Sozialdemokratische Partei Deutschlands in the late 1960s, elements of a contracts approach were introduced to secure a high degree of fiscal discipline.

10. It is interesting to note in this context that the former attempt of the United States to reduce budget deficits under the Gramm Rudman Hollings Act failed, as the majority party in the legislature decided to ignore the specified deficit targets. This is consistent with our conjecture that a contracts approach is inadequate for single-party majority settings.

References

ACIR (Advisory Council for Interstate Relations). 1987. "The Effect of Constitutional Restraints on Government Spending." In *Significant Features of Fiscal Federalism*. Washington, DC: Advisory Council for Interstate Relations.

Alesina, Alberto, and Roberto Perotti. 1995. "Fiscal Expansions and Adjustments in OECD Countries." *Economic Policy* 21: 207–48.

Alesina, Alberto, Reza Baqir, and William Easterly. 1997. "Public Goods and Ethnic Divisions." NBER Working Paper 6009, National Bureau of Economic Research, Cambridge, MA.

Annett, Anthony. 2000. "Social Fractionalization, Political Instability, and the Size of Government." IMF Working Paper 00/82, International Monetary Fund, Washington, DC.

Crain, Mark, and James C. Miller. 1990. "Budget Process and Spending Growth." *William and Mary Law Review* 31: 1021–46.

de Haan, Jakob, and Jan-Egbert Sturm. 1994. "Political and Institutional Determinants of Fiscal Policy in the European Community." *Public Choice* 80: 157–72.

Duverger, Maurice. 1954. *Political Parties: Their Organization and Activity in the Modern State*. New York: Wiley.

Eichengreen, Barry. 1990. "One Money for Europe?" *Economic Policy* 10: 117–87.

Eichengreen, Barry, and Jürgen von Hagen. 1996. "Fiscal Policy and Monetary Union: Federalism, Fiscal Restrictions, and the No-Bailout Rule." In *Monetary Policy in an Integrated World Economy,* ed. Horst Siebert, 211–31. Tübingen, Germany: JCB Mohr.

Feld, Lars P., and Gebhard Kirchgässner. 1999. "Public Debt and Budgetary Procedures: Top Down or Bottom Up?" In *Fiscal Institutions and Fiscal Performances,* ed. James Poterba and Jürgen von Hagen, 151–80. Chicago: University of Chicago Press.

Hallerberg, Mark. 2000. "The Importance of Domestic Political Institutions: Why and How Belgium and Italy Qualified for EMU." ZEI Discussion Paper, Zentrum für Europäische Integrationsforschung, University of Bonn, Germany.

Hallerberg, Mark, and Jürgen von Hagen. 1998. "Electoral Institutions and the Budget Process." In *Democracy, Decentralization, and Deficits in Latin America,* ed. Kiichiro Fukasaku and Ricardo Hausmann. Paris: OECD Development Centre.

———. 1999. "Electoral Institutions, Cabinet Negotiations, and Budget Deficits in the EU." In *Fiscal Institutions and Fiscal Performance,* ed. Jim Poterba and Jürgen von Hagen, 209–32. Chicago: University of Chicago Press.

Inman, Robert. 1993. "Presidential Leadership and the Reform of Fiscal Policy: Learning from Reagan's Role in TRA 86." NBER Working Paper 4395, National Bureau of Economic Research, Cambridge, MA.

Inman, Robert, and Michael A. Fitts. 1990. "Political Institutions and Fiscal Policy: Evidence from the U.S. Historical Record." *Journal of Law, Economics, and Organization* 6: 79–131.

Jones, Mark P., Pablo Sanguinetti, and Mariano Tommasi. 1999. "Politics, Institutions, and Public Sector Spending in the Argentine Provinces." In *Fiscal Institutions and Fiscal Performance,* ed. James Poterba and Jürgen von Hagen, 135–50. Chicago: University of Chicago Press.

Katzenstein, Peter. 1984. *Small States in World Markets: Industrial Policy in Europe.* Ithaca, NY: Cornell University Press.

Kiewiet, D. Roderick, and Kristin Szakaly. 1996. "Constitutional Limits on Borrowing: An Analysis of State Bonded Indebtedness." *Journal of Law, Economics, and Organization* 12: 62–97.

Kirchgässner, Gebhard, Lars P. Feld, and Marcel R. Savioz. 1999. *Die direkte Demokratie.* Basel, Germany: Helbing and Lichtenhahn.

Kontopoulos, Yianos, and Roberto Perotti. 1999. "Government Fragmentation and Fiscal Policy Outcomes: Evidence from OECD Countries." In *Fiscal Institutions and Fiscal Performance,* ed. James Poterba and Jürgen von Hagen, 81–102. Chicago: University of Chicago Press.

Lao-Araya, Kanokpan. 1997. "The Effect of Budget Structure on Fiscal Performance: A Study of Selected Asian Countries." IMF Working Paper, International Monetary Fund, Washington, DC.

Lijphart, Arend. 1984. *Democracies: Patterns of Majoritarian and Consensus Government in Twenty-One Countries.* New Haven, CT: Yale University Press.

———. 1994. *Electoral Systems and Party Systems: A Study of Twenty-Seven Democracies 1945–1990.* Oxford, UK: Oxford University Press.

Matsusaka, John G. 1995. "Fiscal Effects of the Voter Initiative: Evidence from the Last 30 Years." *Journal of Political Economy* 103: 587–623.

Millar, Jonathan. 1997. *The Effect of Budget Rules on Fiscal Performance and Macroeconomic Stabilization.* Bank of Canada Working Paper 97–15, Bank of Canada, Ottawa.

Molander, Per. 2000. "Reforming Budgetary Institutions: Swedish Experiences." In *Institutions, Politics, and Fiscal Policy,* ed. Rolf Strauch and Jürgen von Hagen, 191–214. Dordrecht, Netherlands: Kluwer Academic Publishers.

Persson, Torsten, and Guido Tabellini. 1999. "The Size and Scope of Government: Comparative Politics with Rational Politicians." *European Economic Review* 43: 699–735.

———. 2004. "Political Economics and Public Finance." In *Handbook of Public Finance,* ed. Alan Auerbach and Martin Feldstein. Amsterdam: North-Holland.

Persson, Torsten, Gérard Roland, and Guido Tabellini. 1997. "Separation of Powers and Political Accountability." *Quarterly Journal of Economics* 112: 1163–202.

———. 2000. "Comparative Politics and Public Finance." *Journal of Political Economy* 108: 1121–61.

Persson, Torsten, Guido Tabellini, and Francesco Trebbi. 2003. "Electoral Rules and Corruption." *Journal of the European Economic Association* 1: 958–89.

Pommerehne, Werner. 1978. "Institutional Approaches to Public Expenditure: Empirical Evidence from Swiss Municipalities." *Journal of Public Economics* 9: 255–80.

———. 1990. "The Empirical Relevance of Comparative Institutional Analysis." *European Economic Review* 34: 458–69.

Poterba, James. 1994. "State Responses to Fiscal Crises: The Effects of Budgetary Institutions and Politics." *Journal of Political Economy* 102: 799–821.

Roubini, Nouriel, and Jeffrey D. Sachs. 1989. "Political and Economic Determinants of Budget Deficits in the Industrial Democracies." *European Economic Review* 33: 903–38.

Seabright, Paul. 1996. "Accountability and Decentralization in Government: An Incomplete Contracts Model." *European Economic Review* 40: 61–89.

Stein, Ernesto, Alejandro Grisanti, and Ernesto Talvi. 1999. "Institutional Arrangements and Fiscal Performance: The Latin American Experience." In *Fiscal Institutions and Fiscal Performance,* ed. James Poterba and Jürgen von Hagen, 103–34. Chicago: University of Chicago Press.

Stienlet, Georges. 2000. "Institutional Reforms and Belgian Fiscal Policies in the 90s." In *Institutions, Politics, and Fiscal Policy,* eds. Rolf Strauch and Jürgen von Hagen, 215–34. Dordrecht, Netherlands: Kluwer Academic Publishers.

Strauch, Rolf R. 1998. "Budget Processes and Fiscal Discipline: Evidence from the U.S. States." ZEI Working Paper, Zentrum für Europäische Integrationsforschung, University of Bonn, Germany.

Strauch, Rolf R., and Jürgen von Hagen. 1999. "Tumbling Giant: Germany's Experience with the Maastricht Criteria." In *From EMS to EMU,* ed. David Cobham and George Zis. London: Macmillan.

Taagepera, Rein, and Matthew Soberg Shugart. 1989. *Seats and Votes: The Effects and Determinants of Electoral Systems.* New Haven, CT: Yale University Press.

———. 1993. "Predicting the Number of Parties: A Quantitative Model of Duverger's Mechanical Effect." *American Political Science Review* 87 (2): 455–64.

Tabellini, Guido. 2000. "Constitutional Determinants of Government Spending." Working Paper, Innocenzo Gasparini Institute for Economic Research, Bocconi University, Milan, Italy.

Velasco, Andres. 1999. "Debts and Deficits with Fragmented Fiscal Policymaking." In *Fiscal Institutions and Fiscal Performance,* ed. James Poterba and Jürgen von Hagen, 37–58. Chicago: University of Chicago Press.

von Hagen, Jürgen. 1991. "A Note on the Empirical Effectiveness of Formal Fiscal Restraints." *Journal of Public Economics* 44: 199–210.

———. 1992. "Budgeting Procedures and Fiscal Performance in the European Communities." European Commission Economic Paper 96, European Commission, Luxembourg.

———. 1997. "The Economics of Kinship." In *Going Global,* ed. Padma Desai, 173–208. Boston: MIT Press.

———. 1998. "European Experience with Fiscal Initiatives: Fiscal Institutions, Maastricht Guidelines, and EMU." In *Fiscal Targets and Economic Growth,* ed. Thomas J. Courchene and Thomas A. Wilson, 331–50. Kingston, ON: John Deutsch Institute, Queen's University.

von Hagen, Jürgen, and Barry Eichengreen. 1996. "Federalism, Fiscal Restraints, and European Monetary Union." *American Economic Review* 86 (May): 134–38.

von Hagen, Jürgen, and Ian Harden. 1994a. "Budget Processes and Commitment to Fiscal Discipline." *European Economic Review* 39: 771–79.

———. 1994b. "National Budget Processes and Fiscal Performance." *European Economy, Reports and Studies* 3: 315–418.

———. 1996. "Budget Processes and Commitment to Fiscal Discipline." IMF Working Paper, International Monetary Fund, Washington, DC.

Weaver, R. Kent. 1986. "The Politics of Blame Avoidance." *Journal of Public Policy* 6: 371–98.

2

Performance-Based Budgeting Reform
Progress, Problems, and Pointers

MATTHEW ANDREWS

The past decade has seen many governments attempting to establish a results-oriented (or performance-based) budgeting approach. The emphasis on results or performance in the budget process reflects a new belief that public sector accountability should focus on what government does with the money it spends, rather than just how it controls such expenditure (Osborne and Gaebler 1992). In the parlance of new institutionalism, results-oriented or performance-based budgeting reforms introduce rules and norms that make it culturally appropriate for or induce (through positive and negative incentives) public representatives and managers to concentrate on outcomes and outputs rather than inputs and procedures.[1] There are two valid questions at this juncture: How well have reforms worked in introducing a results orientation into budgeting processes (with representatives and managers being accountable for results), and where should reformers be concentrating to improve such effects?

This chapter examines these questions in light of recent experience with budget reforms around the globe. It begins by providing examples of governments moving (either gradually or aggressively) toward a performance-based budgeting approach, and a short explanation of the new kind of accountability patterns expected to arise when performance-based budgeting is in place. It then takes a critical look at the adoption of reforms in a setting considered one of "best practice" in the developing world, the South African government. Its Department of Health budget is used as a representative example of the general path of reform progress in this setting. In looking at the budget's structure, it is apparent that the government has gradually moved from a purely line-itemized budget to a medium-term program budget and finally to a budget with performance-based elements in it—a progression that mirrors developments in other governments as well (in developed and developing countries, and in subnational and national governments).

The core question in this and other settings is this: Given the reforms over the past period, how close is the government to developing a true performance-based accountability system? (Or, as asked above: How well have reforms worked in introducing a results orientation into budgeting processes?) Considering the state of affairs in countries such as South Africa (as reflected in budget documents up to 2003), the answer is less than sanguine, for three reasons:

■ First, even though performance targets are now being developed, they are generally kept separate from the actual budget (in South Africa as well as in countries such as Malaysia and Singapore, and in most U.S. states), which undermines their legitimacy and entrenches a "specialization" and "separation" culture common in governments (in which planners, development experts, and performance-minded evaluators do certain tasks and accountants and budgeters do other tasks, never to communicate across their professional boundaries).

■ Second, performance information in the South African case suffers weaknesses commonly alluded to in the literature related to other settings. For example, outputs are confused with inputs and outcomes remain unconsidered. Targets appear to have been technocratically identified and thus lack real-world value. Targets are poorly detailed, making actual measurement unlikely. It is unclear exactly how the targets will be reached, with no connection between outputs and activities in some cases and arguments as to why poor service could lead to target achievement in others. This information fails to create results-oriented bottom lines, leaving political representatives and managers no reason or incentive to meet them.

■ Third, and possibly most important, is the lack of a relational design in the budget itself. Even where effective targets are provided, the budgets in South Africa and many other nations moving toward this kind of system commonly fail to specify who should be accountable for these results, who should hold them accountable, and how. Very little thought appears to have been given to the process of institutionalizing political or managerial accountability for the targets identified in these budgets. Where results-oriented mechanisms create accountability relationships in the personnel system (such as where chief executives are appointed on the basis of performance contracts), they are typically disconnected from the results-oriented elements in the budgeting process.

The final section of this chapter provides some pointers for reform progress, building on the marked improvements made in countries such as South Africa and addressing some of the problems still observed. The discussion centers on a proposed budget structure that links fiscal allocations to clearly defined and measurable performance targets at the project level and identifies those accountable for outputs (managers) and for outcomes (political representatives)—all in one document. The proposed approach is seen as a progression beyond the current reform position toward the entrenchment of results-oriented accountability in governments (with a series of bottom lines that have meaning, and that can be evaluated and enforced).

Introduction

Results-oriented or performance-based budgeting has been gradually adopted as a key public sector reform in developing and developed countries alike. Examples include Australia and Malaysia (Xavier 1998), Organisation for Economic Co-operation and Development (OECD) countries generally (Shand 1998), commonwealth countries (Kaul 1997), and Singapore (Jones 1998). The reform is adopted so as to transform public budgeting systems from an input and output orientation to an output and outcome orientation, introducing a new results-oriented accountability into public organizations. It does this by changing the rules of budgeting—influencing both budgetary processes and budgetary roles. "The use of performance measurement in budgeting means changes in governments' operations, personnel, structures, and even cultures" (Wang 2000, 113). These changes are designed to alter how budgets are developed, who does what in the budgetary process, and how the budget influences those allocating or receiving money through it. Through such influences, it is argued, the reforms focus public officials on results and performance, with new results-oriented accountability relationships and incentives. Ammons (2002) asserts, "[This] accountability argument for performance measurement is powerful and persuasive. How can government be truly accountable if it only tracks the dollars moving through its system and barely mentions the services rendered through the use of these resources?" (344).

The new accountability relationships entrenched in performance-based budgeting link the performance of political representatives and managers to budget allocations, as shown in the results chain in figure 2.1 (Shah 2000).

In the figure, results-oriented or performance-based budgeting can be seen to focus governments on the right-hand side of the results chain. Concern for results requires representatives to consider what kinds of outcomes and impacts government will target as it spends citizens' money. A political results orientation thus involves the definition of specific policy goals or objectives, often referred to as outcomes. An outcome example, related to education provision, could relate to an increase in the pass rate of school-leaving students (with the impact being improved quality of the workforce and economic growth).[2] The budget is then used as a vehicle to allocate money on the basis of such an outcome goal, with representatives and administrators determining which kinds of activities, inputs, and projects are required to achieve the goal, and what kind of project-level performance targets (related to actual production) would most likely facilitate such achievement. These performance targets are communicated in terms of outputs, facilitating the measurement and evaluation of results toward the end of the budgetary cycle. Output examples could relate to the number of classes taught or other areas of production. At the end of the budgetary cycle the departmental manager would be responsible for showing whether outputs were met.

By introducing such a results-oriented approach, performance-based budgeting links the money coming into government with the results of government activities, through implicit and explicit performance-based contracts or agreements. These contracts or agreements show what citizens can expect from their political representatives (the outcome goals as communicated through plans), how government is going to get there (the programs, projects, and activities it intends to fund), how much it will cost (the inputs), and what administrative entities are expected to produce with their funds (the output goals). Such information is the basis of new accountability relationships, as reflected in budget documents, which influence the incentives, that budgeters face, in particular motivating legislators, executives, and program and project managers to be more results and performance oriented.

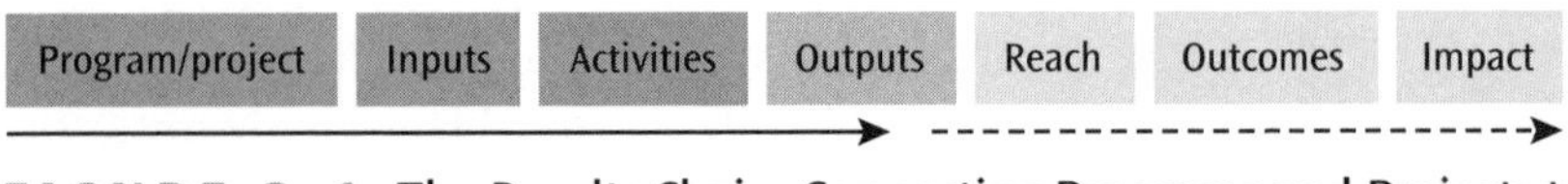

FIGURE 2.1 The Results Chain, Connecting Programs and Projects to Outputs and to Outcomes

Performance-based budgeting is meant to influence allocation behavior, so that new allocations are based on results. Objective information on output achievement and implications for outcomes improves planning and decision making at the legislative and executive levels and enhances the accountability allocation resource for decisions (Broom and McGuire 1995; Martin 1997). Civil society can observe how the process toward outcomes is progressing, who is to blame for failures along the way (whether the problem is slow output production or poor planning), and how political representatives treat different levels of performance (whether rewards and redress are offered, and whether funds are allocated for improved performance). In short, performance-based budgeting institutions involve "contractual" commitments that bind politicians to communicated outcomes and the provision of information about those outcomes and their generation. In so doing, they produce a results-oriented accountability for executive and legislative decision makers. This kind of results-oriented political accountability demands that political leaders

- set outcome goals
- link allocations to these goals (ensuring a logical sequence from outputs to outcomes in programs and projects funded)
- have the information to enforce achievement of output targets
- have the incentive to actually enforce achievement of output targets
- are called to account for both the amount of money they spend and their results (how well their administration produces outputs and realizes the achievement of outcomes)

Performance-based budgeting is also meant to influence how managers view their roles in the budget process (and how they manage). In complete form, performance-based budgeting gives managers significant flexibility in overseeing their resources while holding them accountable for program results and promising reward or redress on the strength of such results. Formal methods of reward include increased transfer authority, increased contract authority, reduced budget oversight, gain sharing, or a pay bonus for key staff members. The promise of reward or redress also extends to potential civil society responses to strong or weak managers whose performances are now open to public scrutiny. These reward and redress options are meant to bind managers to promises of performance in the budget, and to provide an incentive for managers to change their approach to management, adopt new methods of providing services, and become more results oriented and efficient. This kind of results-oriented managerial accountability demands that managers

■ set targets (for outputs and efficiency)
■ understand that money is linked to targets
■ are called to account for both the amount of money they spend and their performance in terms of targets

Progress

As argued, the potential for a new accountability approach has led many countries to attempt to adopt results-oriented or performance-based budgeting in the last decade. South Africa's progress toward results-oriented or performance-based budgeting is representative of best practices in the developing world, with its increased emphasis (through legislation such as the 1999 Public Finance Management Act) on "outputs alongside spending plans" providing "a basis for assessing the value for money of spending and its alignment with government objectives" (National Treasury 2002, 2).[3] The progress is evident when examining changes to the structure of the budget document and the kind of accountability relationships developed through such changes. This structure has progressed from reflecting traditional line items to showing programs and subprograms and performance targets. This progression has been fairly gradual (phased in over 5 years as of 2003, when this assessment was done), with the National Treasury choosing to adopt an incremental reform approach similar to that of Singapore (Jones 1998; Schick 1998).

A Starting Point: The Traditional Line-Item Format

As in many developing and developed countries, the South African government traditionally structured its budgets to show money spent by line item. Table 2.1 is an example, showing the national Department of Health's 2001/02 appropriations.

The line-item budget entrenches a process-oriented accountability in the public sector, focusing administrators on the inputs to which money is allocated (such as equipment) and the process of disbursement. This control emphasis developed in the early part of the century in tandem with theories of bureaucratic government and as a response to problems of financial irregularity in government, as explained by Mikesell (1995, 165):

> Traditional budgets emphasize control of fund use and have not been structured to facilitate resource-allocation decisions. That emphasis exists largely because public budgeting emerged in a period where concern was, purely and simply, prevention of theft.... Modern governments have moved beyond that stage, but too much of budgeting remains in that old orientation.

TABLE 2.1 South African Department of Health Budget, Main Appropriations for 2001–2, by Line Item (thousands of rand)

Expenditure item	Appropriation
Personnel	152,000
Administrative	78,207
Inventories	100,203
Equipment	18,395
Land and buildings	16,200
Professional and special services	69,628
Transfer payments	6,176,736
Total expenditure	6,611,369

Source: Adapted from National Treasury 2002.

As mentioned by Mikesell, while the line-item approach facilitates control, it also thwarts the development of a results-oriented accountability, in which the following kinds of questions are relevant: What is government doing with the money it receives? What are the goals of government interventions? Is government reaching its goals, or at least moving toward achievement of them? How much money is government spending, and is it spending more than is needed to achieve its goals? Who is responsible for spending behavior and outcomes? Such questions increasingly inform new accountability concepts in the public sector. The first three questions relate to how money is being translated into services, an issue that the line-item budget fails to address. It is impossible, for example, for citizens to see how much money the government is spending on HIV/AIDS prevention and treatment (a key national policy area) or what kinds of new facilities are being built to facilitate the expansion of health care service. The fourth question relates to spending efficiency, and again the line-item budget is found wanting, providing no means of assessing how well money is spent. The fifth question relates to the *who* of a basic accountability structure: Who is held accountable for expenditures in the Health Department? The line-item budget again provides no information to facilitate effective accountability.

The Program Budget: An Advancement

A generally accepted first step beyond the line-item budget involves identifying who is spending money and on what. The move to program budgeting in the U.S. states reflected such a step, as did the 1990s' move toward reporting budgets in terms of spending agencies and programs in countries such as Australia, Malaysia, and Singapore. The focus of program budgeting was (and is) the identification of planning and spending objectives, and the budget is seen as a statement of policy—representing the combined and goal-directed activities of the many interdependent parts of complex public organizations. Through it one can see who is spending public resources (the department or agency given funds) and what they are spending the money on (the programs to which resources are allocated).

In the latter half of the 1990s, with the introduction of the medium-term expenditure framework (MTEF) reforms, the South African government began restructuring its budget format to show the programs toward which its departments were allocating funds. Table 2.2 provides an example of this kind of reporting over the medium term.

The budget in table 2.2 constitutes an improvement from the line-item budget in that it allows the broad identification of how government is spending its money (over a medium-term period). In the case of the South African Department of Health three large programs are identified: administration, strategic health, and health service delivery. Within these large programs various subprograms are identified. In the strategic health program, there are six subprograms (or projects/activity areas) through which the government is spending money on HIV/AIDS prevention or treatment: HIV/AIDS (nongovernmental organizations [NGOs]), the Government AIDS Action Plan (NGOs), the South African National AIDS Council, the HIV/AIDS Conditional Grant, Love Life, and the South African AIDS Vaccine Initiative. In this budget structure the amount spent on HIV/AIDS prevention and eradication as a percentage of the entire health budget (to assess the importance of the policy area) is 5 percent. This calculation was impossible to make in the line-item budget and certainly enhances budgetary accountability. In the health service delivery program, one can identify three more specific projects: disease prevention and control, hospital services, and non-personnel health services. Specific activities within each subprogram allow even greater insight into what the department is doing with its allocation—in hospital services, for example, the department is (among other things) constructing hospitals in Durban and Pretoria.

This kind of budget shows significant progress toward the achievement of results-oriented accountability in the public sector (the goal driving much public sector reform). It suggests that the department has conceptualized its operations in terms of what it does, rather than what inputs it uses (as reflected in the line-item budget). This kind of conceptualization forms the basis of linking appropriations with performance in programs, projects, and activities. The budget shows, for example, that 50 million rand is allocated

TABLE 2.2 The 2001–2 South African Health Department Budget: Estimates per Program (thousands of rand)

Programs/subprograms	Revised appropriation 2001–2	2002–3 estimated appropriation	2003–4 estimated appropriation
Administration	–	–	–
Policy analysis	–	–	–
Strategic Health	853,426	996,765	1,113,827
District Health Systems			
Financial assistance to NGOs	–	–	–
Health Monitoring and Evaluation			
Medical Research Council	127,221	145,498	152,270
Health Systems Trust	2,000	2,000	2,000
South African Institute for Medical Research	287	287	287
Maternal, Child, and Women's Health			
Primary School Nutrition	582,411	582,411	582,411
Poverty Relief	10,000	12,000	15,000
South African Vaccine Producers	4,052	–	–
Financial Assistance to NGOs	100	310	350
Medicines Regulatory Affairs			
Medicines Control Council	–	–	–
Mental Health and Substance Abuse			
Financial Assistance to NGOs	1,000	1,377	1,410
HIV/AIDS and Tuberculosis			
South African Tuberculosis Association	25	–	–
HIV/AIDS (NGOs)	12,190	50,500	43,250
Government AIDS Action Plan (GAAP) (NGOs)	22,357	–	–
South African National AIDS Council	10,000	10,000	15,000
HIV/AIDS Conditional Grant	54,198	157,209	266,576
Love Life	25,000	25,000	25,000
Tuberculosis—Financial Assistance to NGOs	–	2,500	2,600
South African AIDS Vaccine Initiative	–	5,000	5,000
Medical Schemes			
Medical Schemes Council	2,585	2,673	2,673
Health Service Delivery	5,370,528	5,708,318	6,019,155
Disease Prevention and Control			
Council for the Blind	350	400	400
National Health Laboratory Services	260	394	407
Medical Legal	10,000	35,000	52,000
Hospital Services			
Hospital Rehabilitation	500,000	520,000	543,400

(continued)

TABLE 2.2 The 2001–2 South African Health Department Budget: Estimates per Program (in rand) (*continued*)

Programs/subprograms	Revised appropriation 2001–2	2002–3 estimated appropriation	2003–4 estimated appropriation
Hospital Construction— Durban Academic Hospital	103,800	–	–
Hospital Construction— Umtata Hospital	–	–	–
Hospital Construction— Pretoria Academic Hospital	50,000	70,000	90,000
National Tertiary Services	3,459,594	3,666,842	3,892,849
Health Professionals Training and Development	1,234,090	1,279,248	1,299,475
Hospital Management Improvement Grant	–	124,000	130,000
Non-personnel Health Services			
Compensation Commissioner	11,434	11,434	9,624
Environmental Health (NGOs)	–	–	–
Health Promotion (NGOs)	1,000	1,000	1,000
Total	**6,223,954**	**6,705,083**	**7,132,982**

Source: Adapted from National Treasury 2002.
– denotes not available.

to the construction of the Pretoria Academic Hospital in 2001/02. This allows political representatives and citizens to ask, "What is being done on the construction site with that money during that year?" In answering the question, one has the makings of a performance-based accountability agreement and the rudiments of an incentive system based on results rather than process and input management (as has traditionally been the case with the line-item budget).

Adding a Results/Performance Focus: Further Advancement

Following the example of countries such as Australia and the general progression toward a results-oriented, performance-based form of accountability, the South African National Treasury most recently added a third kind of table to its Estimates of National Expenditure, indicating the key outputs, indicators, and targets related to each program area. In 2001/02, departments were required to identify "targets for service delivery in main output areas" (National Treasury 2002, 1). This is an important step toward fulfilling the requirement in terms of the Public Finance Management Act (1 of 1999) that measurable objectives for main spending programs be submitted to Parliament (National Treasury 2002, 38). The performance measures are due to be formalized in the 2003 budget and are presented as a separate table in the 2001/02 Estimates of National Expenditure to show the progress of the reform. Table 2.3 presents the outputs, indicators, and targets as they relate to the strategic health program.

Some governments (including those of Malaysia and most of the U.S. states) are at the point of budget development suggested in table 2.3—attempting to introduce measurable goals that could be used to focus managerial and political behavior on results in already identified programs, subprograms, and activities. In these cases (as in the table), it is apparent that officials are being called to think about more than just the kinds of programs to which money is being allocated. They are being called to conceptualize the kinds of performance these programs should achieve.

In identifying outputs, output measures, or indicators and targets associated with what the South African Treasury calls *subprogrammes,* managers are starting to provide more information that facilitates results-oriented accountability. As part of the HIV/AIDS prevention initiative, for example, the government has identified the number of condoms distributed as an important indicator of performance and has committed to provide 472 million to citizens annually by 2004/05. When such commitments are open to evaluation and enforcement, they constitute effective levers for the development of results-oriented incentives and accountability mechanisms in the public sector. Table 2.3 thus provides detail to the budget that further aids the progress of reform toward results-oriented or performance-based accountability. The progress is marked, when one considers how much more information is provided in table 2.3 than is available in table 2.1 (and thus in traditional line-item budgets).

Problems

Governments around the world typically find their reforms lying somewhere along the line stretching from conventional line-item budgets, to program budgets, to budgets in which performance information is included. The South African budget reform progress, as evidenced in changes (or additions) to budget publications (such as the Estimates of National Expenditure), has advanced to a point where the government now has all three types of budgets reported in one place—line item, program type, and performance type (National Treasury 2002). This position is similar to that of

TABLE 2.3 Key Outputs, Indicators, and Targets Related to Strategic Health Allocations in South Africa

Strategic health programs

Subprogram	Output	Output measure/indicator	Target
District Health Systems	Improved equity in access to primary health care services	Proportion of primary health care facilities that render the full package of essential services	Full implementation by 2003/04
	Fully functional clinics and community health centers	Number of existing and new facilities that have water, sanitation, electricity, and roads	All facilities to have services by 2003/04
	Primary health care delivery by local government regulated by service agreements	Number of municipalities rendering comprehensive health services and with service agreements with provinces	Service agreements to be signed by September 2002
Health Monitoring and Evaluation	Full implementation of district health information system	Proportion of districts implementing the health information system	100% by 2004/05
Maternal, Child, and Women's Health	Improved immunization coverage	Number of cases of indigenous measles	Indigenous measles eliminated
		Immunization coverage of 1-year-olds	90% coverage of 1-year-olds by 2004 (minimum 80% in each province)
		Schools visited for routine school vaccination	90% coverage by 2004

Improved child health	Provinces implement the National Plan of Action for Children and Integrated Management of Childhood Illnesses Strategy	Implementation in all nine provinces
	Prevalence of wasting and stunting among children, and being underweight for their age among children under 6	Reduce prevalence of wasting from 2.6% to 1%, stunting from 23% to 15%, and under-weight children from 9% to 5% by 2004
Improved youth and adolescent health	Guidelines for youth and adolescent health published and distributed	Guidelines implemented in all provinces
	Teenage pregnancy rate	Reduce teenage pregnancies
	Substance abuse rates among adolescents	Reduce substance abuse
Improved women's health and reduced maternal mortality	Number of districts that have implemented the national program for cervical and breast cancer awareness and screening	Program implemented in all districts by 2004
	Number of clinics that have implemented antenatal clinic protocols	Antenatal clinic protocols implemented by all facilities by 2004

(continued)

43

TABLE 2.3 Key Outputs, Indicators, and Targets Related to Strategic Health Allocations in South Africa (*continued*)

Strategic health programs

	Output	Output measure/indicator	Target
		Number of districts with intersectoral plans to tackle the causes of poverty and poor nutrition	All districts to implement intersectoral action
		Legislation to ensure food fortification	Legislation in place by 2002
HIV/AIDS and Tuberculosis	Improved strategies to deal with the HIV/AIDS epidemic	Incidence of HIV	Leveling off of epidemic with fall in number of infected under 20-year-olds
		Cases of sexually transmitted infections effectively treated in public and private sectors	50% of cases treated effectively by 2001
		Condoms distributed	472 million annually by 2004/05
		Development of packages of affordable care and support for infected and affected persons	Packages available nationally

44

Strengthen the tuberculosis program	Cure rate	85% in new smear positive cases
	Smear conversion rate (sputum test change from positive to negative)	Achieve smear conversion rate of at least 85% in new cases by December 2003
	Expansion of short course programme on directly observed treatment	Short courses in all districts
	Percentage decline in Multidrug-resistant tuberculosis	Reduce Multidrug-resistant tuberculosis to less than 1% in all new cases
Essential Drugs Lists and Standard Treatment Guidelines for all levels of health service delivery	Completion of Essential Drugs List for primary health care	December 2002

Source: Adapted from National Treasury 2002.

many U.S. states and countries such as Malaysia, where traditional and new budget approaches exist side by side (OPPAGA 1997; Xavier 1998). Problems still exist in such situations, however, which limit the potential of such mixed-budgeting systems to effect the achievement of a true performance-based accountability system.

There are three main areas in which reforms, as generally adopted in South Africa and other similar settings, are still problematic:

1. Budgets still do not provide a clear link between performance and allocation, limiting any results-oriented accountability connections in budgets.
2. Performance measures are especially problematic and do not constitute an effective basis for results identification, measurement, and management.
3. The budgets still fail to identify who is responsible for performance and resource use, making it difficult to know who is accountable.

What Is the Basis of Accountability? The Money/Results Connection

At the core of a results-oriented accountability approach are assumptions that managers understand that money is linked to targets, that political representatives have the information to impose output targets, and that political representatives have the incentive to actually enforce achievement of output targets (being accountable for linked outcomes). All three of these important requirements are unmet when budgets fail to effectively connect money to results, as is the case in South Africa and in many other examples of performance-based budgeting reform. In situations where the performance part of the budget is kept separate from the money part of the budget (as in South Africa, where allocation amounts are included in the line-item budget presentation in table 2.1 and the summary of estimates per program in table 2.2 but not in the table 2.3, the table on key outputs, indicators, and targets), neither political representatives nor managers are given a clear message to connect results and allocations. This problem is worsened by the fact that the programs identified in the summary of transfers and subsidies per program do not match the programs identified in the table of key outputs, indicators, and targets—limiting the ability to match performance targets with allocations. Examples from the South African Department of Health budgets include the following:

- Medicines Regulatory Affairs is listed as a program in the summary of estimates but is not listed in the table on key outputs, indicators, and targets.

- District Health Systems has zero allocations, but specific outputs are identified for it.[4]
- Pharmaceutical Policy and Planning is listed as a subprogram in the table on key outputs, indicators, and targets but has no allocation in the table showing program allocations.

The poor connection between actual allocations and performance targets in so-called performance-based budgets is also evident in Malaysia. The government has various budget documents, with the main appropriations document showing limited performance data and the separate Programme and Performance Budget Estimates Book used as a source of information on the programs and activities of ministries, departments, and statutory bodies of the federal government for each budget year. "Parliamentarians are the main users of the book gathering information and explanations of all major Programmes and Activities carried out by Ministries/Departments and Statutory Bodies that receive allocation for operating expenditure from the Federal Government. This book is a supporting document to the Federal Budget Book that is presented annually in October to Parliament" (Treasury of Malaysia 2002, 1).

Separating details of funding from performance measures has the effect of de-emphasizing the importance of results, as managers continue to view the results emphasis as an add-on instead of the core focus of the budget. Managers and political representatives in such situations are likely to continue focusing on allocations control instead of performance—especially when their internal accounting systems are more conducive to line itemization than to performance-based budgeting, which is commonly the case, or when internal and external audit and lending agents continue to focus on questions of expenditure control instead of performance. Separating the question of how well money is spent from how money is spent also negates the development of managerial incentives necessary for a results-oriented accountability structure. The budget does not show how much money is allocated to the achievement of individual outputs, making it difficult to hold political representatives or managers accountable—and limiting any kind of results-oriented incentives associated with allocation behavior. This is the case with HIV/AIDS and tuberculosis, where funds are allocated to various programs in the summary of estimates table, and specific targets are identified in the table on key outputs, indicators, and targets, but no reference is given to link individual programs (and responsible agencies) with individual targets.

A final consequence of introducing results information separately from actual allocations is the entrenchment of a specialization and separation culture common in governments (in which planners, development experts, and performance-minded evaluators do certain tasks and accountants and budgeters do other tasks, never communicating across their boundaries). This kind of culture has been known to limit the role of planners in local government planning and budgeting reforms (Andrews 2002) and of development experts in MTEF-type reforms in Africa.[5] When performance targets are not directly connected to allocations in the budget document and process, personnel working on monetary allocations lack incentive to engage with personnel working on performance management issues.

What Is the Basis of Accountability? Problems with Identifying Results

Even where performance measures can be related to actual projects in the South African case, there is a question as to whether the results identified can actually stimulate a results-oriented accountability in government. Wang (2000, 109) states, "Performance measurement depends on developing clear, consistent organizational goals." His comment is universally agreed upon, with the general sentiment that results-oriented accountability demands the identification of results that are relevant, clear, and measurable. In many cases (including the South African one) the results identified do not meet these criteria—outcomes are unconsidered, outputs are confused with inputs, and targets lack a real-world value and are poorly detailed and disconnected from activities and projects needed to achieve them.

The first observation to be made from table 2.3 is that there are no outcomes. As shown in figure 2.1 (the results chain, connecting programs and projects to outputs to outcomes), outcomes are the goals of policy that usually appear in political manifestos and reflect political goals. These are the goals that are relevant in creating results-oriented political accountability (as they relate to the election manifestos that politicians espouse). If such goals are not included somewhere in the budget, it will be impossible to hold political representatives accountable—whether they are members of the executive in a parliamentary system (the minister of health in South Africa, for example) or the presidential cabinet in a presidential system.

The second observation to be made from table 2.3 is that the outputs identified are very often questionable. While it is understood that the definition of output is itself variable, it appears as if many of the outputs identified in the table are in fact inputs in the production process. These outputs seem to be technocratically identified, relating to the implementation of systems or the development of guidelines. They may seem like outputs within a bureaucratic process, but they have no such meaning in a broader service environment (where they are inputs into the production process). Such goals are not only poorly defined, they are also socially irrelevant and fail to focus managers on the external production of services and on performance within such context. Such problematic goals include the following:

- In the health monitoring and evaluation subprogram, the output identified is "full implementation of district health information system," which relates more to an input in a production process than an output of one. An output of such implementation would involve improved information access or ability to evaluate and monitor district health provision—not simply the implementation of a system.
- In the maternal, child, and women's health subprogram, the output measure or indicator identified is "guidelines for youth and adolescent health published and distributed." These are once again inputs into a production process, not outputs of one. The measure fails to capture the essence of youth and adolescent health responsibilities and cannot be expected to enhance accountability for achieving improved youth and adolescent health.
- In the maternal, child, and women's health subprogram, the output "improved women's health and reduced maternal mortality" is associated with four indicators: number of districts that have implemented the national program for cervical and breast cancer awareness and screening, number of clinics that have implemented antenatal clinic protocols, number of districts with intersectoral plans to tackle the causes of poverty and poor nutrition, and legislation to ensure food fortification. Implementing programs and protocols and developing plans and legislation are not outputs that show improved women's health and reduced maternal mortality. Indeed, the literature shows that giving managers such procedural goals can take their focus off actual service provision.[6]

The third observation one can make about the performance targets is that they generally lack the kind of detail that makes them measurable and evaluable. Outputs, measures, and targets typically do not relate the actual measure, quantity, location, date, cost per unit, or quality measure relevant for evaluation. The output "improved child health" is associated with an appropriately detailed output measure and target, "prevalence of wasting and stunting among children, and being underweight for their age among children under 6," and "reduce prevalence of wasting from 2.6 percent to 1 percent, stunting from 23 percent to 15 percent, and underweight children from 9 percent to 5 percent by 2004." Other measures fail to meet this kind of standard. An example relates to the output "improved youth and adolescent health," which is associated with two measures: "teenage pregnancy rate" and "substance abuse rates amongst adolescents." The relevant targets are "reduce teenage pregnancies" and "reduce substance abuse." These output measures and indicators lack the detail necessary to give them meaning or to make them effective vehicles for creating results-oriented accountability profiles. Questions managers could ask when being evaluated on the targets, as written, include the following: In which population groups was the teenage pregnancy rate meant to drop? By how much was it meant to decline? By when was it meant to decrease? Substance abuse rates declined for some substances, but not others—but we were just targeting broadly, were we not?

A final problem with most of the outputs, indicators, and targets in the Department of Health's budget is that they are not meaningfully linked to any kind of activity or project (a point similar to that discussed earlier, related to the money/results disconnect). In a number of cases outputs, indicators, and targets seem totally unrelated, leaving one to question exactly what the department is aiming at (and in fact what they are doing). In other cases the outputs identified appear generic and do not seem to relate to what the department is doing, suggesting that managers have not developed unique and relevant measures and targets that they are indeed focusing on. In these cases one has to ask what meaning the performance measures have, even internally, and to question the potential such measures have to focus managers on results:

- Under HIV/AIDS and Tuberculosis, an indicator is "cases of sexually transmitted infections effectively treated in public and private sectors" with a target being 50 percent of cases treated effectively by 2001. What is meant by "cases of sexually transmitted infections" and "effective treatment"? A more applied measure would state what kind of infections are being targeted and with what kinds of treatments.
- Under HIV/AIDS and Tuberculosis, an output is "improved strategies to deal with the HIV/AIDS epidemic," an indicator is "incidence of HIV," and a target is "leveling off of epidemic with fall in number of infected under 20-year-olds." The major problem is that the incidence of HIV is not necessarily associated with good medical service. It is possible that the epidemic could level off (with a decline in HIV-positive cases) because of deaths in cases where the disease was first reported in previous years.

When measures are vague, technocratic, and unrelated to results, they have limited potential to stimulate a results-oriented accountability. This is because they fail to create a results-oriented bottom line that is relevant to the activities and mission of the organization, that can be measured, and that can be enforced. Managers lack the incentive to produce results because the results identified are weak, often unrelated to activities, and poorly detailed. "Performance measurement" such as this "produces information that confuses, rather than reinforces, decision makers and the public" (Wang 2000, 103).

Who Is Accountable?

The third area in which the South African situation suffers weakness (also common in other cases) is in the relational side of performance-based accountability. Even if money is connected to performance and performance measures are of a high standard, one still needs to know who is accountable for performance (and who will hold them accountable and how) before a performance-based accountability system can be said to exist.

The South African government so far has failed to show these kinds of details in its budgets. Under HIV/AIDS and Tuberculosis, for example, the following are identified as fund recipients: the South African Tuberculosis Association HIV/AIDS (NGOs), the Government AIDS Action Plan (GAAP) (NGOs), the South African National AIDS Council HIV/AIDS Conditional Grant, Love Life, Tuberculosis—financial assistance to NGOs, and the South African AIDS Vaccine Initiative. The following are among the output targets identified: "leveling off of (HIV) epidemic with fall in number of infected under 20-year-olds," "50 percent of (sexually transmitted disease) cases treated effectively by 2001," and "472 million (condoms distributed) annually by 2004–5." In trying to connect the individual projects and cost centers with targets, the public is left asking, "Who is responsible for which targets?" and "If one of the targets is not met, which project manager is responsible?" These questions show that the budget effectively fails to create an organizational bottom line because it does not identify who is accountable for generating results at different points in the organization, or in the public production process.

The failure of the budget to identify or affirm accountability relationships in countries such as South Africa is curious, because such countries often have civil service policies that require chief executives (and other senior appointees) to be hired on the basis of performance contracts. The national civil service reforms are focused on a goal similar to that of the budget reforms: "To build a performance culture in the civil service, starting with the top management echelons" (Fraser-Moleketi 2000). Furthermore, the civil service reforms have required that (since 2000) "all managers sign performance contracts aligned to appropriate reward structure" (Fraser-Moleketi 2000). The civil service performance contracts and reward structures are seemingly unrelated to the performance-based budgeting exercises, however, with no reference in the Estimates of National Expenditure to managerial performance contracts and no in-budget identification of such contracts. Furthermore, the Estimates of National Expenditure provide no guidance as to who will measure performance and enforce targets (or what mechanisms will be used to do so). There is also no political performance accountability link (and no outcome targets have been developed).

No one is identified in the budget as being accountable for results and no one is identified as having the role of holding agents accountable. These factors make it impossible to hold anyone accountable for results.

Points for Proceeding

The example of recent budget reform in South Africa shows that—even with positive reform progress—a best-practice government can still face problems in the move to develop results-oriented bottom lines and accountability constructs in their budgets. Although the budget process has changed significantly in the past five years, it is still unlikely to provide the basis for performance-based accountability in the public sector. What are the next steps for a country such as South Africa, and pointers for countries behind South Africa in performance-based budgeting reform?

The aim of reforms such as those in South Africa is to change the institutional constructs influencing the nature of public sector accountability. In the words of the South African Minister of Public Service and Administration, such reforms are intended to "build a performance culture" (Fraser-Moleketi 2000) or at least to introduce incentives that focus individuals on performance in the public sector.[7] To continue reforms and stimulate the development of such a performance-based culture or of performance-based incentives, budget reformers should think about the following points for progress:

- Mainstream performance budgets by linking allocations to results requirements.
- In developing performance criteria, ensure relevance, readability, and realism.
- Clarify accountability relationships by creating results-oriented bottom lines.
- Make accountability relationships enforceable by creating appropriate institutions.

These four points were all considered in developing table 2.4, a proposed budget structure that links fiscal allocations to clearly defined and measurable performance targets at the project, program, and departmental levels and identifies those accountable for outputs (managers) and for outcomes (political representatives)—all in one document.

Mainstream Performance Budgets by Linking Allocations to Results Requirements

The first problem identified with the South African budget as it stands in 2002 (and with budgets in countries such as Malaysia and Singapore) is that the performance element is separate from the actual allocations part of the budget. It is difficult to assess how much money is being allocated to the production of which outputs. This is corrected in table 2.4, where obvious connections are shown between budgetary allocations, the department, program, subprogram, and project/activity in which allocations are to be spent, and the output targets associated with each entity in the public production process. The spending entities identified are those directly responsible for outputs.[8] Entity identities and outputs are broken down in a way conducive to performance management in hierarchical structures (like public organizations), with project or activity areas identified as responsible for the production of specific outputs (such as the condom distribution project) and tied to subprograms in which officials are responsible for overseeing output production in related project or activity areas (such as HIV/AIDS prevention) and then to programs where officials oversee related subprograms (such as strategic health programs) and finally, to the department, where the head is responsible for overseeing performance in all programs (as in the Department of Health).

Table 2.4 mainstreams a performance-type accountability by tying budget allocations directly to results requirements. This kind of approach mirrors the way in which countries such as Australia insert performance requirements into their standard budgets, fostering an understanding that results and finances are tied, and that results should be considered as centrally in the management process as basic disbursement control. Consider, for example, a segment from the health budget in Australia (shown in table 2.5).

The small section from the Australian budget shows exactly which program money is going to the Department of Health and Ageing over a medium-term period. It then ties the allocations to an explanation of the program which, if read carefully, sets out output requirements fairly directly (building new facilities, for example). Furthermore, the actual allocations are connected, through the production targets, to broader social outcomes—

TABLE 2.4 Proposed Results-Oriented Budget Format for the South African HIV/AIDS Program, 2001–2* (thousands of rand)

DEPARTMENT Program Subprogram Project/activity	2001/02		2002/03		2003/04		Official responsible	Related outcomes
	Budget (in rand)	Output target: Quantity, location, date	Budget (in rand)	Output target: Quantity, location, date	Budget (in rand)	Output target: Quantity, location, date		
Strategic Health	853,426	All outputs targeted in the program	996,765	All outputs targeted in the program	1,113,827	All outputs targeted in the program	Ms. G	All related to program
HIV/AIDS prevention	*62,000*	*A and B below*	*124,000*	*A and B below*	*169,000*	*A and B below*	*Mrs. A*	*outcome targets 1 and 2 below*
					70,000		Mr. B	
Condom distribution	30,000	A. 200 million condoms to be distributed with learning pamphlets through public clinics and hospitals annually by March 2002 (at least half distributed in rural areas).	55,000	A. 350 million condoms to be distributed with learning pamphlets through public clinics and hospitals annually by March 2003 (at least half distributed in rural areas).		A. 472 million condoms to be distributed with learning pamphlets through public clinics and hospitals annually by March 2004 (at least half distributed in rural areas).		1

Mother-to-child HIV/AIDS treatment	32,000	B. All pregnant women tested for HIV/AIDS in the nation by December 2002. 90% of HIV positive women (anticipated = 5,000) treated with antiretrovirals on a daily basis for entire period of pregnancy by March 2002.	69,000	B. All pregnant women tested for HIV/AIDS in the nation. All HIV positive women (anticipated = 7,000) treated with antiretrovirals on a daily basis for entire period of pregnancy by (and from) March 2003.	99,000	B. All pregnant women tested for HIV/AIDS in nation. All HIV positive women (anticipated = 9,000) treated with antiretrovirals on a daily basis for entire period of pregnancy over entire period.	Dr. X	2
Department of Health	Whole budget	All outputs targeted in the department	Whole budget	All outputs targeted in the department	Whole budget	All outputs targeted in the department	Minister of health	All

(continued)

TABLE 2.4 Proposed Results-Oriented Budget Format for the South African HIV/AIDS Program, 2001–2* *(continued)*

DEPARTMENT Program *Subprogram* Project/activity	2001–2		2002–3		2003–4		
	Budget (in rand)	Output target: Quantity, location, date	Budget (in rand)	Output target: Quantity, location, date	Budget (in rand)	Output target: Quantity, location, date	Official responsible	Related outcomes

Outcomes Targets:

1. Citizens engaging in safe sex increases from 50% to 60% by March 2003 and to 70% by March 2004.

2. Number of HIV infections among newborn babies declines from 5,000 per year to 1,000 per year in 2002 (evaluated March 2002) and to 500 per year in 2003 (evaluated March 2003) and to 100 per year in 2004 (evaluated March 2004).

Impact (longer-term outcome):

Decrease in incidence of new HIV cases from 10,000 per annum in 2002 to 1,000 per annum in 2005.

Evaluation method, evaluator identity, date of evaluation publication:[a]

Annual survey (to be conducted in early March each year) of sexually active citizens, by HSRC, with results submitted to Auditor General's Office and published by April 30 of each year.

Babies' HIV status tested at birth and recorded on birth records at each public facility, examined in March each year by Auditor General's Office, with report issued by April 30 each year.

Recorded death status, examined in March 2005 by Auditor General's Office, with report issued by April 30 of that year.

Note: *The table's detail is based upon, but not necessarily representative of, detail in National Treasury (2002). For example, money spent on HIV/AIDS is split into two programs (and projects within such) in this table, with funding to each calculated as a portion of the amount being spent in the various subprogram (123,745 in 2001–2, 247,709 in 2002–3, 354,826 in 2003–4). This kind of split is not the same as that in National Treasury (2002), but is offered as a more appropriate way of developing a performance-based budget—linking projects, finances, and targets more directly than in National Treasury (2002).

a. The issue of who pays for and manages evaluations is key to developing an effective results orientation.

TABLE 2.5 An Example of Program Identification in Australian Budgets, with Related Detail (in millions of Australian dollars)

Health and Ageing	2002–3	2003–4	2004–5
Better treatment for cancer patients	13.1	18.8	20.4

Explanation: "The Government will improve patient access to radiation oncology services, particularly in rural and regional areas, through building up to six new facilities outside the capital cities and funding their operation. Part of the funding will also be allocated to measures designed to attract and retain appropriately trained staff to the new facilities through the provision of ongoing professional education and training designed to keep staff up to date with international best practices."

Related outcomes: *Outcome 2:* Access through Medicare to cost-effective medical services, medicines, and acute health care for all Australians. *Outcome 9:* Knowledge, information, and training for developing better strategies to improve the health of all Australians.

Source: Commonwealth of Australia 2002.

enhancing the legitimacy of these political performance requirements. In this case, like the idea envisioned in table 2.4, the steps of allocating money, setting goals, evaluating goals, and rewarding or penalizing managers in the production hierarchy are unified into one budgeting process (rather than two disparate processes, one for budgeting and one for performance management). In so doing, performance is legitimized into the public production and management process.

Develop Performance Criteria Carefully, Ensuring Relevance, Readability, and Realism

Mainstreaming performance into the standard budget will facilitate performance-based accountability only if the performance goals and information are themselves useful and organizationally relevant, readable, and realistic. Berman (2002) stresses the importance of useful measures. Problems identified in the South African Department of Health outputs and indicators are typical of many governments and combine to limit their influence on managerial and political behavior. In HIV/AIDS care, for example, the output and indicator combination of "improved strategies to deal with the HIV/AIDS epidemic" and "incidence of HIV" do not combine to facilitate effective performance management. Effective targets identify outputs and outcomes that are relevant to the organization's mission and can be evaluated.

Table 2.4 shows output targets for a medium-term budget (with targets stepped up in each year) that meet all relevant criteria. They are directly tied to the projects (in the condom distribution project, for example, the output relates to specific numbers of condoms distributed—a production target linked directly to the project mission). The project is then related to an outcome target (in this case, an increase in the number of citizens engaging in safe sex), which would commonly be a related outcome of other projects and programs as well, and for which the departmental minister will ultimately be held responsible. Outcomes are then related to impacts (longer-term outcomes) such as "decrease in incidence of new HIV cases from 10,000 per annum in 2002 to 1,000 per annum in 2005." This kind of identification needs to be informed by an analysis of the organizational mission and structure, as well as an understanding of the meanings of terms such as inputs, outputs, and outcomes and the logical process of connection between all three. Standard literature defines inputs as resources invested in a process, program, or activity; outputs as the amount of work produced by a process, program, or activity; and outcomes as the extent to which stated objectives are met. Impacts could be defined as longer-term outcomes that relate to political promises at election time.

Figure 2.2 connects project choice, input use, outputs, outcomes, and impacts in a results chain as an exercise that forces identification of the logical progress of the public production and management process. Weak performance measures suggest either poor understanding of performance management or a lack of buy-in to the performance management idea. Working through the results chain is useful in both situations, because it assists managers who are used to a controlling approach to better understand the results concept and the process for achieving results, and it disciplines unwilling managers to consider target identification in a way that is immediately relevant to the organization's production process. The approach also facilitates easy explanation of targets and communication of the links between projects, programs, and the overall mission of the organization.

Because performance-based budgeting is critically linked to results-oriented management, the process of results targeting needs to be linked to other areas of management. Indeed, to ensure that results measures are realistic, it is imperative that officials perform a risk assessment when setting targets. A risk is anything that could jeopardize the achievement of an output or outcome. Asking the following kinds of questions helps identify risks: What could go wrong? How could we fail? What must go right for us to succeed? Where are we vulnerable? How could our operations be disrupted? What activities are most complex? On the basis of such questioning,

Sub-program	Inputs	Projects/activities	Outputs	Reach	Outcomes	Impact
HIV/AIDS/ STD prevention	62,000[a]					
	30,000	Condom distribution	350 million condoms to be distributed with "learning pamphlets" through public clinics and hospitals annually by March 2003 (at least half distributed in rural areas).	Citizens in rural and urban areas, through public facilities	Citizens engaging in safe sex increases from 50% to 80% by March 2004.	Decrease in incidence of new HIV cases from 10,000 per annum in 2002 to 1,000 per annum in 2005.
	32,000	Mother-to-child HIV/AIDS treatment	All pregnant women tested for HIV/AIDS in the nation by December 2002. 90% of HIV positive women (anticipated 5,000) treated with antiretrovirals on a daily basis for entire period of pregnancy by March 2002.	Citizens in rural and urban areas, through public facilities	Number of HIV infections among newborn babies declines from 5,000 per year to 1,000 per year in 2002 (evaluated March 2002) (and related in future years).	Decrease in incidence of new HIV cases from 10,000 per annum in 2002 to 1,000 per annum in 2005.

Note: This example's detail is developed without direct reference to the South African study, which lacks detail sufficient to identify the connection between inputs and outputs and outcomes.

a. Note calculation as per that in table 2.4.

FIGURE 2.2 Connecting Inputs, Outputs, and Outcomes in the Results Chain

officials can assess risk and identify control activities needed for managing the risk (as shown in table 2.6).

Assessing risk related to performance targets helps ensure that such targets are realistic and that they will be considered binding when the time comes for performance evaluation. Getting managers and executives (in the case of government these are often political appointees) to think about these threats up front should strengthen the targets themselves. It should also facilitate effective "managing for results" (whereby managers can focus on results and manage factors that threaten to yield poor performance). This kind of assessment is required in the Commonwealth of Virginia, where agencies complete internal assessments as part of the performance-budgeting process (Virginia Department of Planning and Budget 2002). In these assessments they identify risks related to external trends, internal process requirements, new legislation, and other factors.

Another step beyond identifying output and outcome goals should also be pointed out. It involves tying outputs and outcomes targets to efficiency and quality measures. These kinds of ties should strengthen management in the production process. It is the kind of link that should develop from internal control processes but go beyond to include an emphasis on alternative methods of production—with the goal being to reach targeted performance (with targeted quality) in the most cost-effective way (Andrews and Moynihan 2002). No such measures are incorporated in table 2.4, because of space considerations and also because this kind of identification comes after relevant, readable, and realistic outputs and outcomes have been identified.

TABLE 2.6 Assessing Risk in a Performance-Based Budgeting Approach

Outputs and outcomes	Risks	Control activities
List clearly defined and measurable outputs and outcomes	For each output and outcome, list all significant risks (likely to occur and with large potential impacts)	For each risk, list: 1. Actions taken to manage the risk, 2. Control activities which help to ensure that the actions to manage the risk are carried out properly and in a timely manner, 3. Sources of information, methods of communication, and monitoring activities

Make Accountability Relationships Obvious by Creating Results-Oriented Bottom Lines

A third pointer for countries in South Africa's position is this: To entrench performance-based accountabilities in a public organization, redefine relationships in the organization so as to reflect an emphasis on results.

Budgets and financial documents communicate the core responsibilities and accountability relationships in a public organization (Mikesell 1995). The important questions about accountability and responsibility are "By whom?" "To whom?" and "For what?" In standard budget formats (and indeed in the systems in place in countries such as South Africa) it is apparent that answers to these questions are unclear. (There are no references to specific accountability links in budget documents.) Where such relationships do exist, the "For what?" answer always reflects a control emphasis instead of a performance one. The emphasis on spending within budget is, for example, the dominant answer in most countries. In such instances, results targets and measures have limited influence on accountability structures, because specific individuals or organizational parts are not held accountable for them.

If performance-based budgets are to herald a new kind of accountability structure, governments need to replace the ex ante control emphasis in hierarchical public sector accountability structures with an ex post performance emphasis. This new emphasis lends itself to a hierarchical structure in which officials down the rungs of the organization are tied together by their performance in producing public goods. This is shown in table 2.4, for example:

1. Individuals in charge of specific projects are made accountable for the specific outputs of those projects. (Mr. B is responsible for the outputs identified in the condom distribution project, for example.)
2. Individuals in charge of subprograms are held accountable for output clusters produced in projects under their care. (Mrs. A is accountable for the outputs of the condom distribution and mother-to-child HIV/AIDS treatment projects, both of which fall under the subprogram HIV/AIDS prevention, for example.)
3. Individuals in charge of programs are held accountable for output clusters produced in them. (Ms. G, the head of the strategic health program, is held accountable for the outputs produced in the HIV prevention and HIV treatment subprograms, for example.)
4. The executive in charge (in this case, the minister) is accountable for all outputs, and the way outputs combine to affect outcomes (as, in the example, the bottom line of the budget shows the minister responsible for all outputs and outcomes).

By identifying officials accountable for results, the budget format in table 2.4 creates a series of bottom lines that should have the effect of making results-based accountability the driving form of accountability in public organizations. This identification becomes the basis of external accountability constructs—enabling legislators and citizens to see exactly which officials are responsible for producing which results. It also becomes the basis of internal accountability relationships, with officials connected by expectations of performance in the production process. This kind of relational accountability is important for better understanding individual roles in the performance-based organization—an understanding that also becomes the basis for managerial strategy. Figure 2.3 shows such a relational structure in a four-layer hierarchy.

The figure clearly shows the results connections between officials in a typical organization. If the officials at the top of the organizational hierarchy (the head of the political executive and the executive leadership) set policy based on targeted outcomes, they need to manage those responsible for the programs that are focused on achieving those outcomes. Program managers similarly need to manage the project managers appointed, hired, or contracted to produce specific outputs. Accountability relationships arise when program managers hold project managers accountable for producing specific outputs, ministers or secretaries similarly hold program managers accountable for output clusters related to the achievement of specific outcomes, and the president (or executive head) holds ministers

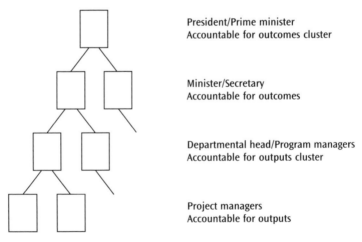

President/Prime minister
Accountable for outcomes cluster

Minister/Secretary
Accountable for outcomes

Departmental head/Program managers
Accountable for outputs cluster

Project managers
Accountable for outputs

FIGURE 2.3 Results-Based Accountability Relationships Inform Managerial Structures

or secretaries accountable for outcome production. In table 2.4, for example, the health minister would be held accountable annually for outcomes such as "citizens engaging in safe sex increases from 50 percent to 60 percent by March 2003 and to 70 percent by March 2003 and to 80 percent by March 2004" and for an impact at the end of an electoral cycle, "decline in HIV incidence."

Make Accountability Relationships Enforceable by Creating Appropriate Institutions

Having identified who is accountable for what and how accountability relationships interact in the production process, governments intent on introducing effective results-oriented accountability need to institutionalize processes by which accountability relationships are enforced. In particular, this involves institutionalizing

- internal and external performance evaluation
- performance management incentives
- avenues of political results accountability

Internal and External Performance Evaluation

In order to enforce performance-oriented accountability, it is vital that governments be able to evaluate performance. This means more than having measurable indicators, however (Wang 2000; Virginia Department of Planning and Budget 2002). It means identifying who will evaluate performance, when, how, and with what kind of evaluation distribution. The aim is to create incentives for managers to manage for performance and for politicians to take their outcome targets seriously. With such an aim in mind, there is a strong argument for independent, external evaluation of outputs and outcomes results. In table 2.4 outcomes results are slated for external evaluation by the Auditor General's Office, for example. One could also look to a dedicated office under the president to evaluate such results. This would make sense given that the president is the one responsible for checking ministerial performance (at least in this model). The keys are that the entity be created through legislated means (formally institutionalized) as independent of established departments, and that it have its own budget to be used exclusively for measuring and reporting on performance.

There is also a strong argument that results should be published at the same time as they are sent for executive analysis, to ensure transparency in the reward or redress offered by the executive. Outputs should be evaluated by independent agencies, but there is a rationale to hold such evaluation in-house as well. The rationale is simply that program managers' performance depends on project managers' performance (as in figure 2.3), and regular internal evaluation (say, quarterly) could highlight potential performance shortfalls in particular projects. In this way performance measurement facilitates performance-based management and organizational learning, as managers intervene to refocus their subordinates on the targets at hand.

Performance Management Incentives

A key argument in new institutionalism is that behavior changes when incentives created by institutions change (Poterba 1996). In most governments, officials—managers and politicians—are not given incentives to perform but are instead rewarded for fiscal prudence, discipline, and adherence to rules. To engage officials to produce results, it is vital that reward and redress structures be reset to create incentives that foster effective performance management (reorienting officials toward the production of targeted results). Performance management incentives have at least two dimensions: incentives for individuals to manage so as to maximize their own performance, and incentives for individuals to manage in relationship with others so as to maximize organizational performance. Prominent incentive mechanisms focused on both dimensions include pecuniary-based reward structures and moral suasion and civic pressure devices.

Pecuniary-based reward structures involve using formal contracts to tie individual or organizational compensation to performance. The South African government has such contracts in place for senior managers, but it does not appear to place these contracts in the context of organizational targets set out in the performance-based budget. This means that officials in only some layers of the organizational hierarchy face incentives to perform. This situation is problematic when considering the hierarchical nature of the public sector production process: If a program manager has a performance contract but those above or below her do not, it is virtually impossible for that official to manage across levels of the organization and ensure that results are produced.[9] In order to orient managers (and managerial relationships) toward performance, contracts need to be set throughout the organizational hierarchy, from the minister down. In terms of figure 2.3, this involves the president setting outcomes-based contracts with ministers or secretaries (in the U.S. system), while these officials set output cluster targets for program managers, who then set output targets for project managers. These contracts inform compensation decisions throughout the organization, with managerial welfare connected through the logical connection of results dependence (if a manager fails at the bottom of the hierarchy, she faces lower compensation, but her performance also affects the compensation of superiors). Such logical connection creates incentives for superiors to manage lower layers in the way most appropriate for producing performance, (allowing appropriate discretion while monitoring performance).

Similar contracts are in place in governments such as those of Florida and Virginia in the United States (OPPAGA 1997; Fuchs 1998; Virginia Department of Planning and Budget 2002).[10] The Virginia experience is generally considered best practice in the U.S. context, with individual contracts reinforced by organizational gain-sharing agreements—whereby departments producing results within budget are allowed to keep surplus funds and use them to benefit the entire organization. This kind of reward option creates incentives for individuals to work toward personal performance maximization and to contribute to departmentwide discussions of policy selection, production technique, and so forth—all with the focus on ensuring maximized performance. This kind of incentive appeals to the assumed budgetary discretion preference of bureaucratic managers who desire control over as much of their budget as possible (Kraan 1996).

The second kind of incentive mechanism used in relation to performance-based budgeting initiatives (in countries such as the United Kingdom and Malaysia) involves publicizing results commitments so as to effect a moral pressure on officials to perform. Mission and objective statements must be identified at all levels of the Malaysian government to state what services are offered and furnish a time frame for completion of them. Such statements are incorporated into a results-based budget as well as a client's charter, and are displayed prominently. The charter is described as having "encouraged a change in the mind-set of public officials, who are now required to search for more efficient and effective methods for the delivery of public services that satisfy customers" (Chiu 1997, 175). The changed mind-set has gone a long way in improving the performance of the Malaysian public sector, with officials having an incentive to perform as promised or face public questioning and discipline (Mohamad 1997). The Ugandan government, while far from adopting a performance-based budget, has also shown the effectiveness of civic interest in creating budgetary incentives. "Monthly transfers of public funds to districts are now reported in the main newspapers and broadcast on radio . . . transfers to primary education (are) displayed on public notice boards in each school and district center" (Reinikka 1999, 3). The results are clear, as reflected in a 1998 survey of the Ministry of Education budget, which "found major improvements in the flow of funds" (Reinikka 1999, 3).

Avenues of Political Results Accountability

Performance-based accountability is certainly enhanced by enforcing managerial bottom lines through pecuniary and moral suasion mechanisms. Performance-based accountability is further enhanced by creating effective avenues of political results accountability. In terms of table 2.4, this involves enforcing the ministerial bottom line, whereby ministers (or equivalent officials) are held accountable for departmental performance (especially regarding outcomes). These avenues also relate to enforcement of presidential performance—where the president is held accountable for disciplining poorly performing members of the executive, and for the way she manages the executive (and the outcomes it produces).

Avenues for political accountability at the local level are often grafted onto legislation pertaining to local governance. Legislation such as the South African Local Government Transition Acts of 1993 and 1996 spell out the responsibilities of political representatives in local governments, for example. In some settings such responsibilities are limited to adherence to rules in the budgeting process, but in others they extend to issues of representative morality. These kinds of requirements are sometimes evident at the national level as well, where constitutions set out a code of conduct for presidents, members of the executive, and other legislators. This kind of legislation (whether introduced in the constitution or in civil service laws pertaining to political representatives and particularly members of the executive) could be used to create avenues of political performance accountability. Presidents could be legally required, for example, to publicly evaluate ministerial performance on an annual basis—against set contracts—and to reward or penalize ministers accordingly (with high performers receiving monetary rewards for their policy-making and managerial achievements but poor performers facing monetary penalties or perhaps even replacement for their policy-making and managerial shortcomings). Legislation could similarly require that presidents be transparent with the electorate regarding their own policy performance, thereby facilitating voting based on performance.

Conclusion

Accountability is the theme of all public sector financial management. In the performance-based reform movement, accountability is still the core theme. Fundamental questions for reformers are, "How well have reforms worked in introducing a results orientation into budgeting processes (with representatives and managers being held accountable for results), and where should reformers be concentrating to improve such effects?"

With reference to the example of South Africa as a best-practice developing country, this chapter shows that performance-based (or results-oriented) accountability is difficult to establish through budget reforms. Indeed, reforms entail a progression from one form of governance (and one kind of accountability) to another. There are many steps in this progression, and many new institutions have to be set in place and new capacities developed to facilitate transformation from the traditional process and control-based accountability structures to performance-based accountability structures.

The South African example is considered best practice partly because of success with generic models (like MTEF), but also because of the apparent wisdom exhibited with regard the sequencing of reforms. This chapter tracked that sequencing through the development of program identities in medium-term budgets (to answer questions about who is spending and on what) to the identification of outputs, measures, and targets (to provide information about what agencies can be expected to produce). It then suggested problems that still limit the potential of the budgeting model to foster a results-oriented accountability culture or results-oriented incentives for managers and political representatives, as well as steps required to stimulate the development of such culture or incentives. In the South African case these include the need to mainstream performance into the budget; to ensure that performance targets are relevant, readable, and realistic; to identify who is responsible for performance; and to introduce institutions necessary to enforce accountability relationships (both managerial and political).

These steps are likely appropriate for other countries as well. All countries intent on developing a performance-based budgeting approach need to understand the sequences involved in introducing results-based governance—and to know general points for effective reform—because bad performance-based reform is probably worse than a good line-item budget. Bouckaert and Peters (2002) emphasize this in saying, "Implementing an inadequate system of performance management can provide a false sense of security and accomplishment and in the process will misdirect resources and activities. Inadequate performance management can become the Achilles' heel of the modernization process itself" (344). This chapter has aimed to show that the move to performance-based accountability is progressing well in some countries, but that work is still required to ensure that it is an asset and not a managerial liability (or an Achilles' heel for public sector managers).

Notes

1. The two institutional effects reflect the different theoretical perspectives on institutionalism. The sociological branch (and elements of the political science wing) argues that institutions (especially norms) shape cultures and make certain kinds of behavior appropriate, while the economics approach holds that institutions shape transactions costs and incentives in processes of decision making and interaction (see Andrews 2002).
2. The definitions of input, output, and outcome follow common approaches in Hatry (1977), Nayyer-Stone (1999), Weist and Kerr (1999), and Schaeffer (2000). The same definitions inform the approach taken in governments such as the Commonwealth of Virginia (Virginia Department of Planning and Budget 2002). They are explored in more detail later.
3. World Bank (1998) presents the South African medium-term expenditure framework reforms as a best practice. The National Treasury shows, in legislation such as the Public Finance Management Act, that MTEF is part of a general move toward a results-oriented accountability structure in the budgeting process.
4. The outputs identified include improved equity in access to primary health care services, fully functional clinics and community health centers, and primary health care delivery by local government regulated by service agreements.
5. The last point is frequently discussed in the development community, which promotes such reforms. Where MTEFs are developed and published separately from the annual budget, they tend to have very little meaning, and the developmental side of the process is held distinctly separate from the accounting and reporting and control side.
6. Andrews (2002) finds, in a study of South African local governments, that many municipalities adhered to the legal requirement to develop local plans without developing meaningful plans or using such plans to drive their budgets (the intended direction of plan development). In such instances the incorrect performance target (creating plans) had an unintended consequence of focusing managers on the task of developing plans instead of providing services.
7. The cultural/incentives arguments are reflected throughout institutionalist literature (see Poterba 1996, 28 and Andrews 2002). In the first instance, results-oriented rules (such as the requirement that department heads set targets) constitute a benchmark and structure for budget deliberations, an objective approach that yields certain types of behavior (results targeting) culturally appropriate and others (a pure control concentration, for example) culturally inappropriate. Kaul (1997, 15) says of this kind of change in the Malaysian context: "The concern for quality and the increasing identification with the public concerns are important aspects of the new culture. This gives rise to the possibility that a new public service value system is emerging in which quality, like probity more traditionally, is taken as moral as much as regulatory." In the second instance results-oriented rules that link performance to future allocations or compensation provide a promise of repercussion associated with certain behavior (lower compensation because of poor performance), creating incentives for specific behavior (a greater performance focus).
8. This overcomes the problem of identifying subprograms and projects by the agents spending the money but not necessarily responsible for outputs. Instead of saying that money is going to the South African Government AIDS Action Plan (GAAP), the South African National AIDS Council, the HIV/AIDS conditional

grant, Love Life, Tuberculosis—financial assistance to NGOs, and the South African AIDS Vaccine Initiative, the present approach favors showing how money is being allocated to subprograms that are connected by definition to specific outputs (for example, AIDS treatment and AIDS prevention).

9. Consider, for example, the situation in which a program manager is contracted to produce specific output cluster results but there is no way of appointing project managers to similar contracts. The program manager would have no way to ensure subordinate project managers perform effectively and, because program results are tied to project results, the program manager's own performance would be related to those of the project managers.

10. In other governments (as in the U.S. state of Texas) these incentive mechanisms been difficult to introduce because of legal constraints on the type of compensation that government employees can earn (legal constraints are an important consideration for reformers).

References

Ammons, David N. 2002. "Performance Measurement and Managerial Thinking." *Public Performance and Management Review* 25 (4): 344–47.

Andrews, Matthew. 2002. "Fiscal Institutions Adoption in South African Municipalities." Paper presented at the Center for Science and Industrial Research, Pretoria, March 15, 2002.

Andrews, Matthew, and Don Moynihan. 2002. "Why Reforms Do Not Always Have to 'Work' to Succeed." *Public Performance and Management Review* 25 (3): 282–97.

Berman, Evan. 2002. "How Useful Is Performance Measurement?" *Public Performance and Management Review* 25 (4): 348–51.

Bouckaert, Geert, and B. Guy Peters. 2002. "Performance Measurement and Management: The Achilles' Heel in Administrative Modernization." *Public Performance and Management Review* 25 (4): 359–62.

Broom, Cheryle, and Lynne A. McGuire. 1995. "Performance-Based Government Models: Building a Track Record." *Public Budgeting and Finance* 15: 3–17.

Chiu, Ng Kam. 1997. "Service Targets and Methods of Redress: The Impact of Accountability in Malaysia." *Public Administration and Development* 17: 175–80.

Commonwealth of Australia. 2002. "Budget Measures 2002." 2002/03 Budget Paper 2. Commonwealth of Australia, Canberra. http://www.dofa.gov.au/budget/2002–03/bp2/html/01_BP2Prelims.html#P40_867.

Fraser-Moleketi, Geraldine. 2000. "Briefing on February 10, 2000."http://www.polity.org.za/govdocs/speeches/2000/sp0210i.html.

Fuchs, Larry. 1998. "Florida Department of Revenue: The Sharp Side of the Leading Edge." *New Public Innovator* (May–June): 92.

Hatry, Harry P. 1977. *How Effective Are Your Community Services?* Washington, DC: Urban Institute.

Jones, David Seth. 1998. "Recent Budgetary Reforms in Singapore." *Journal of Public Budgeting, Accounting, and Financial Management* 10: 279–310.

Kaul, Mohan. 1997. "The New Public Administration: Management Innovations in Government." *Public Administration and Development* 17: 13–26.

Kraan, Dirk-Jan. 1996. *Budgetary Decisions: A Public Choice Approach.* Cambridge, U.K.: Cambridge University Press.

Martin, Lawrence L. 1997. "Outcome Budgeting: A New Entrepreneurial Approach to Budgeting." *Journal of Public Budgeting, Accounting, and Financial Management* 9: 108–26.

Mikesell, John L. 1995. *Fiscal Administration,* 4th ed. New York: Wadsworth.

Mohamad, Mustapha. 1997. "Public Service Management: Management Appraisal, Incentives, and Sanctions." *Asian Review of Public Administration* 1 (January–June).

National Treasury. 2002. Vote 16, Department of Health. "In *Estimates of National Expenditure,* 347–70. Pretoria: South African National Treasury." http://www.finance.gov.za/.

Nayyar-Stone, Ritu. 1999. *Budget Reference Manual for Bulgaria.* Washington, DC: Urban Institute.

OPPAGA (Office of Program Policy Analysis and Government Accountability, State of Florida). 1997. *Performance-Based Program Budgeting in Context: History and Comparison.* Tallahassee: State of Florida.

Osborne, David, and Ted Gaebler. 1992. *Reinventing Government.* Reading, MA: Addison-Wesley.

Poterba, James M. 1996. "Budget Institutions and Fiscal Policy in the U.S. States." *American Economic Review* 86 (2): 395–408.

Reinikka, Ritva. 1999. "Using Surveys for Public Sector Reform." World Bank PREMnotes 23, World Bank, Washington, DC.

Schaeffer, Michael. 2000. *Municipal Budgeting Toolkit.* Washington, DC: World Bank.

Schick, Allen, 1998. "Why Most Developing Countries Should Not Try New Zealand Reforms." *World Bank Research Observer* 13: 123–31.

Shah, Anwar. 2000. "Governing for Results in a Globalized and Localized World." Paper presented at the International Conference on Federalism, Monterrey, Mexico, March. http://www.federalism.ch/FTP-Mirror/summer_university_03/week_2/Shah-governing-for-results.pdf.

Shand, David. 1998. "Budgetary Reforms in OECD Member Countries." *Journal of Public Budgeting, Accounting, and Financial Management* 10 (1): 63–88.

Treasury of Malaysia. 2002. "Programme and Performance Budget Estimates Book." http://www.treasury.gov.my/englishversion/f_2nd_penerbitan.htm.

Virginia Department of Planning and Budget. 2002. "Virginia's Planning and Performance Handbook." http://www.dpb.state.va.us/VAResults/HomePage/PMMaterials.html.

Wang, Xiaohu. 2000. "Performance Measurement in Budgeting: A Study of County Governments." *Public Budgeting and Finance* 20: 102–18.

Weist, Dana, and Graham Kerr. 1999. "Budget Execution, Monitoring, and Capacity Building." Decentralization Briefing Notes, World Bank, Washington, DC.

World Bank. 1998. *Public Expenditure Management Handbook.* Washington DC: World Bank.

Xavier, John Anthony. 1998. "Budget Reform in Malaysia and Australia Compared." *Public Budgeting and Finance* 18 (1): 99–118.

3

Simple Tools for Evaluating Revenue Performance in a Developing Country

MAHESH PUROHIT

R evenue performance indicates the relative change in yield from tax and nontax revenue of national or subnational governments. It takes into account the changes in rates, base, and coverage related to the structure of revenue sources. It also incorporates issues related to efficiency in governance of tax and nontax sources.

Various concepts and techniques are used for the measurement of absolute and relative revenue performance indicators. For a more coherent appreciation, this chapter first presents an analysis of the issues related to concepts. The second part presents the concepts and methodology adopted for estimating revenue performance. The third part gives illustrative results with the help of recommended simple tools. The fourth part presents a summary of conclusions as to the choice of methodology and policy imperatives.

Introduction

Research organizations working at the national level or as think tanks of the ministry of finance[1] and international agencies engaged in monitoring the fiscal health of nations[2] attempt to analyze the revenue performance of governments. These organizations try to find out whether government revenue is increasing sufficiently over a period of time. They also attempt to ascertain whether the tax revenue of a government is increasing at a rate higher than the rate of increase of the gross domestic product (GDP). Efforts are also made to find out whether the generated revenue is sufficient to finance capital formation, to increase the rate of economic growth in the short run, and to impart automatic stability to the economic system in the medium run.

An analysis of these aspects enables one to estimate the revenue performance of the country concerned. Performance is considered satisfactory on a given measuring scale if the available revenue sources provide increasing revenue year after year. The sources should also be income elastic with reference to their base. They should, in addition, enable government to raise the level of spending so as to provide better public services.

Most governments use a variety of sources for raising resources. These sources include tax and nontax sources. Tax revenue sources include taxes on income and property, as well as taxes on commodities and services. The nontax sources cover avenues such as contributions from public enterprises (commercial and noncommercial), interest receipts, revenue from economic and fiscal services, external grants, user charges, and other sources. Although the magnitude of tax and nontax revenue depends on the performance of each source, tax revenue in most cases accounts for a major proportion of the total. Also, the structure of direct and indirect taxes affects revenue performance overall. It also discloses how the potential tax bases have best been tapped through the revenue effort of a country.

In developed countries the production structure is characterized by large business undertakings, especially multinational companies. The government is able to obtain a major part of its tax revenue through direct taxes. Income tax, in particular, takes in a major chunk in the character of a mass tax, partly because the average income in these countries is quite high, and partly because broad wage employment enables the collection of income tax on salaries at a minimum cost through the system of withholding. In developing countries, on the contrary, there exists a greater reliance on taxes on commodities and services, and a major part of revenue is drawn from these taxes. The importance of the contribution depends on the type of sales or turnover taxes in existence. While in the short run larger revenues could be raised from cascade-type sales taxes, their adverse effects on the economy might result in low revenue performance in the medium term. Also, in most cases, the surplus from public undertakings arises from the monopoly of natural resources, from which a major part of the revenue is drawn.

Concepts and Methodology

Revenue performance is measured by various methods. The most convenient method is to find out the change in revenue over the past year as a percentage relative to the base year or successive years. This method helps in
assessing the rate of growth in revenue. Another method to estimate growth
in relation to the base is the coefficient of buoyancy or income elasticity of
the revenue. This method takes into account the changes in revenue with
reference to the changes in the tax base. Yet another method—revenue
effort—relates to identifying the conspicuous efforts of governments to
mobilize resources, such as any move to rationalize the rate structure, eliminating unwanted and misused exemption provisions or provisions that
make the administration of the tax structure complex and complicated. As
a final method, an attempt is made to prepare a comprehensive index of the
revenue performance of the governmental unit concerned. The methods
enumerated here adopt a variety of techniques—some rudimentary and
others advanced—and provide specific results, as explained below.

Growth Rate

An important and widely used measure of revenue performance is an estimate of its growth rate. This estimate may be made with reference to the preceding year or with reference to the preceding time period. When it is
estimated with reference to the past year, it is calculated as the percentage
change over the year. This is calculated as $\Delta R/R$, where Δ represents the
change over the past year and R represents revenue collections. This method
uses a ratio of change in revenue in the current year over the total revenue
of the past year.

When the growth rate is estimated over a period of time, the trend rate
is calculated through the following regression equation :

$$R = ab^t \tag{3.1}$$

where $b = (1 + r)$, r is the growth rate of R, and t varies from 1 to n. The
growth rate calculated through the regression technique estimates the compound growth rate.

This is the simplest method of measuring revenue performance. It can
provide estimates for total revenue or for individual components of revenue.
However, its significance is limited in analyzing the causal relationship that
suggests which variables have contributed to growth. This is especially true

of variables such as price change, tax effort, or variation in GDP that affect the growth rate.

Buoyancy of Revenue

Another way of measuring the relative growth of revenue is to compute the percentage change in revenue that has taken place for a 1 percent change in GDP. Such a measure is known as buoyancy or the income elasticity of revenue. Buoyancy is a measure of the responsiveness (of the tax or any revenue measure) to changes in the base (such as income), including the effects of changes in the structure of the tax. Income elasticity refers to a change in revenue without any discretionary changes in the rate, base, or coverage of the tax structure. It assumes the tax base to be constant (Sahota 1961; Purohit 1978).

The growth rate method estimates revenue performance independent of any other factor that might contribute to growth. Buoyancy instead is judged in relation to independent quantifiable economic variables (such as national income or GDP). Buoyancy relates the growth rate of revenue to the growth of the base of the revenue sources, which is normally GDP. It attributes the growth rate of revenue to the responsiveness of the revenue base (that is, normal automatic growth in revenue due to the growth in the base). The buoyancy of a revenue source with respect to its base shows the ratio of relative change in the base. It is computed as a percentage change in revenue relative to a 1 percent change in GDP (or the base of the revenue). Symbolically, this could be expressed as $\Delta R/R \div \Delta Y/Y$. If this coefficient comes out to be greater than unity, revenue is said to be buoyant. The revenue performance of the governmental unit is supposed to be productive, giving a higher yield as GDP grows.

The functional form used to measure buoyancy is of the type

$$R = aY^b \tag{3.2}$$

When this exponential form is transformed into a logarithmic form, it changes to:

$$\log R = \log a + b \log Y$$

where R is revenue, Y is GDP, and b is buoyancy coefficient. This relationship shows the percentage change in revenue with respect to the percentage change in GDP.

Relative Revenue Effort

Although a higher coefficient of buoyancy indicates that the relative growth of the yield from revenue has been good, it is important to examine whether this is owing to the greater effort of a government to mobilize resources. Revenue performance would be considered better in a country that puts out greater efforts for given resources.

Revenue effort is measured through an ordinal concept of relative effort. In this approach, the revenue performance of a governmental unit is judged against the average performance of its counterparts, after making due allowance for variations in factors affecting their revenue effort. The revenue effort measure is thus concerned with comparing the actual performance of governments in raising revenue against their estimated capacity to do so. Also, the revenue effort of a nation largely determines the scope for increase in the level of revenue in that particular governmental unit.

The relative revenue effort can be measured by two methods. These are stochastic and nonstochastic. The stochastic method is a derivative of the revenue ratio analysis, wherein the revenue ratio (R_y) is defined as the ratio of total actual revenue collection (R) to gross national product (Y). Revenue efforts of various countries, at a point in time, are systematically related to the factors affecting their taxable capacity. That is,

$$R/Y = f(X_1, X_2, X_3, \cdots X_n) \tag{3.3}$$

where X_i are the factors affecting revenue-generating capacity.

These factors need not necessarily be the revenue base. The index of revenue effort (E), based on the revenue-generating capacity and revenue effort, is measured as a proportion of actual and estimated revenue ratios, as shown below:

$$E = R_y \big/ R_y^* \tag{3.4}$$

where R_y = actual revenue and R_y^* = estimated revenue. The index of revenue effort, as derived above, reflects the extent to which the revenue-generating capacity of a country has been exploited by the government.

One way of measuring revenue effort is to estimate the average degree of relationship between revenue ratios in different countries and their revenue-generating capacities. This can be worked out through regression. The resultant revenue ratios represent the ratio that a country would have had if it used its capacity to an average extent. Comparison of the estimated ratio with the actual revenue ratio will indicate whether that country that is making the average degree of effort or showing positive or negative deviations from the average.

From the equation 3.4, the index of revenue effort can be expressed as a ratio of actual revenue collection to the potential revenue collection that would have been expected given the country's capacity at an average level of raising revenue. For carrying out this exercise, a number of factors are selected that a priori could be important indicators of revenue-generating capacity:

- gross national product
- population
- proportion of income from industrial and commercial sectors of total state domestic product
- degree of urbanization

These factors could be incorporated in the relationship given below:

$$R/Y = \alpha + b_1 \, Y/P + b_2 U_i \tag{3.5}$$

where Y/P is the per capita income, U is the degree of urbanization, and b is the estimate of coefficient.

Empirical studies indicate that when the total income ratio is regressed on all the capacity factors, per capita income and urbanization come out to be important factors. They explain most of the variations.

A different method to estimate relative effort is based on measuring the revenue potential of a country. One could also use the effective rate of raising resources through tax or nontax sources. In so doing, one could derive the revenue potential by applying the average effective rates to the potential base in each country.

Performance Index

Although coefficients of growth rate, buoyancy, and revenue effort indicate revenue performance by a national or subnational government, it is difficult to assimilate the different measures. Sometimes the results drawn from the growth rate could be different from those derived from buoyancy or from revenue effort. It is therefore important to prepare a comprehensive index to estimate revenue performance of a country. In preparing such an index, one could use a variety of variables, such as changes in

- gross domestic product
- population
- real per capita tax revenue
- tax revenue
- composition of taxes
- nontax revenue
- real per capita revenue
- changes in tax structure of direct and indirect taxes
- top personal income tax rate
- openness of the economy
- top corporate income tax rate
- top sales tax or value added tax rates

Using such indicators, the Fraser Institute has attempted to estimate a fiscal performance index for the Canadian provinces (Emes 1999). The revenue subindex is composed of 10 variables. The methodology has been derived from a U.S. study conducted by the Cato Institute on the fiscal performance of 46 U.S. governors (Moore and Stansel 1998).

The index prepared on the basis of the above listed variables requires assigning weights to different variables. The weights being subjective, any change in the weights would also change the index.

Method of Principal Components

It is possible to avoid making subjective judgments and assigning weights by using the entire set of variables, through the method of principal components. This method takes into account all indicator variables related to revenue performance.

With a view to examining the causal relationship of revenue realized and the factors affecting its growth, the revenue performance model is given by the relationship

$$Rp = f(x) \tag{3.6}$$

where Rp is the revenue performance and x is the composite vector of causal variables.

In this framework, it is clear that revenue performance is a composite variable consisting of several components. Sales tax revenue, for example, is affected by the components of GNP related to trade and the manufacturing sector. Similarly, agricultural income tax has a direct bearing on the agriculture component of the GDP, and the number of motor vehicles registered in a state directly affects taxes on passengers and goods, as well as taxes on motor vehicles.

In addition, through revenue effort, a country could evolve changes in its rates or the base of the taxes and the governance of taxes. All these factors contribute considerably to the performance of revenue and are intimately interconnected. It is impossible to isolate the effect of each of the variables on revenue performance. This paradox makes the system very complex. It is important to maintain the identity of the individual variables because when a particular country is interested in raising its revenue, the policies to mobilize resources would have to be geared toward each of the variables.

The method of principal components helps in studying the combined impact of such variables. It is a special case of the more general method of factor analysis (see Koutsoyiannis 1979). Its aim is to construct out of a set of variables x_js ($j = 1, 2, \ldots k$), some new variables (p_i) called principal components, which are linear combinations of the xs:

$$z_j = a_{j1}x_1 + a_{j2}x_2 + \cdots a_{jk}x_k \qquad (3.7)$$

where $i = 1, 2, \ldots p$, and $p \leq k$.

The method could be applied by using the original values of x_j or their deviations (loadings) from their means $X_j = x_j - \bar{x}_j$, or the standardized variables (measured as the deviations of x_j from the means and subsequently divided by the standard deviations ($z_j = X_j/s_{xj}$). For the sake of convenience one could use the latter method, which is a more general method (being a unit-free number) and could be applied to variables measured in different units.

Database and Empirical Estimates

With the idea of presenting illustrative results of revenue performance of national and subnational governments, this chapter measures revenue performance of 34 developing countries using data on gross national product, trade balance, and population for the period 1992–98. It is based on the IMF's *International Financial Statistics* (IMF 1999a). Data on total tax revenue and nontax revenue have been collected from *Government Finance Statistics Yearbook* (IMF 1999b) of the IMF. The system of common definitions and classification found in the IMF's *Manual on Government Finance Statistics* (IMF 1985) has been used for each country.

Revenue performance of these countries has been measured with the help of each methods enumerated in the earlier part of the chapter: growth rate, buoyancy, and the method of principal components (MPC). The results appear in table 3.1.

TABLE 3.1   Revenue Performance of Selected Developing Countries, 1992–98

Country	Growth rate	Buoyancy	MPC
Bolivia	19.1	1.22	88.7
Botswana	11.8	0.84	77.9
Burundi	3.2	0.34	86.4
Cameroon	−4.0	0.30	74.6
Chile	17.9	1.06	81.4
China	31.1	1.08	96.5
Colombia	29.3	0.94	95.1
Congo, Dem. Rep. of	11.1	0.10	79.0
Costa Rica	26.3	1.08	72.4
Croatia	33.7	0.82	67.4
Dominican Republic	18.4	1.16	96.1
Egypt, Arab Rep. of	17.6	1.13	92.5
Estonia	29.7	1.08	75.5
Hungary	18.4	0.82	80.8
Indonesia	18.5	1.03	89.1
Iran, Islamic Rep. of	42.9	1.25	57.3
Jordan	12.4	1.26	72.1
Kenya	21.7	1.17	93.8
Madagascar	17.5	0.81	75.5
Malaysia	9.9	0.89	95.6
Mauritius	10.3	0.83	91.8
Mexico	22.1	0.97	73.1
Morocco	9.3	1.39	84.1
Nepal	19.8	1.46	82.8
Panama	5.1	1.12	76.7
Pakistan	14.5	0.35	77.3
Peru	33.7	0.53	96.6
Philippines	15.0	1.19	77.4
Sierra Leone	24.7	1.34	95.3
South Africa	13.5	0.90	75.0
Sri Lanka	13.3	0.25	87.9
Syrian Arab Rep.	17.3	1.03	87.9
Thailand	12.0	1.10	89.4
Tunisia	9.9	0.99	74.2

Source: IMF 1985, 1999a, 1999b.
Note: MPC refers to method of principal components.

It can be observed from the results that the growth rate of developing countries could be classified in three groups. Six countries have recorded growth rates of less than 10 percent, 18 have recorded rates of 10 to 20 percent, and 10 have achieved more than 20 percent growth in revenue. This indicates good performance by the majority of the developing countries. In similar fashion, the results for buoyancy of revenue indicate that the buoyancy coefficient is more than unity in 19 countries. It is in fact equally distributed among countries having a coefficient higher than one and countries having a coefficient lower than one. The method of principal components—using variables such as total revenue, population, gross national product, and trade balance (reflecting openness of the economies) —indicates that in a majority of the countries the variations are explained by the first component.

Summary of Conclusions and Policy Prescriptions

Revenue performance denotes the relative change in the yield from tax and nontax sources. It encompasses changes in rates, bases, and governance of revenue measures. Performance is said to be satisfactory if the given revenue sources provide increasing revenue year after year. Although the magnitude of revenue depends on the performance of each source, the structure of direct and indirect taxes also affects the overall performance. It also depends on how best the potential revenue bases have been tapped through a country's effort to raise revenue.

Various methods are used in measuring revenue performance. One important method is to estimate the growth rate of revenue. This can provide estimates for total revenue or for individual components of revenue. A straightforward way of obtaining a measure of relative growth is to compute the percentage change in revenue that has taken place for a 1 percent change in revenue base. Such a measure is known as buoyancy or the income elasticity of revenue. In general, buoyancy refers to the growth rate of revenue (or the responsiveness) to the tax base (that is, automatic growth in revenue as a result of growth in the base).

A different method for estimating revenue performance is to calculate the relative revenue effort of a country. This method compares the actual performance of governments in raising actual revenue against their estimated capacity. One way of measuring revenue effort is to estimate the average degree of relationship between revenue ratios in different governmental units and their capacity to generate resources. One could also use the effective rate of raising resources through tax or nontax measures.

Another method is to prepare a comprehensive index to estimate the revenue performance of a government. A variety of variables can be used: changes in income, population, real per capita tax revenue, tax revenue, composition of taxes, nontax revenue, real per capita revenue, changes in the tax structure of direct and indirect taxes, top personal income tax rates, top corporate income tax rates, sales tax rates, gas tax rate, and urbanization. On the basis of all these variables, an index could be prepared. This, however, requires assigning weights to the different variables. Because the weights are subjective, changing the weights could change the index.

To avoid subjective judgment in assigning weights, one can use the entire set of variables in the method of principal components. This method takes into account all causal variables related to performance of revenue. In this framework, revenue performance is a composite variable consisting of several components. It is important to maintain the identity of the individual variables because, when a government is interested in raising its revenue, its policies to mobilize resources would need to be geared toward each of the variables.

The method of principal components helps one study the combined impact of such variables. For the sake of convenience one could use this method, which is a more general method (being a unit-free number) and could be applied to variables measured in different units.

The results presented in the study in this chapter are based on a comparative picture of 34 developing countries across the globe. The results suggest that a similar exercise could be attempted for any single country or its subnational governments. Also, it suggests that one could use a variety of variables in preparing an index of revenue performance.

Notes

1. Such organizations exist in many countries. Some such organizations are the Institute of Fiscal and Monetary Policy in Tokyo; the National Institute of Public Finance and Policy in New Delhi; and the Fraser Institute in Vancouver, British Columbia, Canada.
2. These international agencies include the International Monetary Fund, the World Bank, the Asian Development Bank, and others.

References

Chelliah, Raja J., and Narain Sinha. 1982. *Measurement of Tax Effort of State Governments 1973–76.* Mumbai: Somaiya Publications.

Dalvi, M. Q., and M. M. Ansari. "Measuring Fiscal Performance of the Central and the State Governments in India: A Study in Resource Mobilisation." *Indian Economic Journal* 33 (4): 106–22.

Emes, Joel. 1999. *Fiscal Performance Index, 1999.* Vancouver: Fraser Institute.

———. 2000. *The Budget Performance Index 2000: Comparing the Recent Fiscal Conduct of Canadian Governments.* Vancouver: Fraser Institute.

Hinrichs, Harley H. 1966. *A General Theory of Tax Structure Change during Economic Development.* Cambridge, MA: Law School of Harvard University.

IMF (International Monetary Fund). 1985. *Manual on Government Finance Statistics.* Washington, DC: International Monetary Fund.

———. 1999a. *International Financial Statistics.* Washington, DC: International Monetary Fund.

———. 1999b. *Government Finance Statistics Yearbook.* Washington, DC: IMF.

Koutsoyiannis, Anna. 1979. *Theory of Econometrics.* London: Macmillan.

Krishnaji, N. 1989. "Measuring Tax Potential—A Note on Ninth Finance Commission's Approach." *Economic and Political Weekly* 24 (February 4): 265–67.

Legler, John B., and Perry Shapiro. 1968. "The Responsiveness of State Tax Revenue to Economic Growth." *National Tax Journal* 21 (1): 46–56.

Mansfield, Charles Y. 1972. "Elasticity and Buoyancy of a Tax System: A Method Applied to Paraguay." *IMF Staff Papers* 19 (2): 425–43.

Moore, Stephen, and Dean Stansel. 1998. "A Fiscal Policy Report Card on America's Governors: 1998." Cato Policy Analysis 315, Cato Institute, Washington, DC.

Purohit, Mahesh C. 1978. "Buoyancy and Income Elasticity of State Taxes in India." *Artha Vijnana* 20: 244–87.

Raghbendra, Jha, M. S. Mohanty, and Somnath Chatterjee. 1995. "Fiscal Efficiency in the Indian Federation." Department of Economic Analysis and Policy, Reserve Bank of India, Bombay, June 19.

Sahota, G. S. 1961. *Indian Tax Structure and Economic Development.* Delhi: Institute of Economic Growth.

4

Evaluating Public Expenditures

Does It Matter How They Are Financed?

RICHARD M. BIRD

H71
H72
H50
H61

E62

Economic analysis and popular opinion often conflict. An example is the connection between the revenues and expenditures of the public sector. Common sense suggests that there should be a strong and logical connection between the two sides of the budget. For example, if an average citizen in any country is asked what he or she thinks about the desirability of a particular expenditure increase, the answer is often related to how the respondent thinks the increase will be financed. Similarly, although most people do not like tax increases, again their attitudes seem likely to depend to at least some extent on what they think will be financed.[1]

People are right. Revenues and expenditures are inextricably linked. Indeed, as Musgrave (1969a) has long emphasized, "a theory of public finance remains unsatisfactory unless it comprises both the revenue and expenditure sides of the fiscal process" (797). Nonetheless, despite this admonition, and despite common sense, most formal economic analysis of either tax or expenditure changes traditionally has been conducted under the assumption that there is no connection between what happens on one side of the budget account and what happens on the other side. This chapter explores a few of the issues that arise when we take seriously the need to consider both sides of the budget in evaluating public expenditures.

There are, of course, excellent reasons why economists operate the way they do. Life is complicated. The only way one can begin to make sense of it is to take that complexity apart in some logical way and to analyze it piece by piece. It would be far too confusing, for example, to analyze the incidence of an increase in the income tax while also taking into account the distributive effects of the expenditures assumed to be financed by the new revenues. The combined incidence of the tax and expenditure changes (*balanced-budget incidence*) would obviously differ depending on the nature of the expenditures financed and might tell us little about the effects of the tax change alone if the latter is our primary interest.[2] Matters would be even more complicated if allowance were made for the effects of such budgetary changes on such macroeconomic variables as the rate of inflation (*specific incidence*). For these reasons, following Musgrave (1959), economists concerned with fiscal incidence now commonly analyze what is called the *differential incidence* of tax (and expenditure) changes—that is, the effects on the distribution of income assuming that some other tax is simultaneously altered so as to maintain constant both the real level of revenues and expenditures and the real level of aggregate demand.

In reality, of course, such precise substitutions almost never occur. Real-world tax changes are thus likely to affect the level (and perhaps the composition) of expenditures, as well as to have implications for the macroeconomy. Depending on the nature of the problem being analyzed, all three incidence concepts just mentioned might therefore be relevant in analyzing the effects of tax (or expenditure) changes. Specific incidence analysis, for instance, is required to answer questions relating to the distributional impact of tax increases unaccompanied by expenditure increases or measures to offset effects on aggregate demand. Similarly, balanced-budget incidence analysis is required to analyze the distributional effect of tax increases that finance specified expenditure increases (Break 1974). Nonetheless, the only tool we have to deal directly with the distributional effects of taxation (or expenditure) alone is the differential incidence concept. Therefore, it is not surprising that this type of analysis dominates the academic literature on tax incidence.

Even in this case, however, no unique answer emerges since, by definition, differential incidence compares the distributional effects of any particular change with some other change. The results will thus depend on the nature of the changes being compared. One might perhaps think of comparing any tax change with a precisely offsetting change in an equal yield set of perfectly neutral taxes (so-called lump-sum taxes) that affect neither distribution nor allocation decisions. Since no such set of taxes can exist, however, in practice differential incidence analysis is usually carried out by comparing a proposed change in taxes (or transfers) to an equal-yield change in a comprehensive proportional income tax (or occasionally, as in Shoup [1969], some other general levy such as a uniform value added tax). Despite the many conceptual and empirical problems with such analysis, it is the best we can do—and so that is what we do.

Analogous problems arise in analyzing the effects on allocative efficiency of alternative ways of financing public expenditures. Unsurprisingly, in the traditional economic literature these problems have been resolved, to the extent they have been resolved at all, in a similar fashion— although in this case, unlike that of incidence analysis, most analysts seem to have fewer qualms about positing the existence of an alternative "perfectly efficient" tax system. I first consider briefly the orthodox treatment of financing in evaluating public expenditures, and then note a few questions that have been raised about both the conceptual and empirical applications of this approach. In the rest of the chapter I then review several issues that should be considered with respect to how particular public expenditures are or might be financed. Although no clear general guidelines emerge from this review, it is nonetheless apparent that in many instances these matters are too critical to be neglected and that more explicit consideration of the relevant fiscal institutions will, in this as in other areas of public policy, generally improve analysis. This point is developed briefly in the final section.

The Orthodox Tradition

The formal analysis of the marginal cost of public funds began with Pigou (1928), who noted that public expenditure "ought plainly to be regulated with some reference to the burden involved in raising funds to finance them" (30). In a famous quotation very much in the utilitarian spirit he went on to say, "If a community were literally a unitary being, with the government as its brain, expenditure should be pushed in all directions up to the point at which the satisfaction obtained from the last shilling expended is equal to the satisfaction lost in respect to the last shilling called up on government service" (31). Of course, as Pigou recognized, no community is a unitary being in this sense. Governments must thus in practice extract resources coercively through taxation. The costs of doing so—both the administrative and compliance costs and the excess burden or deadweight loss of taxation— ought, he argued, to be taken explicitly into account in determining the appropriate level of public expenditure.

It has thus long been clearly understood that whether a particular expenditure is worthwhile depends to some extent on how it is financed. In particular, since as a rule the economic cost of raising public funds will be larger than the number of tax dollars raised, the optimal size of the public budget is less than it would be with a more efficient tax system. This message is found in many modern texts in public finance. For example, Cullis and Jones (1992) note that "failure of policy makers to appreciate the full costs of taxation . . . will lead to 'excessive' government expenditure" (199). Stiglitz (2000) concurs, saying that "since it becomes more costly to obtain public goods when taxation imposes distortions, normally this will imply that the efficient level of public goods is smaller than it would have been with nondistortionary taxation" (148). "Indeed," Stiglitz continues, "it appears that much of the debate about the desirable level of public goods provision centers around this issue. Some believe that the distortions associated with the tax system are not very great, while others contend that the cost of attempting to raise additional revenues for public goods is great" (148–49).[3]

Serious empirical attempts to determine the costs of taxation began with Harberger (1964) and were subsequently extended by Browning (1976) and numerous others. While it is by no means easy to determine the precise relation between the many estimates produced over the years by different authors, Ballard and Fullerton (1992) have usefully distinguished between two related but distinct approaches. The first approach they call the Pigou-Harberger-Browning approach to estimating the marginal cost of funds (MCF). The alternative approach, favored by the more theoretically inclined, was launched by Stiglitz and Dasgupta (1971) and developed further by Atkinson and Stern (1974). As Ballard and Fullerton (1992) note, although each uses different terminology, each of these approaches essentially estimates the same thing but assumes, in effect, that a different sort of public expenditure is being financed. The traditional (Pigou-Harberger-Browning) approach assumes that the public goods provided will compensate consumers so that only substitution effects remain, while the more modern approach—to use the terminology of Brent (1996, chapter 9)—allows for the income effect of the public good but assumes it has no effect on labor supply. In reality, of course, both income effects and effects on labor supply often accompany fiscal changes, so in principle "the MCF ultimately depends not just on the tax, but also on the nature of the government expenditure under consideration" (Ballard and Fullerton 1992, 125).

Despite such observations, the orthodox tradition has continued to focus solely on the excess burden imposed by taxation. Moreover, the numbers reported in MCF studies have tended to creep up over time. Ballard,

Shoven, and Whalley (1985), for example, came up with a range of MCF estimates for the United States ranging from $1.17 to $1.56 for each dollar of revenue raised. Using a different methodology, Browning (1987) estimated an MCF between $1.10 and $4.00 per dollar of marginal revenue. A recent review and summary by Feldstein (1997) of the extensive subsequent literature estimating the distortionary costs of taxation in the United States concludes, "The total cost per incremental dollar of government spending, including the revenue and the deadweight loss, is thus a very high $2.65. Equivalently, it implies that the marginal distortionary costs per dollar of revenue are $1.65" (211). In another recent survey, Diewert, Lawrence, and Thompson (1998) suggest, somewhat more modestly, that an MCF of at least 23 percent should be added to the monetary costs of tax-financed government spending.

To some extent the initial impetus for much of this work was intended, in line with Pigou's initial observation, to provide a basis for evaluating whether a particular increase in expenditure was worthwhile. Interestingly, over time estimates of the marginal social cost of taxation have come to be considered primarily in the context of tax policy reform (for example, in Myles 1995, 190–92). For example, the most detailed studies of the deadweight losses of taxation in developing countries have been developed almost entirely in this context (Newbery and Stern 1987; Ahmad and Stern 1991).[4] Perhaps for this reason, for the most part the estimated marginal costs of public funds have not been explicitly factored into cost-benefit or project evaluation exercises. Instead, in most treatments of cost-benefit analysis (as in Dinwiddy and Teal 1996, for example), attention has been focused on the related but distinct question of the social opportunity cost of capital—an approach that focuses not on the MCF, but rather on the intertemporal consequences of withdrawing resources from private consumption and from investment, respectively.[5]

If capital markets are perfect and government and private discount rates are the same, the source of finance will be irrelevant because the opportunity cost of the resources used for any project will be the same in any case. But if discount rates differ, as many have argued they do (and should), or if capital markets are less than perfect, as is invariably the case in developing countries, this is no longer true. In general, therefore, it seems plausible that the costs of finance will be greater when the resources used for public purposes would otherwise have been invested. Moreover, these costs will vary depending on both the precise investments displaced and the nature of the expenditure. From this perspective, as Musgrave (1969a) noted, loan-financed projects would, as a rule, appear to be more costly than tax-financed projects because they are more likely to displace private investment. In any case, exactly how expenditures are financed—through loans or taxes (and what kind of taxes)—will thus determine to some extent whether and to what extent private consumption or investment is displaced.

Although this is not the place to review this complex subject,[6] different views on this issue have led different authors to advocate different guidelines on how the opportunity cost of public investment and the discount rate should be determined. To this extent at least, links between the nature of revenues and the desirability of expenditures have traditionally been taken into account in project analysis. Nonetheless, on the whole it seems fair to say that in practice the usual assumption in expenditure analysis has been simply to take the revenue side as given. In particular, despite the origins of much of this discussion in Pigou's early treatment, and despite the numerous estimates that have been made in other contexts of the marginal cost of public funds, it has not been usual in assessing expenditures to take explicit account, in the words of Pigou (1928), of "the burden involved in raising funds to finance them" (30).

Traditionally, perhaps the main concrete recognition of this point in expenditure analysis has been the common assumption that investment projects will be financed, and should be financed, by loan finance.[7] As Musgrave (1997) has argued, if people are to be able to make rational fiscal decisions, they need to be able to compare the benefits and costs of such decisions, which means they have to take into account both the expenditures to be carried out and the way in which they are financed. If the expenditure in question is one that will yield a future stream of benefits—that is, an investment in either physical or human capital—it would be rational for a private individual to borrow to finance it. The same is true for a society. Thus the use of loan finance for public capital formation—along with procedures such as capital budgeting to make the link clear—has much to be said for it as a means of ensuring that the political process through which public goods are provided yields the desired time path of total (public plus private) consumption.

As with many sound ideas, the actual practice of such separate budgeting has left much to be desired. Yet the principle seems sound: finance public consumption by taxes and public investment by loans, and keep the two separate. Nonetheless, separate capital budgets have long been out of favor with budgetary experts. As Premchand (1993) noted, most experts consider capital budgeting to be "an anachronism" (292). More recently, however, the same author has said that even "countries and governments hitherto critical of capital budgets now see advantages in them" (Premchand 1998, 336) and suggested that "the existence of a separate capital budget may prove to be a handy asset" (353). Although the prevailing orthodoxy remains very much against such budgets (World Bank 1998), there is much to be said for this argument. Similarly, to the extent that the expenditure projects being analyzed may properly be considered to constitute "investment," there is much to be said for the traditional procedure in cost-benefit analysis of treating the source of financing as a loan—even, in the case of many developing countries, a loan from foreign sources.

Recently, however, Devarajan, Squire, and Suthiwart-Narueput (1996, 1997) have introduced a new element into the traditional mix by arguing strongly for explicitly taking into account the marginal social cost of public funds in evaluating projects that call for net flows of budgetary funds. They illustrate this point by citing as a minimal correction the lowest estimate for the United States in the Ballard, Shoven, and Whalley (1985), of an MCF of $1.17, noting that this cost is likely to be higher in developing countries with more limited, and generally more distorting, tax systems.[8] Unless such a "shadow price of public finance" (Squire 1989, 1122) is explicitly included in the evaluation of public expenditure projects, they argue, the net present value of such projects will be systematically overvalued. Hence, as suggested by the textbook wisdom cited earlier, the public sector will be inappropriately expanded. Their conclusion on this point is worth reproducing in full:

> When . . . fiscal cost arises from an expansion in supply beyond what would have been forthcoming from the private sector, it represents the price that society has to pay to reap the benefits underlying the rationale for public intervention. If the government is not charging the maximum amount that the private sector is willing to pay, there is an additional fiscal cost—a *transfer*. Both the expansion and the transfer constitute additional burdens on the budget. To the extent that governments have to rely on (distortionary) taxation, raising the required revenue will entail real costs. These costs, as well as the marginal cost of public funds, need to be incorporated in project appraisal wherever possible. (Devarajan, Squire, and Suthiwart-Narueput 1997, 45)

At least four aspects of this conclusion are worth singling out:

1. Public expenditure may have a sound rationale in terms of providing benefits that would not otherwise be forthcoming, but it still gives rise to a fiscal cost.
2. This fiscal cost will be higher if correct user prices are not charged.
3. Raising additional funds is itself costly.

4. Both these costs and the costs imposed by distortionary taxes need to be taken into account in appraising public expenditures.

All these points may be found in Pigou (1928), so it appears that we have, in a sense, closed the circle and once more explicitly linked the evaluation of public expenditures to their financing. What is particularly interesting about the recent revival of this approach, however, is that Harberger (1997), long an advocate of the standard convention of assuming that the marginal source of funds is borrowing in the capital market—which meant in practice that the issue was essentially dealt with in terms of the discount rate—has now also explicitly accepted this case for applying at least a minimal shadow price of fiscal funds to all cash flows to and from governments. It thus now seems to be widely accepted among leading practitioners of project evaluation that, in the words of Boadway and Bruce (1984, 306), "the deadweight loss due to the financing . . . should be included as one of the costs of introducing the project." Theory and practice now seem to agree.

Before exploring this apparent meeting of the minds further, however, it may be interesting to note how at least some World Bank–sponsored analysis of this matter has evolved over the years. In the early heyday of planning, when, in the words of Kirkpatrick and Weiss (1996) governments were still seen as "engines of development" (10). Adler (1964), for example, argued in effect for exactly the opposite correction in the sense of attaching additional weight to expenditures that would generate increased public revenues. While this "production principle of public finance" (40), as he called it, was primarily stated in terms of increased output, he explicitly noted also that projects that yielded larger revenue feedback were to be preferred if it could be presumed, as he seemed prepared to do, that the additional revenue would be used for further productivity-enhancing public expenditure.[9] In other words, public revenue was held to be important because there was thought to be a public savings constraint that made additional dollars of public income more valuable than additional private consumption. Along these lines, Squire and van der Tak (1975) explicitly assumed that an additional dollar of government revenue was as valuable as an additional dollar of private savings. To a limited extent such arguments are sometimes seen at the macro level—consider, for example, the treatment of the public savings constraint. However, in yet another instance of the discord between the macro and micro treatments of public finance highlighted by Musgrave (1997), such notions appear long ago to have vanished from traditional expenditure evaluation techniques.[10]

Before accepting the recent revival of the MCF factor in project analysis, several important considerations need to be discussed further:

■ What precisely is to be included in the social marginal cost of public funds? Is it deadweight losses alone (as in Feldstein 1997)? Should it include also administrative costs (as in Pigou 1928, and as implied by Devarajan, Squire, and Suthiwart-Narueput 1997)? Should it be expanded further to include a variety of other costs involved in raising public revenues (Usher 1991)?

■ No matter how the MCF is defined, it is clearly not a fixed number or independent of how a particular project is financed. If taxes were set optimally, the MCF would be the same for all tax sources. In fact, as Ahmad and Stern (1987, 1991) demonstrate in detail for India and Pakistan, the MCF may vary considerably from tax to tax and may even be less than one (whether or not distributional weighting is used). As Brent (1996) notes, it is therefore critical either to assume that the marginal expenditure will be financed in the same way as the average expenditure is now financed—which is what Devarajan, Squire, and Suthiwart-Narueput (1997) appear to suggest—or to make some other explicit assumption about the source of finance (such as the traditional assumption associated with Harberger 1972 that the funds will be borrowed).

■ What if the expenditures being considered are funded from taxes that are not distorting (Ng 2000a)? Or from user charges (Devarajan, Squire, and Suthiwart-Narueput 1997)? Or from debt (Feldstein 1972)? Or from earmarked taxes (Drèze and Stern 1987; Squire 1989) or other specified taxes, such as those levied by local governments (Stiglitz 1994)? Even apart from such specific cases, the tenor of most recent discussion is clearly that, as Brent (1996) says, the traditional view (found, for example, in Devarajan, Squire, and Suthiwart-Narueput 1997) is that the shadow price of public funds obtained by raising taxes—the MCF—"*must be* greater than 1; while in the modern approach it *can be* less than 1" (230). Ballard and Fullerton (1992) similarly conclude their summary as follows: "Economists should set aside the apparent presumption that the marginal benefits of a tax-financed public good must exceed its dollar cost" (129).

■ Finally, is it correct to treat the efficiency costs of public revenues as costs without taking into account any distributional benefits that may be associated with such costs (Kaplow 1996)?

The balance of this chapter considers these and some related points. It concludes with a brief consideration of the importance of fiscal institutions that link expenditures and revenues in determining fiscal efficiency.

The Marginal Cost of Public Funds

Most real-world tax systems impose distortionary costs. As Feldstein (1997) notes, taxes may (a) reduce the supply of labor, (b) reduce the supply of capital, (c) induce the substitution of untaxed fringe benefits for cash income, and (d) induce more spending on tax deductible items such as charity and health care. Extending this list, Usher (1991) adds such other "hidden costs" as (e) the overhead costs of tax collection and provision of services, (f) the concealment costs incurred in tax, and (g) the enforcement costs of dealing with these problems and constraining corruption.[11] As Usher notes, all of these latter costs are likely to be higher in countries that have less developed public administrations. However, as Diewert, Lawrence, and Thompson (1998) point out, the deadweight loss of taxes is of course highest when behavioral responses are highest. This may suggest that, in the more fragmented markets typical of developing countries, and despite the more distortionary (less general) nature of the tax systems prevalent in such countries, the MCF might nonetheless be lower than would otherwise be expected. However, as Ahmad and Stern (1987, 1991) demonstrate in detail for India and Pakistan, it is still likely to be quite high in developing countries.

Most studies of MCF, such as Feldstein (1997), focus mainly or exclusively on the deadweight losses associated with distortionary taxes. Sometimes, as noted in both Pigou's (1928) original discussion and in the recent paper by Devarajan, Squire, and Suthiwart-Narueput (1997), mention is also made of administrative and compliance costs, but that is about as far as it goes. Alm (1999), like Usher (1986, 1991), emphasizes the importance of incorporating evasion costs, and Das-Gupta and Mookherjee (1998) consider compliance and enforcement issues in detail. On the whole, however, few attempts have been made to incorporate such costs—including the additional excess burdens associated with them (Collard 1989)—into any formal analysis. This omission is less surprising than it may appear at first, however, because there have been surprisingly few empirical studies of such costs (Sandford 1995) and almost none for developing countries, apart from the work of Das-Gupta and Mookherjee (1998).

As Ballard and Fullerton (1992) argue, in principle the relevant MCF will depend on both the particular tax or taxes levied and the expenditures financed. As Atkinson and Stern (1974) demonstrated, for example, an excise tax on a normal commodity will always have a net distortionary effect (because the income and substitution effects reinforce one another), but a tax on wages may (by inducing increases in work effort through its income effect) actually lower the marginal cost of public funds. Similarly, if the public expenditure financed is complementary to taxed activities, such as public transit, it may also increase labor supply and hence reduce the MCF, while if it is a substitute (such as a park), it may reduce work effort and hence increase the MCF. As Kaplow (1996) notes, however, although such effects should— if important—be taken into account in appraising particular expenditures, they do not appear to justify any general adjustment of the MCF used in expenditure analysis.

Are Public Funds Always Costly?

In fact some have argued that it is always a gross simplification to apply any uniform MCF—or "corrective premium" as Devarajan, Squire, and Suthiwart-Narueput (1996, 45) call it—to public revenues. Three sorts of revenue may, for example, possess the magic quality of being burdenless. The first is the lump-sum tax, as famed in theory as costless as it is conventionally assumed to be nonexistent in practice. But this is clearly an overstatement. As Ng (1987) has argued—and indeed as Henry George (1879) had noted long before—there are some taxes that have no substitution effects and hence impose no deadweight cost. Taxes on economic rent or pure profits have this characteristic, as do poll taxes (or other lump-sum taxes). Such taxes may not always be considered equitable, but they are more widespread than seems normally to be recognized. To some extent, for example, taxes on land (Tideman 1994) and, in less than perfect markets, on profits fall on rents (Mintz and Seade 1991). Moreover, from the perspective of any particular country, taxes that are borne by foreigners—whether exported by monopoly producers or imposed on the location rents accruing to foreign owners—are similarly burdenless (Bruce 1992).[12]

More importantly, economists have long recognized—at least since Pigou (1920)—that some taxes may correct market distortions by forcing economic agents to take social costs into account and hence improve market efficiency. Ballard and Medema (1993), for example, estimated in a model with pollution that a Pigouvian tax internalizing the externality would have an MCF of only $0.73—that is, that each dollar of revenue would produce, as it were, an excess benefit of $0.27. The recent literature on environmental taxation has reinforced recognition of this argument in the form of the "double dividend" of such corrective taxes, namely, that they not only improve the efficiency of resource allocation directly, but may also do so indirectly to the extent that the revenues they yield enable more distorting taxes to be reduced (Goulder 1995). In this case, since the marginal social cost of public funds raised by such taxes is not positive but negative, the implication would appear to be, in line with the Pigouvian principle stated initially, that an expansion of public sector activity might be warranted. Ng (2000a) thus concludes, for this and other reasons, that "the usual method of estimating the optimal level of public spending (equating the sum of individual marginal evaluations to the marginal cost, *with or without taking into account the distortionary costs of taxation*) is likely to lead to a sub-optimal level" (263, italics added).[13]

Finally, since no tax system in the world is now optimal, it follows that in any country there are many possible tax changes that would reduce distortion and hence lower the MCF. Ahmad and Stern (1987, 1991), for example, provide detailed quantitative estimates of the potential efficiency gains to be had from reforming the tax systems of India and Pakistan. A tax change that would both produce revenue and reduce efficiency losses in many countries would be to abolish or reduce tax incentives that distort investment and savings choices. Fullerton and Henderson (1989), for instance, estimated that reducing the investment tax credit in the United States would have an MCF of only $0.62. As Kaplow (1998) puts it: "If we finance a public good, say, by closing an inefficient tax loophole or reducing an inefficient subsidy, it would be possible that total distortion would be even less than if we used a lump-sum tax" (124). Considerations such as these led Ballard and Fullerton (1992) to conclude that "economists should set aside the apparent presumption that the marginal benefits of a tax-financed public good must exceed its dollar cost" (129).

Even those, such as Devarajan, Squire, and Suthiwart-Narueput (1997), who appear to argue the contrary also seem to accept that, when expansions in public sector activities are financed by correctly set user charges, any MCF correction should be applied only to the net burden financed from the public budget. This exclusion of expenditure financed by user charges from the world of shadow pricing is understandable. As has often been argued, properly designed user charges, like any efficient price, by definition give rise to no excess burden or distortion. As Brent (1996) puts this argument, "When taxes incur an excess burden over and above the revenue they produce, user fees are an alternative source of funds that could reduce the inefficiency of that taxation. One should therefore expect user fees to be important when the MCF is high" (297).

Indeed, admittedly with more caution, a similar blessing might be extended even to other sources of finance that, however approximately, establish some meaningful link between those who enjoy the benefits from any public service and those who pay for it. Well-designed earmarked taxes, for example, even when not as strictly linked to the precise usage of a service as a well-designed user charge, may impose smaller efficiency losses on society than taxes that are not earmarked (Bird 1997). In many respects good local taxes are similar to earmarked benefit taxes, in that the taxes are paid and the benefits enjoyed by the same group of people. This same line of reasoning would appear to suggest that expenditures financed out of local revenues should, as a rule, impose smaller deadweight losses than similar expenditures financed out of general revenues (Kaplow 1996). Clearly, neither the earmarking nor the local finance case is as strong as the user charge case, since there can be many variations in benefits and burdens within the affected groups and hence some distortions exist.[14] Nonetheless, there is a presumption that financing derived from properly designed local taxes and earmarked benefit taxes implies a lower MCF than general fund financing and that properly designed user charges imply that the shadow price and the nominal price of funds are equal.

The key words in this conclusion are *properly designed*. As has recently been emphasized (Thirsk and Bird 1993; Bird 1997; Bird and Tsiopoulos 1997), in practice most user charges and earmarked taxes, even in developed countries, fall far short of this standard. With respect to municipal water pricing in Canada, for example, Renzetti (1999) has shown that not only does marginal cost exceed price in each of 77 municipal utilities examined but that, in addition, as might be expected, the result of this underpricing was significant overconsumption. One reason for this outcome was that residential water supply was often not metered. Another was that accounting of costs was incomplete. And a third was that the pricing rules applied "have relatively little to do with the economic cost of supplying potable water and treating waste water" (Renzetti 1999, 699). The result was that the estimated deadweight loss associated with water and sewage service provision financed through user charges was significant, ranging from Cdn$0.42 per dollar charged for nonresidential water supply to a high of Cdn$6.39 for sewage treatment. Because water pricing is one of the most developed forms of user charging in the public sector, and Canada is a highly developed country, it would seem unduly unrealistic to expect better results from the actual user charge systems in developing countries.

Another serious problem in many countries is that the revenues from even properly designed user charges are often not explicitly linked through the budgetary process to the expenditures with respect to which they are levied. As Bird and Tsiopoulos (1997) emphasize, such a link constitutes an essential institutional feature of any sound user charge. The same might be said of earmarked benefit taxes, as demonstrated in Thirsk and Bird (1993). As hinted earlier with respect to capital budgeting, it thus seems time to rethink the traditional reluctance of budgetary experts to condone such specific budgets. The many ills to which such practices admittedly gave rise in the past in some countries should not preclude more careful consideration of more explicit expenditure-revenue links in the future. Such links may not only be essential to determining good policy outcomes in a democratic setting. They may also prove to be an important way in which the preferences of the people who are allegedly being served by the state can gradually enter more explicitly into the determination of state policies.

Decentralization is one of the major methods now being used around the world, in part to achieve this objective (Burki and Perry 2000). This is not surprising since in many ways decentralizing decisions to local governments is in principle—to the extent such decisions are locally financed—similar to decentralizing them to a public enterprise financed by user charges or a special agency financed by a benefit tax, such as a road fund. Problems similar to those arising with respect to user charges and benefit taxes may arise with local taxes. Apart from land taxes, all other forms of local taxes are likely to give rise to some distortionary costs, although efforts can be made to reduce the magnitude of such costs by, for example, limiting the range of possible rate variation (Bird 2000). Similar arguments may be made with respect to many benefit taxes, even those with "market-correcting" features, such as the gasoline tax. Hughes (1987) shows, for example, that although gasoline taxes may often be progressive in developing countries, they may also give rise to efficiency losses. While higher gasoline taxes may have a corrective effect by reducing the use of motor vehicles in congested urban areas, a similar reduction in rural areas may have a perverse effect.

Efficiency and Equity

Finally, virtually all treatments of the MCF issue neglect distributional issues. Either they are conducted in single consumer (or representative consumer) frameworks, where distribution is not an issue, or they explicitly assume, as do Ballard and Fullerton (1992), that all taxpayers are both equal and treated equally. Although the need to thus simplify reality is analytically understandable, this is not how the world works. The reality of the assumptions used to derive analytical conclusions must always be carefully considered—and, if necessary, the conclusions adjusted—before applying them to real-world policy issues.

A quite different approach leading to a quite different conclusion has recently been put forth in an important paper by Kaplow (1996). He argues, in effect, that the best general way to treat the distortionary cost of taxation in evaluating public expenditures is to ignore it—that is, to treat the social marginal cost of public funds as equal to their nominal cost. In other words, the economic cost of raising an additional dollar of public revenue is, in his analysis, exactly equal to the dollar raised. The key to his argument is that he assumes that the distortionary cost of taxes is, for the most part, a reflection of the attempt to redistribute income through the tax system.[15] In this circumstance, as Kaplow (1996, 520) puts it:

> Knowledge that the aggregate reform—the public good and the tax adjustment, taken together—causes distortion thus provides little guidance, because the existence of distortion is associated with greater redistribution. Whether the net effect is good or bad depends upon the extent of preexisting redistribution and the policymaker's judgment about the optimal extent of redistribution.

This argument was subsequently strongly criticized by Browning and Liu (1998) as unduly downplaying the distortionary cost of taxes. It is in any case clearly overstated—perhaps especially for developing countries—since many distortions cannot plausibly be associated with any distributive aim. It is nonetheless, as Ng (2000a) demonstrates, not only convincing but fully compatible with even such high measures of such costs as found in Feldstein (1997) and others.

This apparently paradoxical result—that there can be a high marginal excess burden of taxation that need not, and should not, be taken into account in expenditure analysis—can be simply explained, although the extent to which the explanation seems appropriate depends very much on the particular circumstances being analyzed. Essentially, what Kaplow (1996) suggests is that the best procedure as a rule is—contrary to the position recently taken by Devarajan, Squire, and Suthiwart-Narueput (1997), and accepted by Harberger (1997)—not to make any adjustment for the MCF. Instead, Kaplow assumes that the source of finance will be an income tax adjustment that will roughly offset the benefits from the public goods at each income level. When such benefit taxation is used, he argues, there is no need to adjust for distortionary costs, because by definition there will not be any distortion.

To this point, this is simply a variant of the more specific benefit tax argument noted earlier (and is subject to similar qualifications). Kaplow (1996) goes on to argue, however, that what is required to achieve this result is not pure benefit taxation adjusted to each individual's preferences, but rather the much more feasible benefit taxation by income level. While there would still be some redistribution under such a system, it would be within income groups, depending on individual preferences, and hence, he argues, unlikely to have significant distortionary effects on labor supply.[16] He further argues that since it seems reasonable to consider that the tax system in place in any country at any time reflects some relative stable distributional equilibrium, it is not unreasonable to assume that, on the whole, marginal changes in taxes are likely to be relatively distributionally neutral.

Of course, to the extent that other forms of finance are employed, efficiency losses may arise. Even so, Kaplow argues, in many instances such costs will be offset by redistributive benefits. As he puts the point elsewhere: "If an identified method of finance involves greater distortion . . . this is precisely because that method of finance involves greater redistribution" (Kaplow 1998, 124). This argument, is most applicable with respect to progressive income taxes: therefore, it seems less plausible in countries in which such taxes are unimportant. Nonetheless, Kaplow (1998) is surely right when he concludes that it is wrong to "focus entirely upon the distortionary costs of the income tax, ignoring that the *raison d'être* of redistributive taxation is to redistribute income" (124).[17] Just as a feasible lump-sum tax with no distortionary cost—such as a poll tax—might be considered undesirable on distributional grounds, so an increase in a progressive income tax might be considered worthwhile, even though it clearly increases distortion. Of course, this reasoning also suggests that if the source of finance both caused efficiency losses and affected the poor adversely, as would many excise taxes,[18] it would be doubly undesirable.

It is important to understand what is being argued here. The point is not that there are not often real and sometimes large efficiency costs connected with raising public funds. The mere fact that such costs arise, however, does not mean that the benefit-cost ratio for an acceptable project should be calculated using a shadow price of fiscal funds. As Kaplow (1996) demonstrates, if the finance comes from (good) benefit taxes then by definition the shadow and nominal prices are the same, and if it comes from other taxes it may still be considered worthwhile if the distributive effect of such taxes is considered desirable. As Ng (2000a) correctly notes, however, Kaplow's analysis does not deal with some of the distortionary costs mentioned earlier, such as the inducement to inefficient expenditure choices cited by Feldstein (1997) or the inducement to evasion and the consequent need for enforcement costs cited by Usher (1991). Particularly in developing countries, the latter form of distortion seems likely to remain extremely important. Combined with the much smaller likelihood that the tax systems in such countries can be considered to be very redistributive in either intent or outcome (Chu, Davoodi, and Gupta 2000), this consideration suggests that Kaplow's analysis should be viewed cautiously in this context.

Finally, an additional argument introduced by Ng (2000b) deserves brief mention. From the perspective of human happiness—a perspective that, however remote it may appear to the day-to-day work of most economists, underlies economic analysis—it has frequently been noted that relative incomes are often as (if not more) important than absolute incomes. Many expenditures affect relative incomes through, for example, the provision of such "positional goods" (Hirsch 1976) as education (public spending) and automobiles (private spending). Logically, the marginal benefit of expenditures should include such relative income effects, both negative and positive. As Galbraith (1958) noted long ago, the failure to do so on the whole tends to make private expenditure look relatively more beneficial than it really is in welfare terms and public expenditure correspondingly less attractive. While it seems unlikely to be practicable or desirable to attempt to take such relative income effects into account in project analysis, this consideration again casts doubt on the soundness of applying any general MCF rule in such analysis.

The Wicksellian Connection

A wide range of views on how to treat financing issues in the evaluation of public expenditures has been covered in this chapter. Three questions have been considered. First, should the shadow price of public finance be explicitly taken into account in expenditure evaluation? Second, if so, how should this shadow price be estimated? And, third, regardless of the answer to the first question, how much attention needs to be paid to the institutional links between expenditures and revenues—what Breton (1996) has called the *Wicksellian connection* that lies at the heart of an efficient public sector?

The answers to the first and second questions, as have been discussed, are by no means simple and do not easily yield simple rules. For example, when the financing of a project can be firmly linked to a properly designed benefit charge (a user charge, an earmarked benefit levy, or, in some instances, loan finance) or to some other form of burdenless fiscal change (such as a land tax, a Pigouvian tax, or the reduction of a distorting tax "incentive"), the application of an MCF correction—a shadow price of fiscal resources—seems inappropriate. Even when the probable source of budgetary finance is a clearly distorting tax system, the precise level of the correction to be applied will be sensitive to the nature of that system, the nature of the anticipated tax changes, and the nature of the expenditure being financed. To at least some extent, distortions associated with tax finance may reflect the distributional goals of society, and it is arguable that they should not be used to, in effect, unduly restrain the scope and level of public sector activity.

Despite all these considerations, Devarajan, Squire, and Suthiwart-Narueput (1997) might well be right as a practical matter in suggesting that at least a minimal MCF correction may often be called for, unless there is some very good reason not to make such a correction. A useful analogy might be with routine or habitual decisions compared with nonroutine or unique decisions. Most of us go through life using rules of thumb and conventional behaviors to cope with the routine, and as Simon (1959) has argued, it is generally efficient to do so, given the costs of obtaining and processing information. Because most expenditures are likely to be financed from general revenues, an MCF correction on the order of 20 percent or so is unlikely to do any harm and may provide a little counterbalance to the inevitable tendency of advocates to overstate the benefits of particular projects. When the situation is clearly different—as, for example, when an expenditure is to be financed from a well-designed earmarked revenue source—we can and should behave differently.

More basically, perhaps the most important lesson emerging from this brief review of some of these complex issues relates to the third question raised above. Here, the answer seems clear: Much more attention should be paid to links between expenditures and revenues than has been the rule to date in applied economic analysis of the public sector. Several such links have been noted in the course of the preceding discussion: (a) user charges or prices charged for public services, (b) earmarked benefit taxes, (c) local taxes to finance local services, (d) income taxes to finance general public goods, (e) loan finance for investment projects, and (f) proper budgeting procedures (for example, with respect to capital budgets and earmarked funds). Rather than elaborating these points further, I conclude with a few remarks about the general normative framework underlying this discussion and its implications for positive policy.

First, financing matters. It matters for two distinct reasons. The first is that how a project is assumed to be financed can and should affect the net present value of benefits to be expected from it, and hence whether it is worth doing or not. This is properly the principal concern of economic analysts, and, as the preceding discussion suggests, they often face a difficult task in determining how to cost different sources of financing—let alone whether and how to take account of such costs in carrying out quantitative analysis.

The second reason for being concerned about how public expenditures are financed is more basic. It goes to the heart of the central problem of public economics: what should governments do? As Devarajan, Squire, and Suthiwart-Narueput (1997) properly emphasize, determining what governments should do is inseparably entangled with how whatever they do is to be financed. What they perhaps do not stress sufficiently, however, is that (a) the proper treatment of efficiency costs is inextricably related to distributional concerns, and (b) it is critical in determining what governments should do to ensure that the link between expenditure and revenue decisions is as clearly established in the budgetary and political process as possible. As Musgrave (2000, 82–3) puts it:

> Defining the optimal outcome was simple enough, but how to reach it was the critical matter. This linkage between normative and operational analysis goes to the heart of the Wicksellian model. It thereby differs from the Pigouvian approach to budgeting as equating known marginal benefits and costs (Pigou 1928, chapter VII) and Samuelson's formulation whereby the optimal allocation of resources is decided by an omniscient referee (Samuelson 1954).

The distributional aspect was discussed earlier in connection with the argument of Kaplow (1996) for not making an MCF correction, on the grounds that such distortions are simply the cost paid for achieving the distributional goals of the polity. While I am skeptical of the relevance of this argument in the far-from-perfect democracies and the highly distorted tax systems prevalent in many developing countries, some attention should nonetheless be paid to this line of thought. After all, viewed in historical perspective, what Kaplow (1996) is in effect arguing is simply that, as Wicksell (1896) argued a century earlier, allocative decisions in the public sector will be made efficiently if they are financed efficiently—that is, by benefit taxes (or *Lindahl prices* as they are often called, following Wicksell's student, Lindahl [1919]). Wicksell further noted, however, that this mode of financing would be normatively and politically acceptable only if society had already adjusted the distribution of income and wealth to accord with the politically acceptable just distribution of income. A very similar argument was made by Kaplow (1996), who asserts, not implausibly, that it seems reasonable to consider that any proposed new expenditure will be financed in an essentially distributionally neutral fashion, in the sense that the preexisting distributional compromise embodied in the public finance system will not be significantly disturbed.[19]

In many ways, the heart of the financing question is what can be done to make the Wicksellian connection operational. Taking into account the financing side of public expenditures is not something that can or should simply be factored into project evaluation by some (nonexistent) omniscient observer who, on the basis of impartially weighing of the evidence, decides what is best for society, and especially not for someone else's society. Rather, it is an essential component of the process by which good budgetary decisions—decisions that, as closely as is practically feasible, should reflect people's real preferences—can be obtained in any society. As noted earlier, much of the rationale for "good" decentralization—that is, decentralization that increases accountability along the lines sketched, for example, in Bird (1993, 2001)—lies precisely in such arguments.

The same is true of all other devices for linking more closely financing and expenditure decisions discussed above. The point is not, for example, that user charge financing or capital budgeting is always preferable to general fund financing and budgeting. In many instances, indeed, such practices have arguably produced worse results than those that might have emerged with a soundly conceived and executed comprehensive budgetary system and a uniformly applied expenditure evaluation system along the lines sketched by, for example, Devarajan, Squire, and Suthiwart-Narueput (1997). As with decentralization, however, the fact that something has often been done wrongly in no way detracts from the basic argument that it can be done rightly and that, when so done, it will produce outcomes more in accordance with society's wishes and resources.

To put this final point another way, Devarajan, Squire, and Suthiwart-Narueput (1997) correctly stress the importance for good expenditure analysis of carefully specifying the "appropriate counterfactual" and note that this is by no means an easy task. In effect, what I am suggesting here is (a) that it is equally important, and difficult, to specify the appropriate public sector financing counterfactual; (b) that in some (perhaps many) instances that counterfactual may suggest that it is not appropriate to automatically apply an MCF correction to budgetary flows; and (c) and in many ways most importantly, that thinking through correctly the links between expenditures and revenues is critical not just for good project analysis but more fundamentally for good government.

The key to good results lies not in any particular budgetary or financing procedure but rather in implementing a public finance system that, to the extent possible, links specific expenditure and revenue decisions as transparently as possible. It is perhaps somewhat curious, then, that consideration of whether a shadow price of public funds should be taken into account in evaluating proposals for additional expenditures leads me to conclude that—unless one is prepared to adopt the untenable role of the Samuelsonian ethical observer—the ultimate deciders of what should be done should be those who are most directly affected, and that the best that can be done to ensure that the relevant decision makers make the right decision is to ensure that they and all those affected are made as aware as possible of all the relevant consequences.

Notes

1. Politicians are, of course, well aware of this connection, as evidenced by the many taxes that have been implemented over the years by tagging them with such "good" names as health, education, and defense.
2. For a strong argument, drawing on much past thought, that in fact we are and should be mainly interested in the combined effects of tax changes and the related expenditure changes, see Black (1939, chapter 10).
3. Interestingly, despite the apparent importance he attaches to this question, nowhere in the 800 pages of his textbook does Stiglitz (2000) refer to the many quantitative studies that have been made of these distortion costs for the United States.
4. For a recent review of this literature, see Auriol and Warlters (2001) who note the extreme variability of the estimates.
5. For example, Drèze and Stern (1987) explicitly say that "when projects are financed out of general revenue . . . it is not necessary to consider separately how individual projects are financed" (931). However, they go on to note that if there are earmarked taxes then explicit "side constraints" should be introduced into the model.
6. Useful recent reviews may be found, for example, in Layard and Glaister (1994) and Boardman and Greenberg (1998).
7. This argument, of course, predates the so-called Ricardian equivalence view popularized by Barro (1974), which asserts that rational individuals should be indifferent between tax and loan finance because the present value of the debt burden under loan finance is precisely equal to the taxes they would otherwise be assessed. The demanding assumptions required to achieve this equivalence seem most unlikely to hold in any developing country, or perhaps in any country.
8. The taxes on trade that dominate revenue systems in many smaller developing countries, for example, are generally highly distorting, as argued long ago by Dasgupta and Stiglitz (1974). In an earlier paper, Devarajan, Squire, and Suthiwart-Narueput (1996) instead cited the estimates from Browning (1987). It is not clear whether the change to the alternatively derived estimates in the later paper reflects any preference for one method of estimating MCF over another.
9. As Brent (1996) notes, the usual approach neglects revenue feedback by assuming— sometimes explicitly, as in Mayshar (1990)—that there is none. But this assumption need not accord with reality. As Brent goes on to note, to the extent that some benefits accrue to government as additional revenue, they could be said to produce an "excess benefit" by permitting tax rate reductions and hence a reduction in distortionary costs. This point is of course similar to that made by Devarajan, Squire, and Suthiwart-Narueput (1996) with respect to user charges.
10. Nonetheless, Devarajan, Squire, and Suthiwart-Narueput (1996) somewhat curiously use the old terminology of a premium on public income, although they clearly state that such a premium attaches only to revenue from (properly designed) pricing and measure it by the distortionary tax costs avoided. Devarajan, Squire, and

Suthiwart-Narueput (1997) avoid the resulting confusion—see, for example, the comments in Kirkpatrick and Weiss (1996, 10)—by emphasizing instead the MCF.

11. It should perhaps be noted that there is considerable dispute in the scanty literature that has considered such matters as the extent to which the welfare of evaders—or sometimes even avoiders, as in Musgrave (1992)—let alone that of corrupt officials, should be taken into account in summing up the net social benefits of policy actions. It is not sufficient in this context simply to distinguish between pecuniary transfers and real resource costs, because what is at issue is the social evaluation of outcomes and, as noted later, distribution is properly a matter of social concern.

12. Starrett (1988, 188) notes, for example, that if governments can export taxes, the MCF may be less than one.

13. As Sandmo (2001) shows, however, it is far from clear that "green taxes" yield an MCF less than one even if they are they the only source of funds. Sandmo correctly argues that in general the implications of externality-correcting taxes for the MCF depend crucially on the nature of the interaction of markets. It should be noted, however, that the explicit concern of his interesting argument is to define the MCF so that it is the same for all projects (with public goods elements) funded from general tax finance. This is not the perspective taken in this chapter.

14. Kaplow (1996) asserts that this is really a matter of "horizontal inequity" (519), but this seems wrong since it is clearly incorrect to assume that, for example, all those in a locality have equivalent incomes (or utility levels) either before or after the policy change. (For a recent fascinating discussion of the significance of horizontal equity, see the debate between Kaplow [1989, 1992] and Musgrave [1990, 1993]).

15. Other arguments to the effect that the MCF should incorporate some measure of the offsetting distributional gains may be found in, for example, Sandmo (1998) and Dahlby (1998).

16. Ng (1984) makes a somewhat similar argument in a related context.

17. Stiglitz (2000) makes a comment in the same spirit: "The use of distortionary taxes is thus an inevitable consequence of our desire to redistribute income, in a world in which the government can observe the characteristics of individuals only imperfectly (533)."

18. An example, a tax on kerosene, is analyzed in Hughes (1987).

19. In a similar fashion, Head and Bird (1983) refer to the quasi-constitutional nature of tax systems. More broadly, this argument may be related to Musgrave's (1969b) long-standing position that it is essential for clarity of thought to separate the allocative and distributional dimensions of public sector decisions.

References

Adler, John H. 1964. "Fiscal Policy in a Developing Economy." In *Readings on Taxation in Developing Countries,* ed. Richard M. Bird and Oliver Oldman, 31–58. Baltimore: Johns Hopkins.

Ahmad, Ehtisham, and Nicholas Stern. 1987. "Alternative Sources of Government Revenue: Illustrations from India, 1979–80." In *The Theory of Taxation for Developing Countries,* ed. David Newbery and Nicholas Stern, 281–332. New York: Oxford University Press.

———. 1991. *The Theory and Practice of Tax Reform in Developing Countries.* Cambridge, U.K.: Cambridge University Press.

Alm, James. 1999. "What Is an 'Optimal' Tax System?" In *Tax Policy in the Real World,* ed. Joel Slemrod, 363–80. Cambridge, U.K.: Cambridge University Press.

Atkinson, Anthony B., and Nicholas H. Stern. 1974. "Pigou, Taxation, and Public Goods." *Review of Economic Studies* 41: 119–28.

Auriol, Emmanuelle, and Michael Warlters. 2001. "Taxation in Developing Countries: Theory and Evidence." Draft paper for the International Seminar in Public Economics, Cornell University, Ithaca, New York, September.

Ballard, Charles L., and Don Fullerton. 1992. "Distortionary Taxes and the Provision of Public Goods." *Journal of Economic Perspectives* 6: 116–31.

Ballard, Charles L., and Steven G. Medema. 1993. "The Marginal Efficiency Effects of Taxes and Subsidies in the Presence of Externalities: A Computational General Equilibrium Approach." *Journal of Public Economics* 52 (2): 199–216.

Ballard, Charles L., John B. Shoven, and John Whalley. 1985. "General Equilibrium Computations of the Marginal Welfare Costs of Taxes in the United States." *American Economic Review* 75: 128–38.

Barro, Robert J. 1974. "Are Government Bonds Net Wealth?" *Journal of Political Economy* 82: 1095–1117.

Bird, Richard M. 1993. "Threading the Fiscal Labyrinth: Some Issues in Fiscal Decentralization." *National Tax Journal* 46: 207–27.

———. 1997. "Analysis of Earmarked Taxes." *Tax Notes International* 23 (June): 2095–116.

———. 2000. "Subnational Revenues: Realities and Prospects." In *Decentralization and Accountability of the Public Sector,* ed. S. J. Burki and G. Perry, 319–38. Proceedings of the Annual World Bank Conference on Development in Latin America and the Caribbean 1999. Washington, DC: World Bank.

———. 2001. *Intergovernmental Fiscal Relations in Latin America: Policy Designs and Policy Outcomes.* Washington, DC: Inter-American Development Bank.

Bird, Richard M., and Thomas Tsiopoulos. 1997. "User Charges for Public Services: Potentials and Problems." *Canadian Tax Journal* 45: 25–86.

Black, Duncan. 1939. *The Incidence of Income Taxes.* London: Macmillan.

Boadway, Robin W., and Neil Bruce. 1984. *Welfare Economics.* Oxford, U.K.: Basil Blackwell.

Boardman, Anthony E., and David H. Greenberg. 1998. "Discounting and the Social Discount Rate." In *Handbook of Public Finance,* ed. Fred Thompson and Mark T. Green, 269–319. New York: Marcel Dekker.

Break, George F. 1974. "The Incidence and Economic Effects of Taxation." In *The Economics of Public Finance,* ed. Alan S. Blinder, Robert M. Solow, George F. Break, Peter O. Steiner, and Dick Netzer, 119–237. Washington, DC: Brookings Institution.

Brent, Robert J. 1996. *Applied Cost-Benefit Analysis.* Cheltenham, U.K.: Edward Elgar.

Breton, Albert. 1996. *Competitive Governments.* Cambridge, U.K.: Cambridge University Press.

Browning, Edgar K. 1976. "The Marginal Cost of Public Funds." *Journal of Political Economy* 84: 283–98.

———. 1987. "On the Marginal Welfare Cost of Taxation." *American Economic Review* 72: 11–23.

Browning, Edgar K., and Liqun Liu. 1998. "The Optimal Supply of Public Goods and the Distortionary Cost of Taxation: Comment." *National Tax Journal* 51: 103–16.

Bruce, Neil. 1992. "A Note on the Taxation of International Capital Income Flows." *Economic Record* 68: 217–21.

Burki, Shahid Javed, and Guillermo Perry, eds. 2000. *Decentralization and Accountability of the Public Sector.* Proceedings of the Annual World Bank Conference on Development in Latin America and the Caribbean 1999. Washington, DC: World Bank.

Chu, Ke-young, Hamid Davoodi, and Sanjeev Gupta. 2000. "Income Distribution and Tax and Government Social Spending Policies in Developing Countries." IMF Working Paper WP/00/62, International Monetary Fund, Washington, DC.

Collard, David. 1989. "Compliance Costs and Efficiency Costs of Taxation." In *Administrative and Compliance Costs of Taxation,* ed. Cedric Sandford, Michael Godwin, and Peter Hardwick, 273–77. Bath, U.K.: Fiscal Publications.

Cullis, John, and Philip Jones. 1992. *Public Finance and Public Choice.* London: McGraw-Hill.

Dahlby, Bev. 1998. "Progressive Taxation and the Social Marginal Cost of Public Funds." *Journal of Public Economics* 67: 105–22.

Das-Gupta, Arindam, and Dilip Mookherjee. 1998. *Incentives and Institutional Reform in Tax Enforcement.* Oxford, U.K.: Oxford University Press.

Dasgupta, Partha, and Joseph E. Stiglitz. 1974. "Benefit-Cost Analysis and Trade Policies." *Journal of Political Economy* 82: 1–33.

Devarajan, Shanta, Lyn Squire, and Sethaput Suthiwart-Narueput. 1996. "Project Appraisal at the World Bank." In *Cost-Benefit Analysis and Project Appraisal in Developing Countries,* ed. Colin Kirkpatrick and John Weiss, 35–53. Cheltenham, U.K.: Edward Elgar.

———. 1997. "Beyond Rate of Return: Reorienting Project Appraisal." *World Bank Research Observer* 12: 35–46.

Diewert, W. Erwin, Denis A. Lawrence, and Fred Thompson. 1998. "The Marginal Cost of Taxation and Regulation." In *Handbook of Public Finance,* ed. Fred Thompson and Mark T. Green, 135–71. New York: Marcel Dekker.

Dinwiddy, Caroline, and Francis Teal. 1996. *Principles of Cost-Benefit Analysis for Developing Countries.* Cambridge, U.K.: Cambridge University Press.

Drèze, Jean, and Nicholas Stern. 1987. "The Theory of Cost-Benefit Analysis." In *Handbook of Public Economics,* vol. 2, ed. Alan J. Auerbach and Martin Feldstein, 909–89. Amsterdam: North-Holland.

Feldstein, Martin. 1972. "The Inadequacy of Weighted Discount Rates." In *Cost-Benefit Analysis,* ed. Richard Layard, 245–69. Harmondsworth, U.K.: Penguin Books.

———. 1997. "How Big Should Government Be?" *National Tax Journal* 50: 197–213.

Fullerton, Don, and Yolanda K. Henderson. 1989. "The Marginal Excess Burden of Different Capital Tax Instruments." *Review of Economics and Statistics* 71: 435–42.

Galbraith, John Kenneth. 1958. *The Affluent Society.* London: Hamish Hamilton.

George, Henry. 1879. *Progress and Poverty.* Reprint, New York: Robert Schalkenbach Foundation, 1979.

Goulder, Lawrence. 1995. "Environmental Taxation and the 'Double Dividend': A Reader's Guide." *International Tax and Public Finance* 2: 157–83.

Harberger, Arnold C. 1964. "The Measurement of Waste." *American Economic Review* 54: 58–76.

———. 1972. *Project Evaluation: Collected Papers.* London: Macmillan.

———. 1997. "New Frontiers in Project Evaluation: A Comment on Devarajan, Squire, and Suthiwart-Narueput." *World Bank Research Observer* 12: 73–79.

Head, John G., and Richard M. Bird. 1983. "Tax Policy Options in the 1980s." In *Comparative Tax Studies,* ed. Sjibren Cnossen, 3–29. Amsterdam: North-Holland.

Hirsch, Fred. 1976. *Social Limits to Growth.* Cambridge, MA: Harvard University Press.

Hughes, Gordon. 1987. "The Incidence of Fuel Taxes: A Comparative Study of Three Countries." In *The Theory of Taxation for Developing Countries,* ed. David Newbery and Nicholas Stern, 533–59. New York: Oxford University Press.

Kaplow, Louis. 1989. "Horizontal Equity: Measures in Search of a Principle." *National Tax Journal* 42: 139–54.

———. 1992. "A Note on Horizontal Equity." *Florida Law Review* 1: 191–96.

———. 1996. "The Optimal Supply of Public Goods and the Distortionary Cost of Taxation." *National Tax Journal* 49: 513–33.

———. 1998. "A Note on the Optimal Supply of Public Goods and the Distortionary Cost of Taxation." *National Tax Journal* 51: 117–25.

Kirkpatrick, Colin, and John Weiss. 1996. "Cost-Benefit Analysis for Developing Countries." In *Cost-Benefit Analysis and Project Appraisal in Developing Countries,* ed. Colin Kirkpatrick and John Weiss, 3–23. Cheltenham, U.K.: Edward Elgar.

Layard, Richard, and Stephen Glaister, eds. 1994. *Cost-Benefit Analysis,* 2nd ed. Cambridge, U.K.: Cambridge University Press.

Lindahl, Erik. 1919. "Just Taxation—A Positive Solution." In *Classics in the Theory of Public Finance,* ed. Richard A. Musgrave and Alan T. Peacock, 168–76. Reprint, London: Macmillan, 1958.

Mayshar, Joram. 1990. "On Measures of Excess Burden and Their Application." *Journal of Public Economics* 43: 263–89.

Mintz, Jack, and Jesus Seade. 1991. "Cash Flow or Income?" *World Bank Research Observer* 6: 177–90.

Musgrave, Richard A. 1959. *The Theory of Public Finance.* New York: McGraw-Hill.

———. 1969a. "Cost-Benefit Analysis and the Theory of Public Finance." *Journal of Economic Literature* 7: 797–806.

———. 1969b. "Provision for Social Goods." In *Public Economics,* ed. Julius Margolis and Henri Guitton, 124–44. London: Macmillan.

———. 1990. "Horizontal Equity, Once More." *National Tax Journal* 43: 113–22.

———. 1992. "Social Contract, Taxation and the Standing of Deadweight Loss." *Journal of Public Economics* 49: 369–81.

———. 1993. "Horizontal Equity: A Further Note." *Florida Tax Review* 1: 354–59.

———. 1997. "Micro and Macro Aspects of Fiscal Policy." In *Macroeconomic Dimensions of Public Finance,* ed. Mario Blejer and Teresa Ter-Minassian, 13–26. London: Routledge.

———. 2000. *The Foundations of Taxation and Expenditure.* Vol. III of *Public Finance in a Democratic Society.* Cheltenham, U.K.: Edward Elgar.

Myles, Gareth D. 1995. *Public Economics.* Cambridge, U.K.: Cambridge University Press.

Newbery, David, and Nicholas Stern, eds. 1987. *The Theory of Taxation for Developing Countries.* New York: Oxford University Press.

Ng, Yew-Kwang. 1984. "Quasi-Pareto Social Improvements." *American Economic Review* 74: 1033–50.

———. 1987. "Diamonds Are a Government's Best Friend: Burden-Free Taxes on Goods Valued for their Values." *American Economic Review* 77: 186–91.

———. 2000a. "The Optimal Size of Public Spending and the Distortionary Cost of Taxation." *National Tax Journal* 53: 253–72.

———. 2000b. *From Preference to Happiness: Towards a More Complete Welfare Economics.* Working paper. Monash University, Victoria, Australia.

Pigou, Arthur C. 1920. *Welfare Economics,* 4th ed. London: Macmillan.

———. 1928. *A Study in Public Finance,* 3rd ed. Reprint, London: Macmillan, 1947.

Premchand, A. 1993. *Government Budgeting and Expenditure Controls.* Washington, DC: International Monetary Fund.

———. 1998. *Control of Public Money.* Washington, DC: International Monetary Fund.

Renzetti, Steven. 1999. "Municipal Water Supply and Sewage Treatment: Costs, Prices, and Distortions." *Canadian Journal of Economics* 32: 688–704.

Samuelson, Paul A. 1954. "The Pure Theory of Public Expenditures." *Review of Economics and Statistics* 36: 350–56.

Sandford, Cedric, ed. 1995. *Tax Compliance Costs: Measurement and Policy.* Bath, U.K.: Fiscal Publications.

Sandmo, Agnar. 1998. "Redistribution and the Marginal Cost of Public Funds." *Journal of Public Economics* 70: 365–82.

———. 2001. *Bridging the Tax-Expenditure Gap: Green Taxes and the Marginal Cost of Funds.* Working Paper 579, CESifo, Munich.

Shoup, Carl S. 1969. *Public Finance.* Chicago: Aldine.

Simon, Herbert A. 1959. "Theories of Decision Making in Economics and Behavioral Science." *American Economic Review* 49: 253–83.

Squire, Lyn. 1989. "Project Evaluation in Theory and Practice." In *Handbook of Development Economics,* vol. 2, ed. Hollis Chenery and T. N. Srinivasan, 1093–137. Amsterdam: North-Holland.

Squire, Lyn, and Herman G. van der Tak. 1975. *Economic Analysis of Projects.* Baltimore: Johns Hopkins.

Starrett, David A. 1988. *Foundations of Public Economics.* Cambridge, U.K.: Cambridge University Press.

Stiglitz, Joseph E. 1994. "Discount Rates." In *Cost-Benefit Analysis,* 2nd ed., ed. Richard Layard and Stephen Glaister, 116–59. Cambridge, U.K.: Cambridge University Press.

———. 2000. *Economics of the Public Sector,* 3rd ed. New York: W. W. Norton.

Stiglitz, Joseph E., and Partha Dasgupta. 1971. "Differential Taxation, Public Goods, and Economic Efficiency." *Review of Economic Studies* 38: 151–74.

Thirsk, Wayne R., and Richard M. Bird. 1993. "Earmarked Taxes in Ontario: Solution or Problem?" In *Taxing and Spending,* ed. Allan M. Maslove, 129–84. Toronto, ON: University of Toronto Press.

Tideman, Nicolaus, ed. 1994. *Land and Taxation.* London: Shepheard-Walwyn.

Usher, Dan. 1986. "Tax Evasion and the Marginal Cost of Public Funds." *Economic Inquiry* 24: 563–86.

———. 1991. "Hidden Costs of Public Expenditure." In *More Taxing than Taxes?,* ed. Richard M. Bird, 11–65. San Francisco: ICS Press.

Wicksell, Knut. 1896. "A New Principle of Just Taxation." In *Classics in the Theory of Public Finance,* ed. Richard A. Musgrave and Alan T. Peacock, 72–118. London: Macmillan, 1958.

World Bank. 1998. *Public Expenditure Management Handbook.* Washington, DC: World Bank.

5

Guidelines for Public Debt Management

INTERNATIONAL MONETARY FUND AND
WORLD BANK STAFF

What Is Public Debt Management and Why Is It Important?

Sovereign debt management is the process of establishing a strategy for managing the government's debt to raise the required amount of funding, achieve risk and cost objectives, and meet any other sovereign debt management goals that the government may have set, such as developing and maintaining an efficient market for government securities.

In a broader macroeconomic context for public policy, governments should seek to ensure that both the level and rate of growth of public debt are fundamentally sustainable, and that the debt can be serviced under a wide range of circumstances while meeting cost and risk objectives. Sovereign debt managers share fiscal policy advisers' concern that public sector indebtedness remains on a sustainable path and that a credible strategy is in place to reduce excessive levels of debt. Debt managers should ensure that the fiscal authorities are aware of the impact of government financing requirements and debt levels on borrowing costs.[1] Examples of indicators that address the issue of debt sustainability include the public sector debt-servicing ratio and the ratios of public debt to gross domestic product (GDP) and to tax revenue.

109

Debt that is poorly structured in terms of maturity, currency, or interest rate composition and large and unfunded contingent liabilities have been factors in inducing or propagating economic crises in many countries throughout history. For example, irrespective of the exchange rate regime or whether domestic or foreign currency debt is involved, crises have often arisen because of an excessive focus by governments on possible cost savings associated with large volumes of short-term or floating-rate debt. This focus has left government budgets seriously exposed to changing financial market conditions, including changes in the country's creditworthiness, when this debt must be rolled over. Foreign currency debt also poses particular risks, and excessive reliance on foreign currency debt can lead to exchange rate or monetary pressures if investors become reluctant to refinance the government's foreign currency debt. By reducing the risk that the government's own portfolio management will become a source of instability for the private sector, prudent debt management can make countries less susceptible to financial contagion and risk.

A government's debt portfolio is usually the largest financial portfolio in the country. It often contains complex and risky financial structures and can generate substantial risk to the government's balance sheet and to the country's financial stability. As noted by the Financial Stability Forum's Working Group on Capital Flows, "Recent experience has highlighted the need for governments to limit the build-up of liquidity exposures and other risks that make their economies especially vulnerable to external shocks" (Financial Stability Forum 2000, 2). Therefore, sound risk management by the public sector is also essential for risk management by other sectors of the economy "because individual entities within the private sector typically are faced with enormous problems when inadequate sovereign risk management generates vulnerability to a liquidity crisis" (2). Sound debt structures help governments reduce their exposure to interest rate, currency, and other risks. Many governments seek to support these structures by establishing (where feasible) portfolio benchmarks relating to the desired currency composition, duration, and maturity structure of the debt to guide the future composition of the portfolio.

Several debt-market crises have highlighted the importance of sound debt management practices and the need for an efficient and sound capital market. Government debt management policies may not have been the sole or even the main cause of these crises. Yet, the maturity structure and the interest rate and currency compositions of the government's debt portfolio, together with obligations related to contingent liabilities, have often contributed to the severity of the crisis. Even in situations in which there are sound macroeconomic policy settings, risky debt management practices increase the vulnerability of the economy to economic and financial shocks. Sometimes these risks can be readily addressed by relatively straightforward measures, such as by lengthening the maturities of borrowings and paying the associated higher debt-servicing costs (assuming an upward sloping yield curve), by adjusting the amount, maturity, and composition of foreign exchange reserves, and by reviewing criteria and governance arrangements related to contingent liabilities.

Risky debt structures are often the consequence of inappropriate economic policies—fiscal, monetary, and exchange rate—but the feedback effects undoubtedly play out in both directions. However, there are limits to what sound debt management policies can deliver. Sound debt management policies are no panacea or substitute for sound fiscal and monetary management. If macroeconomic policy settings are poor, sound debt management may not by itself prevent any crisis. Sound debt management policies reduce susceptibility to financial contagion and risk by playing a catalytic role for broader financial market development and financial deepening. Recent experience supports the argument, for example, that domestic debt markets can substitute for bank financing when this source dries up (and vice versa), helping economies weather financial shocks (for example, see Greenspan 1999).

Purpose of the Guidelines for Public Debt Management

The guidelines are designed to assist policy makers in considering reforms to strengthen the quality of their public debt management and to reduce their country's vulnerability to international financial shocks. Vulnerability is often greater for smaller and emerging-market countries because their economies may be less diversified, have a smaller base of domestic financial savings and less-developed financial systems, and be more susceptible to financial contagion through the relative magnitudes of capital flows. As a result, the guidelines should be considered within a broader context of the factors and forces affecting a government's liquidity more generally and the management of its balance sheet. Governments often manage large foreign exchange reserves portfolios, their fiscal positions are frequently subject to real and monetary shocks, and they can have large exposures to contingent liabilities and to the consequences of poor balance sheet management in the private sector. Irrespective of whether financial shocks originate within the domestic banking sector or from global financial contagion, prudent government debt management policies, along with sound macroeconomic and regulatory policies, are essential for containing the human and output costs associated with such shocks.

The guidelines cover both domestic and external public debt and encompass a broad range of financial claims on the government. They identify areas in which there is broad agreement on what generally constitute sound practices in public debt management. The guidelines focus on principles applicable to a broad range of countries at different stages of development and with various institutional structures of national debt management. They should not be viewed as a set of binding practices or mandatory standards or codes, nor should their issuance suggest that a unique set of sound practices or prescriptions exists that would apply to all countries in all situations. Building capacity in sovereign debt management can take several years, and country situations and needs vary widely. These guidelines are mainly intended to assist policy makers by disseminating sound practices adopted by member countries in their debt management strategies and operations. Their implementation will vary from country to country, depending on each country's circumstances, such as its state of financial development.

Each country's capacity-building needs in sovereign debt management are different. Each country's needs are shaped by the capital market constraints it faces, its exchange rate regime, the quality of its macroeconomic and regulatory policies, its institutional capacity to design and implement reforms, its credit standing, and its objectives for public debt management. Nevertheless, the guidelines raise public policy issues that are relevant for all countries. Capacity building and technical assistance, therefore, must be carefully tailored to meet stated policy goals while the available policy settings, institutional framework, and technology and human and financial resources are recognized. The guidelines should assist policy advisers and decision makers involved in designing debt management reforms as they raise public policy issues that are relevant for all countries. This is the case whether the public debt comprises marketable debt or debt from bilateral or multilateral official sources, although the specific measures to be taken will differ to take into account a country's circumstances.

Every government faces policy choices concerning what its debt management objectives will be, what its preferred risk tolerance will be, which part of the government balance sheet the government debt managers should be responsible for, how it will manage contingent liabilities, and how it will establish sound governance for public debt management. On many of these issues, there is increasing convergence on what are considered prudent sovereign debt management practices that can also reduce vulnerability to financial contagion and shocks. These practices include recognizing the benefits of clear objectives for debt management, weighing risks against cost considerations, separating and coordinating debt and monetary management objectives and accountabilities, limiting debt expansion, carefully managing refinancing and market risks and the interest costs of debt burdens, and developing a sound institutional structure and policies for reducing operational risk, in which responsibilities and associated accountabilities are clearly delegated to the various government agencies involved in debt management.

Debt management needs to be linked to a clear macroeconomic framework, under which governments seek to ensure that the level and rate of growth in public debt are sustainable. Public debt management problems often find their origins in the lack of attention paid by policy makers to the benefits of having a prudent debt management strategy and the costs of weak macroeconomic management. In the first case, authorities should pay greater attention to the benefits of having a prudent debt management strategy, a framework, and policies that are coordinated with a sound macro policy framework. In the second case, inappropriate fiscal, monetary, or exchange rate policies generate uncertainty in financial markets regarding the future returns available on local currency–denominated investments, thereby inducing investors to demand higher risk premiums. Particularly in developing and emerging markets, borrowers and lenders alike may refrain from entering into longer-term commitments, which can stifle the development of domestic financial markets and severely hinder debt managers' efforts to protect the government from excessive rollover and foreign exchange risk. A good track record of implementing sound macro policies can help to alleviate this uncertainty. This should be combined with building appropriate technical infrastructure—such as a central registry and payments and settlement system—to facilitate the development of domestic financial markets.

Summary of the Debt Management Guidelines

Debt Management Objectives and Coordination

Objectives

The main objective of public debt management is to ensure that the government's financing needs and its payment obligations are met at the lowest possible cost over the medium to long run, consistent with a prudent degree of risk.

Scope

Debt management should encompass the main financial obligations over which the central government exercises control.

Coordination with Monetary and Fiscal Policies

Debt managers, fiscal policy advisers, and central bankers should share an understanding of the objectives of debt management, fiscal, and monetary policies given the interdependencies among their different policy instruments.

Where the level of financial development allows, there should be a separation of debt management and monetary policy objectives and accountabilities.

Debt management, fiscal, and monetary authorities should share information on the government's current and future liquidity needs.

Debt managers should inform the government on a timely basis of any emerging debt sustainability problems.

Transparency and Accountability

Clarity of Roles, Responsibilities, and Objectives of Financial Agencies Responsible for Debt Management

The allocation of responsibilities among the ministry of finance, the central bank, or a separate debt management agency, for advising on debt management policy and for undertaking primary debt issues, secondary market arrangements, depository facilities, and clearing and settlement arrangements for trade in government securities, should be publicly disclosed.

The objectives for debt management should be clearly defined and publicly disclosed, and the measures of cost and risk that are adopted should be explained.

Open Process for Formulating and Reporting of Debt Management Policies

Materially important aspects of debt management operations should be publicly disclosed.

Public Availability of Information on Debt Management Policies

The public should be provided with information on the past, current, and projected budgetary activities, including financing and the consolidated financial position of the government.

The government should regularly publish information on the stock and composition of its debt and financial assets, including their currency, maturity, and interest rate structures.

Accountability and Assurances of Integrity by Agencies Responsible for Debt Management

Debt management activities should be audited annually by external auditors.

Institutional Framework

Governance

The legal framework should clarify the authority to borrow and to issue new debt, invest, and undertake transactions on the government's behalf.

The organizational framework for debt management should be well specified and should ensure that mandates and roles are well articulated.

Management of Internal Operations and Legal Documentation

Risks of government losses from inadequate operational controls should be managed according to sound business practices, including well-articulated responsibilities for staff and clear monitoring and control policies and reporting arrangements.

Debt management activities should be supported by an accurate and comprehensive management information system with proper safeguards.

Staff members involved in debt management should be subject to a code of conduct and to conflict of interest guidelines regarding the management of their personal financial affairs.

Sound business recovery procedures should be in place to mitigate the risk that debt management activities might be severely disrupted by natural disasters, social unrest, or acts of terrorism.

Debt managers should make sure that they have received appropriate legal advice and that the transactions they undertake incorporate sound legal features.

Debt Management Strategy

The risks inherent in the structure of the government's debt should be carefully monitored and evaluated. These risks should be mitigated to the extent feasible by modifying the debt structure, taking into account the cost of doing so.

To help guide borrowing decisions and reduce the government's risk, debt managers should consider the financial and other risk characteristics of the government's cash flows.

Debt managers should carefully assess and manage the risks associated with foreign currency and short-term or floating-rate debt.

Cost-effective cash management policies should be in place to enable the authorities to meet with a high degree of certainty their financial obligations as they fall due.

Risk Management Framework

A framework should be developed to enable debt managers to identify and manage the trade-offs between expected costs and risks in the government debt portfolio.

To assess risk, debt managers should regularly conduct stress tests of the debt portfolio on the basis of the economic and financial shocks to which the government and the country more generally are potentially exposed.

Scope for Active Management

Debt managers who seek to actively manage the debt portfolio so as to profit from expectations of movements in interest rates and exchange rates that differ from those implicit in current market prices should be aware of the risks involved and should be held accountable for their actions.

Contingent Liabilities

Debt managers should consider the impact that contingent liabilities have on the government's financial position, including its overall liquidity, when making borrowing decisions.

Development and Maintenance of an Efficient Market for Government Securities

To minimize cost and risk over the medium to long run, debt managers should ensure that their policies and operations are consistent with the development of an efficient government securities market.

Portfolio Diversification and Instruments

The government should strive to achieve a broad investor base for its domestic and foreign obligations, with due regard to cost and risk, and should treat investors equitably.

Primary Market

Debt management operations in the primary market should be transparent and predictable.

To the extent possible, debt issuance should use market-based mechanisms, including competitive auctions and syndications.

Secondary Market

Governments and central banks should promote the development of resilient secondary markets that can function effectively under a wide range of market conditions.

The systems used to settle and clear financial market transactions involving government securities should reflect sound practices.

Discussion of the Debt Management Guidelines

Debt Management Objectives and Coordination

Objectives

The main objective of public debt management is to ensure that the government's financing needs and its payment obligations are met at the lowest possible cost over the medium to long run that is consistent with a prudent degree of risk. Prudent risk management to avoid dangerous debt structures and strategies (including monetary financing of the government's debt) is crucial, given the severe macroeconomic consequences of sovereign debt default and the magnitude of the ensuing output losses. These costs include business and banking insolvencies, as well as the diminished long-term credibility and capability of the government to mobilize domestic and foreign savings. Box 5.1 provides a list of the main risks encountered in sovereign debt management.

Governments should try to minimize expected debt-servicing costs and the cost of holding liquid assets, subject to an acceptable level of risk, over a medium- to long-term horizon.[2] Minimizing cost, while ignoring risk, should not be an objective. Transactions that appear to lower debt-servicing costs often embody significant risks for the government and can limit its capacity to repay lenders. Developed countries, which typically have deep and liquid markets for their government's securities, often focus primarily on market risk and, together with stress tests, may use sophisticated portfolio models for measuring this risk. In contrast, emerging-market countries, which have only limited (if any) access to foreign capital markets and which also have relatively undeveloped domestic debt markets, should give higher priority to rollover risk. Where appropriate, debt management policies to promote the development of the domestic debt market should also be included as a prominent government objective. This objective is particularly relevant for countries where market constraints are such that short-term debt, floating-rate debt, and foreign currency debt may, in the short run at least, be the only viable alternatives to monetary financing.

Scope

Debt management should encompass the main financial obligations over which the central government exercises control. These obligations typically include both marketable debt and nonmarket debt, such as concessional financing

B O X 5 . 1   Risks Encountered in Sovereign Debt Management

Market risk is the risk associated with changes in market prices such as interest rates, exchange rates, and commodity prices on the cost of the government's debt servicing. For both domestic and foreign currency debt, changes in interest rates affect debt-servicing costs on new issues when fixed-rate debt is refinanced and on floating-rate debt at the rate reset dates. Hence, short-duration (short-term or floating-rate) debt is usually considered more risky than long-term, fixed-rate debt. (Excessive concentration in very long-term, fixed-rate debt also can be risky as future financing requirements are uncertain.) Debt denominated in or indexed to foreign currencies also adds volatility to debt-servicing costs as measured in domestic currency owing to exchange rate movements. Bonds with correct options can exacerbate market and rollover risks.

Rollover risk is the risk that debt will have to be rolled over at an unusually high cost or, in extreme cases, cannot be rolled over at all. To the extent that rollover risk is limited to the risk that debt might have to be rolled over at higher interest rates, including changes in credit spreads, it may be considered a type of market risk. The inability to roll over debt and/or exceptionally large increases in government funding costs can lead to or exacerbate a debt crisis and thereby cause real economic losses, in addition to the purely financial effects of higher interest rates. Therefore, it is often treated separately. Managing this risk is particularly important for emerging-market countries.

Liquidity risk has two types. One type refers to the cost or penalty investors face in trying to exit a position because the number of transactors has markedly decreased or because a particular market lacks depth. This risk is particularly relevant in cases where debt management includes the management of liquid assets or the use of derivatives contracts. The other type of liquidity risk, for a borrower—refers to a situation in which the volume of liquid assets can diminish quickly in the face of unanticipated cash flow obligations and/or a possible difficulty in raising cash through borrowing in a short period of time.

Credit risk is the risk of nonperformance by borrowers on loans or other financial assets or by a counterparty on financial contracts. This risk is particularly relevant in cases where debt management includes the management of liquid assets. It may also be relevant in the acceptance of bids in auctions of securities issued by the government, as well as in relation to contingent liabilities and in derivative contracts entered into by the debt manager.

Settlement risk refers to the potential loss that the government could suffer as a result of failure to settle, for whatever reason other than default, by the counterparty.

Operational risk includes a range of different types of risks, including errors in the various stages of executing and recording transactions, inadequacies or failures in internal controls or in systems and services, reputation risk, legal risk, security breaches, or natural disasters that affect business activity.

obtained from bilateral and multilateral official sources. In a number of countries, the scope of debt management operations has broadened in recent years. The public sector debt that is included or excluded from the central government's mandate over debt management will vary from country to country, depending on the nature of the political and institutional frameworks.[3]

Domestic and foreign currency borrowings are now typically coordinated. Moreover, debt management often encompasses the oversight of liquid financial assets and potential exposures from off–balance sheet claims on the central government, including contingent liabilities such as state guarantees. In establishing and implementing a strategy for managing the central government's debt in order to achieve its cost and risk objectives and any other sovereign debt management goals, the central government should, whenever possible, monitor and review the potential exposures that may arise from guaranteeing the debts of subnational governments and state-owned enterprises. It should also be aware of the overall financial position of private sector borrowers.

The borrowing calendars of the central and subnational government borrowers may need to be coordinated to ensure that auctions of new issues are appropriately spaced.

Coordination with Monetary and Fiscal Policies

Debt managers, fiscal policy advisers, and central bankers should share an understanding of the objectives of debt management and fiscal and monetary policies, given the interdependencies of their different policy instruments. Policy makers should understand the ways in which the different policy instruments operate and their potential to reinforce one another, and how policy tensions can arise.[4] Prudent debt management and fiscal and monetary policies can reinforce one another to lower the risk premiums in the structure of long-term interest rates. Monetary authorities should inform the fiscal authorities of the effects of the government debt levels on the achievement of their monetary objectives. Borrowing limits and sound risk management practices can help to protect the government's balance sheet from debt-servicing shocks. In some cases, conflicts between debt management and monetary policies can arise owing to the different purposes—debt management policy focuses on the cost-risk trade-off, while monetary policy is normally directed toward achieving price stability. For example, some central banks may prefer that the government issue inflation-indexed debt or borrow in foreign currency to bolster the credibility of monetary policy. Debt managers may believe that the market for such inflation-indexed debt has not been fully developed and that foreign currency debt introduces greater risk onto the government's balance sheet. Conflicts can also arise between debt managers and fiscal authorities, for example, on the cash flows inherent in a given debt structure (for example, issuing zero-coupon debt to transfer the debt burden to future generations). For this reason, it is important that coordination take place in the context of a clear macroeconomic framework.

Where the level of financial development allows, the objectives and accountabilities of debt management and monetary policy should be separate. Clarity in the roles and objectives for debt management and monetary policies minimizes potential conflicts. In countries with well-developed financial markets, borrowing programs are based on the economic and fiscal projections contained in the government budget, and monetary policy is carried out independently from debt management. This helps ensure that debt management decisions are not perceived to be influenced by inside information on interest rate decisions and avoids perceptions of conflicts of interest in market operations. A goal of cost minimization over time for the government's debt, subject to a prudent level of risk, should not be viewed as a mandate to reduce interest rates or to influence domestic monetary conditions. Neither should the cost/risk minimization objective be seen as a justification for the extension of low-cost central bank credit to the government—nor should monetary policy decisions be driven by debt management considerations.

Debt management, fiscal, and monetary authorities should share information on the government's current and future liquidity needs. Since monetary operations are often conducted using government debt instruments and markets, the choice of monetary instruments and operating procedures can have an impact on the functioning of government debt markets and potentially on the financial condition of dealers in these markets. By the same token, the efficient conduct of monetary policy requires a solid understanding of the government's short- and longer-term financial flows. As a result, debt management and fiscal and monetary officials often meet to discuss a wide range of policy issues. At the operational level, debt management, fiscal, and monetary authorities generally share information on the government's current and future liquidity needs. They often coordinate their market operations so as to ensure that they are not operating in the same market segment at the same time. Nevertheless, achieving separation between debt management policy and monetary policy might be more difficult in countries with less-developed financial markets, since debt management operations may have correspondingly larger effects on the level of interest rates and the functioning of the local capital market. Consideration needs to be given to the sequencing of reforms to achieve this separation.

Debt managers should inform the government on a timely basis of any emerging-debt sustainability problems. Although the responsibility for ensuring prudent debt levels lies with fiscal authorities,[5] debt managers' analysis of the cost and risk of the debt portfolio may contain useful information for fiscal authorities' debt sustainability analysis (and vice versa).[6] In addition, debt managers play an important role in setting the composition of that debt through their borrowing activity in financial markets on behalf of the government. This places them in direct contact with market participants, and their observations of investor behavior in both primary and secondary markets, as well as their discussions with market participants, may provide useful insights into the willingness of investors to hold that debt. This window on investors' views can be a useful input into fiscal authorities' assessments of debt sustainability and may help policy makers identify any emerging debt sustainability concerns. Thus, debt managers should extract relevant indicators from their debt portfolio cost-risk analysis and should gather and analyze financial market participants' views on the sustainability of the government's debt in a systematic fashion. They should also have the appropriate communication channels in place so that they can share this information with fiscal authorities on a timely basis.

Transparency and Accountability[7]

As outlined in the IMF (1999a) *Code of Good Practices on Transparency in Monetary and Financial Policies: Declaration of Principles* (the MFP Transparency Code), the case for transparency in debt management operations is based on two premises. First, the effectiveness of such operations can be strengthened if the goals and instruments of policy are known to the public (financial markets) and if the authorities can make a credible commitment to meeting them. Second, transparency can enhance good governance through greater accountability of central banks, finance ministries, and other public institutions involved in debt management.

Clarity of Roles, Responsibilities, and Objectives of Financial Agencies Responsible for Debt Management

The allocation of responsibilities—among the ministry of finance, the central bank or a separate debt management agency—for debt management policy advice and for undertaking primary debt issues, secondary market arrangements, depository facilities, and clearing and settlement arrangements for trade in government securities—should be publicly disclosed.[8] Transparency in the mandates and clear rules and procedures in the operations of the central bank and ministry of finance can help resolve these conflicts, strengthen governance, and facilitate policy consistency. Transparency and simplicity in debt management operations and in the design of debt instruments can also help issuers reduce transaction costs and meet their portfolio objectives. They may also reduce uncertainty among investors, lower investors' transaction costs, meet investors' portfolio objectives, encourage greater investor participation, and over time help governments lower debt-servicing costs.

The objectives for debt management policy should be clearly defined and publicly disclosed, and the measures of cost and risk that are adopted should be explained.[9] Some sovereign debt managers also publicly disclose their portfolio benchmarks for cost and risk, although this practice is not universal. Experience suggests that such disclosure enhances the credibility of the debt management program and helps achieve debt management goals. Complementary objectives, such as domestic financial market development, should also be publicly disclosed. Their relationship with the primary objective should be clearly defined.

Clear debt management objectives are essential to reduce uncertainty as to the government's willingness to trade off costs and risks. Unclear objectives often lead to poor decisions on how to manage existing debt and what types of debt to issue, particularly during times of market instability—resulting in a potentially risky and expensive debt portfolio for the government and adding to its vulnerability to a crisis. Lack of clarity with respect to objectives also creates uncertainty within the financial community. This can increase government debt-servicing costs because investors incur costs in attempting to monitor and interpret the government's objectives and policy framework, and they may require higher risk premiums because of this uncertainty.

Open Process for Formulating and Reporting of Debt Management Policies

The IMF (2001) *Code of Good Practices on Fiscal Transparency—Declaration of Principles* (the FT Code) highlights the importance of and need for a clear legal and administrative framework for debt management, including mechanisms for the coordination and management of budgetary and extrabudgetary activities.

Regulations and procedures for the primary distribution of government securities, including the auction format and rules for participation, bidding, and allocation, should be clear to all participants. Rules covering the licensing of primary dealers (if engaged) and other officially designated intermediaries in government securities, including the criteria for their choice and their rights and obligations, should also be publicly disclosed.[10] Regulations and procedures covering secondary market operations in government securities should be publicly disclosed, including any intervention undertaken by the central bank as an agent for the government's debt management operations.[11]

Public Availability of Information on Debt Management Policies

The public should be provided with information on the past, current, and projected budgetary activity, including its financing, and consolidated financial position of the government. Disclosure of information on the flow and stock of government debt (if possible on a cash and accrual basis) is important.[12] Liberalized capital markets react swiftly to new information and developments, and in the most efficient of these markets, participants react to information whether it is published or not. Market participants will attempt to infer information that is not disclosed, and there is probably no long-term advantage to the issuer from withholding materially important information on, for example, the estimated size and timing of new debt issuance. Therefore debt managers most regularly publish projected domestic borrowing programs. Some adhere to set patterns of new issuance while retaining flexibility to fix the amounts and maturities of instruments that will be auctioned until one or two weeks before the auction.

The government should regularly publish information on the stock and composition of its debt and financial assets, including their currency, maturity, and interest rate structures.[13] The financial position of the public sector should be disclosed regularly.[14] Where contingent liabilities exist (for example, through explicit deposit insurance schemes sponsored by the government), information on their cost and risk aspects should be disclosed whenever possible in the public accounts.[15] It is also important that the tax treatment of public securities be clearly disclosed when they are first issued. The objectives and fiscal costs of tax preferences, if any, for government securities should also be disclosed.

Transparency and sound policies can be seen as complements. The MFP Transparency Code (IMF, 1999a) recognizes, however, that there may be circumstances in which it is appropriate to limit the extent of such transparency.[16] For example, a government may not wish to publicize its pricing strategy before debt repurchases, in order to avoid having prices move against it. However, in general, such limitations would be expected to apply on relatively few occasions with respect to debt management operations.

Accountability and Assurances of Integrity by Agencies Responsible for Debt Management

Debt management activities should be audited annually by external auditors. The accountability framework for debt management can be strengthened by public disclosure of audit reviews of debt management operations.[17] Audits of government financial statements should be conducted regularly and publicly disclosed on a pre-announced schedule, including information on operating

expenses and revenues.[18] A national audit body, such as the agency responsible for auditing government operations, should provide timely reports on
the financial integrity of the central government accounts. In addition, there
should be regular audits of debt managers' performance and of systems and
control procedures.

Institutional Framework

Governance

*The legal framework should clarify the authority to borrow and to issue new debt,
invest, and undertake transactions on the government's behalf.* The authority to
borrow should be clearly defined in legislation.[19] Sound governance practices
are an important component of sovereign debt management, given the size of
government debt portfolios.

The soundness and credibility of the financial system can be supported
by assurances that the government debt portfolio is being managed prudently
and efficiently. Moreover, counterparties need assurances that the sovereign
debt managers have the legal authority to represent the government, and that
the government stands behind any transactions onto which its sovereign debt
managers enter. An important feature of the legal framework is the authority to issue new debt, which is normally stipulated in the form of either borrowing authority legislation with a preset limit or a debt ceiling.

*The organizational framework for debt management should be well speci-
fied and should ensure that mandates and roles are well articulated.*[20] Legal
arrangements should be supported by the delegation of appropriate authority to debt managers. Experience suggests that there is a range of institutional
alternatives for locating the sovereign debt management functions across one
or more agencies, including in one or more of the following: the ministry of
finance, the central bank, an autonomous debt management agency, and a
central depository.[21] Regardless of which approach is chosen, the key requirement is to ensure that the organizational framework surrounding debt management is clearly specified, that there is coordination and sharing of
information, and that the mandates of the respective players are clear.[22]

Many debt managers file an annual debt management report, which
reviews the previous year's activities and provides a broad overview of borrowing plans for the current year based on the annual budget projections.
These reports increase the accountability of government debt managers.
They also assist financial markets by disclosing the criteria used to guide the
debt program, the assumptions and trade-offs underlying the setting of
these criteria, and the managers' performance in meeting them.

Management of Internal Operations and Legal Documentation

Risks of government losses from inadequate operational controls should be managed according to sound business practices, including well-articulated sets of responsibilities for staff and clear monitoring and control policies and reporting arrangements. Operational risk, caused by inadequate controls and policy breaches—can entail large losses to the government and tarnish the reputation of debt managers. Sound risk monitoring and control practices are essential to reduce operational risk.

Operational responsibility for debt management is generally separated into front and back offices, with distinct functions and accountabilities and with separate reporting lines. The front office is typically responsible for executing transactions in financial markets, including the management of auctions and other forms of borrowing and all other funding operations. It is important to ensure that the individual executing a market transaction and the one responsible for entering the transaction into the accounting system are different people. The back office handles the settlement of transactions and the maintenance of the financial records. In a number of cases, a separate middle or risk management office has also been established to undertake risk analysis and monitor and report on portfolio-related risks and to assess the performance of debt managers against any strategic benchmarks. This separation helps promote the independence of those setting and monitoring the risk management framework and assessing performance from those responsible for executing market transactions. Where debt management services are provided by the central bank on behalf of the government's debt managers (for example, registry and auction services), the responsibilities and accountabilities of each party and agreement on service standards can be formalized through an agency agreement between the central bank and the government debt managers.

Government debt management requires a staff with a combination of financial market skills (such as portfolio management and risk analysis) and public policy skills. Regardless of the institutional structure, the ability to attract and retain skilled debt management staff is crucial to mitigating operational risk. This can be a major challenge for many countries, especially where there is a high demand for such personnel in the private sector or an overall shortage of such skills generally. Investment in training can help alleviate these problems, but where large salary differentials persist between the public and private sectors for such staff members, government debt managers often find it difficult to retain these skills.

Debt management activities should be supported by an accurate and comprehensive management information system with proper safeguards. Countries that are beginning the process of building capacity in government debt management need to give a high priority to developing accurate debt record-ing and reporting systems. This accuracy is required not only for producing debt data and ensuring timely payment of debt service, but also for improv-ing the quality of budgetary reporting and the transparency of government financial accounts. The management information system should capture all relevant cash flows and should be fully integrated into the government's accounting system. Although such systems are essential for debt management and risk analysis, their introduction often poses major challenges for debt managers in terms of expense and management time. However, the costs and complexities of the system should be appropriate to the organization's needs.

Staff members involved in debt management should be subject to a code of conduct and conflict of interest guidelines regarding the management of their per-sonal financial affairs. This will help allay concerns that staff members' per-sonal financial interests may undermine sound debt management practices.

Sound business recovery procedures should be in place to mitigate the risk that debt management activities might be severely disrupted by natural disas-ters, social unrest, or acts of terrorism. Given that government debt issuance is increasingly based on efficient and secure electronic book–entry systems, comprehensive business recovery procedures, including backup systems and controls, are essential to ensure the continuing operation of the govern-ment's debt management, maintain the integrity of the ownership records, and provide full confidence to debt holders in the safety of their investments.

Debt managers should make sure that they have received appropriate legal advice and that the transactions they undertake incorporate sound legal features. It is important for debt managers to receive appropriate legal advice and to ensure that the transactions they undertake are backed by sound legal docu-mentation. In doing so, debt managers can help governments clarify their rights and obligations in the relevant jurisdictions. Several issues deserve par-ticular attention, including the design of important provisions of debt instru-ments, such as clearly defining events of default, especially if such events extend beyond payment defaults on the relevant obligations (for example, cross-defaults and cross-accelerations); the breadth of a negative pledge clause; and the scope of the waiver of sovereign immunity. Disclosure obli-gations in the relevant markets must be analyzed in detail because they can vary from one market to another.

One issue that has received increasing attention in recent years is the design of collective action clauses (CACs) and the incorporation of such clauses in international bond documentation. If a government is forced to restructure its debt in a crisis, these clauses allow a supermajority to bind all bondholders within the same issue to the financial terms of a restructuring and to limit the ability of a minority of bondholders to disrupt the restructuring process by enforcing such bondholders' claims after a default. In a debt restructuring process, there is a risk that a minority of holdout investors could slow or disrupt an agreement that a supermajority would be prepared to support. By mitigating this risk, CACs could contribute to more orderly and rapid sovereign debt workouts. When issuing sovereign bonds governed by foreign laws, debt managers should consider including these clauses in new borrowings in consultation with their financial and legal advisers.[23] Box 5.2 describes some of the key features of collective action clauses.

Debt Management Strategy

The risks inherent in the government's debt structure should be carefully monitored and evaluated. These risks should be mitigated to the extent feasible by modifying the debt structure, taking into account the cost of doing so. Box 5.3 summarizes some of the pitfalls encountered in sovereign debt management. A range of policies and instruments can be engaged to help manage these risks.

Identifying and managing market risk involves examining the financial characteristics of the revenues and other cash flows available to the government to service its borrowings, and choosing a portfolio of liabilities that matches these characteristics as closely as possible. When they are available, hedging instruments can be used to move the cost and risk profile of the debt portfolio closer to the preferred portfolio composition.

Some emerging-market governments would be well served to accept higher liquidity premiums and thus keep rollover risks under control, since concentrating the debt in benchmark issues at key points along the yield curve may increase rollover risk. However, reopening previously issued securities to build benchmark issues can enhance market liquidity, thereby reducing the liquidity risk premiums in the yields on government securities and lowering government debt-servicing costs. Governments seeking to build benchmark issues often hold liquid financial assets; spread the maturity profile of the debt portfolio across the yield curve; and use domestic debt buybacks, conversions, or swaps of older issues with new issues to manage the associated rollover risks.

Some debt managers also have treasury management responsibilities.[24] In countries where debt managers are also responsible for managing liquid assets, debt managers have adopted a multipronged approach to the management of the credit risk inherent in their investments in liquid financial assets and in financial derivatives transactions.[25] In countries where credit ratings are widely available, debt managers should limit investments to those with credit ratings from independent rating agencies that meet a preset

BOX 5.2   Collective Action Clauses

Although the inclusion of collective action clauses (CACs) in bond documentation has been a long-standing market practice in some jurisdictions (notably including bonds governed by English law), 2003 witnessed a clear shift toward the use of CACs in bonds governed by New York law (which represent a large portion of emerging-market government bond issues). For example, emerging-market countries such as Brazil, Mexico, the Republic of Korea, and South Africa have included CACs in their recent international bond issues governed by New York law. In addition, many developed countries have also committed to including CACs in their international bond issues so as to encourage their adoption as standard practice in the market. These clauses enable a qualified majority of bondholders to make decisions that become binding on all creditors of a particular bond issue, thereby helping to bring about a more orderly and prompt restructuring. They could also help governments avoid the large macroeconomic costs that might ensue if they are unable to restructure unsustainable debts in an orderly and predictable fashion. Though some concern has been expressed that their inclusion might increase borrowing costs for some governments, there has not been any evidence of a premium associated with the use of CACs in bonds issued in 2003.

One of the most important features of CACs is the *majority restructuring provision,* which enables a qualified supermajority of bondholders to bind all bondholders within the same issue to the terms of a restructuring agreement, either before or after a default.[a] Majority restructuring provisions are typically found in bonds governed by English, Japanese, and Luxembourg law, whereas bonds governed by New York law did not include these provisions until very recently. In Germany, though CACs are possible in principle, further legal clarification is under way to facilitate a broader use of CACs in foreign sovereign bond issues.

Another type of CAC is the *majority enforcement provision,* which is designed to limit the ability of a minority of bondholders to disrupt the restructuring process by enforcing their claims after a default but before a restructuring agreement. Two of these provisions can be found in bonds governed by English and New York law: (a) an affirmative vote of a minimum percentage of bondholders (typically representing 25 percent of outstanding principal) is required to accelerate their claims after a default; and (b) a simple or qualified majority can reverse such an acceleration after the default on the originally scheduled payments has been cured. An even more effective type of majority enforcement provision can be found in trust deeds that are governed by English law but that are also possible for bonds issued in other jurisdictions. A key feature is that the right to initiate legal proceedings on behalf of all bondholders is conferred on the trustee, subject to certain limitations.

Further information on collective action clauses can be found in IMF (2002a, b, 2003b). See also Group of 10 (2002).

[a]Thresholds that have been used for amending payment terms have ranged from 66.67 to 85 % of either the outstanding principal or the claims of bondholders present at a duly convened meeting.

B O X   5 . 3   Some Pitfalls in Debt Management

1. *Increasing the vulnerability of the government's financial position by increasing risk, even though it may lead to lower costs and a lower deficit in the short run.* Debt managers should avoid exposing their portfolios to risks of large or catastrophic losses, even with low probabilities, in an effort to capture marginal cost savings that would appear to be relatively low risk.

   ■ Maturity structure. A government faces an intertemporal trade-off between short-term and long-term costs that should be managed prudently. For example, excessive reliance on short-term or floating-rate paper to take advantage of lower short-term interest rates may leave a government vulnerable to volatile and possibly increasing debt-servicing costs if interest rates increase, and the risk of default in the event that a government cannot roll over its debts at any cost. It could also affect the achievement of a central bank's monetary objectives.
   ■ Excessive unhedged foreign exchange exposures. This can take many forms, but the predominant one is directly issuing excessive amounts of foreign currency–denominated debt and foreign exchange–indexed debt. This practice may leave governments vulnerable to volatile and possibly increasing debt-servicing costs if their exchange rates depreciate and to the risk of default if they cannot roll over their debts.
   ■ Debt with embedded put options. If poorly managed, these increase uncertainty for the issuer, effectively shortening the portfolio duration and creating greater exposure to market and rollover risks.
   ■ Implicit contingent liabilities, such as implicit guarantees provided to financial institutions. If poorly managed, they tend to be associated with significant moral hazard.

2. *Debt management practices that distort private versus government decisions, as well as understate the true interest cost.*

   ■ Debt collateralized by shares of state-owned enterprises or other assets. In addition to understating the underlying interest cost, they may distort decisions regarding asset management.
   ■ Debt collateralized by specific sources of future tax revenue. If a future stream of revenue is committed for specific debt payments, a government may be less willing to undertake changes that affect this revenue, even if the changes would improve the tax system.
   ■ Tax-exempt or reduced-tax debt. This practice is used to encourage the placement of government debt. The impact on the deficit is ambiguous, since it will depend upon the taxation of competing assets and whether the after-tax rates of return on taxable and tax-exempt government paper are equalized.

(continued)

BOX 5.3   Some Pitfalls in Debt Management *(continued)*

3. *Misreporting of contingent or guaranteed debt liabilities.* This action may understate the actual level of the government's liabilities.

   ■ Inadequate coordination or procedures with regard to borrowings by lower levels of government, which may be guaranteed by the central government, or by state-owned enterprises.
   ■ Repeated debt forgiveness for lower levels of government or for state-owned enterprises.
   ■ Guaranteeing loans that have a high probability of being called (without appropriate budgetary provisions).

4. *Use of non–market financing channels.* In some cases this practice can be unambiguously distortionary.

   ■ Special arrangements with the central bank for concessional credit, including zero- and low-interest overdrafts or special treasury bills.
   ■ Forced borrowing from suppliers either through expenditure arrears or through the issuance of promissory notes and tied to borrowing arrangements. This practice tends to raise the price of government expenditures.
   ■ Creating a captive market for government securities. For example, in some countries the government pension plan is required to buy government securities. In other cases, banks are required to acquire government debts against a certain percentage of their deposits. Although such liquid asset ratios can sometimes serve as a useful prudential tool for liquidity management, they have distortionary effects on debt-servicing costs, as well as on financial market development.

5. *Improper oversight or recording of debt contracting and payment or of debt holders.* Government control over the tax base and/or the supply of outstanding debt is reduced.

   ■ Failing to record implicit interest on zero-interest long-term debts. Although doing so helps the cash position of the government, if the implicit interest is not recorded the true deficit is understated.
   ■ Too broad an authority to incur debt. This can be due to the absence of parliamentary reporting requirements on debt incurred, or the absence of a borrowing limit or debt ceiling. However, the authority must ensure that existing debt-servicing obligations are met.
   ■ Inadequate controls regarding the amount of debt outstanding. In some countries, a breakdown in internal operations and poor documentation led to more debt being issued than had been officially authorized.
   ■ Onerous legal requirements with respect to certain forms of borrowing. In some countries, more onerous legal requirements with respect to long-maturity borrowings (relative to short-maturity borrowings) have led to disproportionate reliance on short-term borrowings, thus compounding rollover risk.

minimum requirement. All governments, however, should set exposure limits for individual counterparties that take account of the government's actual and contingent consolidated financial exposure to that counterparty arising from management operations related to debt and foreign exchange reserves. Credit risk can also be managed by holding a diversified portfolio across a number of acceptable financial counterparties and also through collateral agreements. Settlement risk is controlled by having clearly documented settlement procedures and responsibilities and often placing limits on the size of payments flowing through any one settlement bank.

To help guide borrowing decisions and reduce the government's risk, debt managers should consider the financial and other risk characteristics of the government's cash flows. Rather than simply examining the debt structure in isolation, several governments have found it valuable to consider debt management within a broader framework of the government's balance sheet and the nature of its revenues and cash flows. Irrespective of whether governments publish a balance sheet, conceptually all governments have such a balance sheet, and consideration of the financial and other risks of the government's assets can provide the debt manager with important insights for managing the risks of the government's debt portfolio. For example, a conceptual analysis of the government's balance sheet may provide debt managers with some useful insights about the extent to which the currency structure of the debt is consistent with the revenues and cash flows available to the government to service that debt. In most countries, these revenues and cash flows mainly consist of tax revenues, which are usually denominated in local currency. In this case, the government's balance sheet risk would be reduced by issuing debt primarily in long-term, fixed-rate, domestic currency securities. For countries without well-developed domestic debt markets, this may not be feasible, and governments are often faced with the choice between issuing short-term or indexed domestic debt and foreign currency debt.

Issues such as the crowding out of private sector borrowers and the difficulties of issuing domestic currency debt in highly dollarized economies also should be considered. But the financial analysis of the government's revenues and cash flows provides a sound basis for measuring the costs and risks of the feasible strategies for managing the government's debt portfolio. The asset and liability management (ALM) approach is summarized in box 5.4.

Some countries have extended this approach to include other government assets and liabilities. For example, in some countries where the foreign exchange reserves are funded by foreign currency borrowings, debt managers have reduced the government's balance sheet risk by ensuring that the currency composition of the debt that backs the reserves—after taking

BOX 5.4   Asset and Liability Management

Some governments are seeking to learn from companies that have successfully managed their core business and financial risks. Financial intermediaries, for example, seek to manage their business and financial risks by matching the financial characteristics of their liabilities to their assets (off as well as on the balance sheet), given their core business objectives. This approach is known as asset and liability management (ALM). For example, a life insurance company is in the business of selling policies that have a relatively stable expected long-term payment structure as determined by actuarial tables of expected mortality. To minimize its financial risk, such a company will invest the proceeds of its policy sales in long-term assets, to match the expected payout on its policies.

In some ways a government resembles a company. It receives revenues from taxpayers and other sources, and it uses them to pay operating expenses, make transfer payments, purchase foreign exchange, invest in public infrastructure and state-owned enterprises, and meet debt-servicing costs. A government may also make loans and provide guarantees, both explicit and implicit. These various government operations may be undertaken to fulfill a broad range of macroeconomic, regulatory, national defense, and social policy objectives. However, in the process a government incurs financial and credit risks, which can be managed by considering the types of risks associated with both its assets and its liabilities.

There are important differences between the role of the government and that of private companies. While some governments have attempted to produce a balance sheet quantifying the value of their assets and liabilities, and more governments may attempt this in the future, this is not essential for the ALM approach. Instead, the objective of the ALM approach is to consider the various types of assets and obligations the government manages and to explore whether the financial characteristics associated with those assets can provide insights for managing the cost and risk of the government's liabilities. This analysis involves examining the financial characteristics of the asset cash flows and selecting, to the extent possible, liabilities with matching characteristics to help smooth the budgetary impact of shocks on debt-servicing costs. If full matching is not possible or is too costly, the analysis of cash flows also provides a basis for measuring the risks of the liability portfolio and measuring cost/risk trade-offs.

Using a conceptual ALM framework for the debt management problem can be a useful approach for several reasons. At a minimum, it grounds the cost-risk analysis of the government's debt portfolio in an analysis of the government's revenues that will be used to service that debt, which in most cases are denominated by the government's tax revenues. It enables the government debt managers to consider the other types of assets and liability portfolios that the government manages, besides its tax revenues and direct debt portfolio. Assessing the main risks around these portfolios can help a government design a comprehensive strategy to help reduce the overall risk in its balance sheet.

(continued)

BOX 5.4   Asset and Liability Management *(continued)*

> The ALM approach also provides a useful framework for considering governance arrangements for managing the government's balance sheet. This could, for example, involve deciding whether the government should maintain an ownership interest in producing particular goods and services, and the best organizational structure for managing the assets it wishes to retain.
>
> The ALM approach to managing the government's exposure to financial risks is discussed in more detail in Wheeler and Jensen (forthcoming).

account of derivatives and other hedging transactions—reflects the currency composition of the reserves. However, other countries have not adopted this practice because of considerations relating to exchange rate objectives and the institutional framework, including intervention and issues related to the role and independence of the central bank.

Debt managers should carefully assess and manage the risks associated with foreign currency and short-term or floating-rate debt. Debt management strategies that include an overreliance on foreign currency or foreign currency–indexed debt and short-term or floating-rate debt are very risky. For example, although foreign currency debt may appear, ex ante, to be less expensive than domestic currency debt of the same maturity (given that the latter may include higher currency risk and liquidity premiums), it could prove to be costly in volatile capital markets or if the exchange rate depreciates. Debt managers should also be aware that the choice of exchange rate regime can affect the links between debt management and monetary policies. For example, foreign currency debt may appear to be cheaper in a fixed exchange rate regime because the regime caps exchange rate volatility. However, such debt can prove to be very risky if the exchange rate regime becomes untenable.

Short-term or floating-rate debt (whether domestic or foreign currency denominated)—which may appear, ex ante, to be less expensive over the long run in an environment in which yield curves are positively sloped—can create substantial rollover risk for the government. It may also constrain the central bank from raising interest rates to address inflation or to support the exchange rate because of concerns about the short-term impact on the government's financial position. However, such actions might be appropriate from the viewpoint of macroeconomic management and, by lowering risk premiums, may help to achieve lower interest rates in the longer run. Macro-vulnerabilities may be exacerbated if there is a sudden shift in market sentiment as to the government's ability to repay, or when contagion effects from other countries lead to markedly higher interest rates. Many emerging-market governments have too much short-term and floating-rate debt. However, overreliance on longer-term fixed-rate financing also carries risks if, in some circumstances, it tempts governments to deflate the value of such debt in real terms by initiating surprise inflation. Any such concerns would be reflected in current and future borrowing costs. Also, unexpected disinflation would increase the ex post debt-servicing burden in real terms. This could create strains in countries that, because of an already heavy debt burden, have to pay a higher risk premium.

If a country lacks a well-developed market for domestic currency debt, a government may be unable to issue long-term, fixed-rate domestic currency debt at a reasonable cost and, consequently, must choose between risky short-term or floating-rate domestic currency debt and longer-term, but also risky, foreign currency debt. Even so, given the potential for sizable economic losses if a government cannot roll over its debt, rollover risk should be given particular emphasis, and this risk can be reduced by lengthening the maturity of new debt issues. Options to lengthen maturities include issuing floating-rate debt, foreign currency or foreign currency–indexed debt, and inflation-indexed debt.[26] Over the medium term, a strategy for developing the domestic currency debt market can relieve this constraint and permit the issuance of a less risky debt structure. This should be reflected in the overall debt management strategy. In this context, gradual increases in the maturity of new fixed-rate domestic currency debt issues may raise cost in the short run, but they reduce rollover risk and often constitute important steps in developing domestic debt markets. However, debt structures that entail extremely "lumpy" cash flows should, to the extent possible, be avoided.

There should be cost-effective cash management policies in place to enable the authorities to meet, with a high degree of certainty, their financial obligations as they fall due. The need for cost-effective cash management recognizes that the window of opportunity to issue new securities does not necessarily match the timing of planned expenditures. In particular, for governments lacking secure access to capital markets, liquid financial assets and contingent credit lines can provide flexibility in debt and cash management operations in the event of temporary financial market disturbances. They enable governments to honor their obligations, and they provide flexibility to absorb shocks where access to borrowing in capital markets is temporarily curtailed or very costly. However, liquid assets are a more secure source of funds than unconditional, contingent credit lines, because financial institutions called on to provide funds under these lines may attempt to prevent their exposures from expanding by withdrawing other lines from the government. Nonetheless, some governments that do have secure access to capital markets prefer to minimize their holdings of liquid financial assets and instead to rely on short-term borrowings and overdraft facilities to manage day-to-day fluctuations in their revenues and cash flows. Sound cash management needs to be supported by efficient infrastructure for payments and settlements, which are often based on dematerialized securities and a centralized, book-entry register.

By its nature, sound cash management combines elements of debt management and monetary operations. Particularly in some developing countries where it is not given a high priority, poor or inadequate cash management has tended to hamper efficient debt management operations and the conduct of monetary policy.[27] Notwithstanding the desirability for a clear separation of debt management and monetary policy objectives and accountabilities, the search for liquidity creates a challenge for cash managers that might be more easily dealt with if debt and cash management functions were integrated in the same institution or worked in close collaboration.[28] Where cash and debt management functions are separately managed—for example, by the central bank and the treasury or ministry of finance, respectively—close coordination and information flows, in both directions, are of paramount importance to avoid short-run inconsistencies between debt and monetary operations. A clear delineation of institutional responsibilities, supported by a formal service agreement between the central bank, the treasury, and debt management officials, as appropriate, can further promote sound cash management practices.

Appropriate policies related to official foreign exchange reserves can also play a valuable role in increasing a government's room for maneuver in meeting its financial obligations in the face of economic and financial shocks. Table 5.1 summarizes some macroeconomic indicators that can be used as a starting point for assessing a country's external vulnerability.[29] More broadly, the level of foreign exchange reserves should be set in accordance with the government's access to capital markets, the exchange rate regime, the country's economic fundamentals and its vulnerability to economic and financial shocks, the cost of carrying reserves, and the amount of short-term foreign currency debt outstanding. Governments that lack secure access to international capital markets could consider holding reserves that bear an appropriate relationship to their country's short-term external debt, regardless of whether that debt is held by residents or by nonresidents. In addition, there are some indicators specific to the government's debt situation that debt managers need to consider. Ratios of debt to GDP and to tax revenue, for example, would seem to be very relevant for public debt management, as would indicators such as the debt-servicing ratio, the average interest rate, various maturity indicators, and indicators of the composition of the debt.

TABLE 5.1 Overview of Indicators of External Vulnerability

Indicators of reserve adequacy	Description
Ratio of reserves to short-term external debt	Single most important indicator of reserve adequacy in countries with significant but uncertain access to capital markets. Should be based on measure of reserves consistent with the *Balance of Payments Manual,* Fifth Edition (IMF 1993), and operational guidelines for *Special Data Dissemination Standard** reserves template, and a comprehensive measure of short-term debt of the public and private sectors on a remaining maturity basis (Kester 2001).
Ratio of reserves to imports	Useful measure for reserve needs for countries with limited access to capital markets; effectively scales the level of reserves to the size and the degree of openness of the economy.
Ratio of reserves to broad money	Measure of the potential impact of a loss of confidence in the domestic currency, leading to capital flight by residents. Particularly useful if the banking sector is weak or credibility of the exchange rate regime remains to be established. (Other potential sources of capital flight also exist.)
Debt-related indicators	Should generally be used in conjunction with medium-term scenarios, which permit the analysis of debt sustainability over time and under a variety of alternative assumptions.
Ratio of external debt to exports	Useful indicator of trend in debt that is closely related to the repayment capacity of the country.
Ratio of external debt to GDP	Useful indicator relating debt to resource base (reflecting the potential of shifting production to exports or import substitutes so as to enhance repayment capacity).
Average interest rate on external debt	Useful indicator of borrowing terms. In conjunction with debt/GDP and debt/export ratios and growth outlook, a key indicator for assessing debt sustainability.
Average maturity	Useful for homogeneous categories, such as non-concessional public sector debt, to track shortening of maturities or efforts to limit future vulnerabilities.
Share of foreign currency external debt in total external debt	Useful indicator of the impact of exchange rate change on debt (balance sheet effect), especially in conjunction with information on derivatives that transform the effective currency composition.

Source: IMF 2000a.
*The Special Data Dissemination Standard is a website/bulletin board that has information and templates on standards for various economic and financial data: http://dsbb.imf.org/Applications/web/sddshome/.

Risk Management Framework

A framework should be developed to enable debt managers to identify and manage the trade-offs between expected cost and risk in the government debt portfolio. The cost of government debt includes two components: (a) the financial cost, which typically is considered to be the cost of servicing the debt over the medium to long run (and may be measured in terms of its effect on the government's fiscal position); and (b) the potential cost of real economic losses that may result from a financial crisis if a government has difficulty rolling over its debt or if it defaults.[30] In the calculation of the expected cost of debt under a particular strategy for managing the portfolio, debt-servicing costs can be projected forward over the medium to long term on the basis of assumptions of future interest and exchange rates and future borrowing needs. To minimize bias in choosing among different strategies, some governments use "market neutral" assumptions of future interest and exchange rates, such as assumptions based on market measures of forward rates, simple assumptions that rates will remain unchanged, and so forth. The expected cost can be evaluated both in terms of the projected financial effect on the government's budget or other measure of its fiscal position and in terms of possible real costs if the projected debt service is potentially unsustainable in terms of its effect on future tax rates or government programs or if there is a potential for default.

Market risk is then measured in terms of potential increases in debt-servicing costs from changes in interest or exchange rates relative to the expected costs. The potential real economic losses that may result from such increases in costs or may result if the government cannot roll over its debt should also be considered. Sovereign debt managers typically manage several types of risk, as summarized in box 5.1. An important role of the debt manager is to identify these risks, assess to the extent possible their magnitude, and develop a preferred strategy for managing the trade-off between cost and risk. Following government approval, the debt manager also is normally responsible for the implementation of the portfolio management and risk management policies. To carry out these responsibilities, debt managers should have access to a range of financial and macroeconomic projections. Where available, debt managers should also have access to an accounting of official assets and liabilities, on a cash or an accrual basis. They also require complete information on the schedule of future coupon and principal payments and other characteristics of the government's debt obligations, together with budget projections of future borrowing requirements.

To assess risk, debt managers should regularly conduct stress tests of the debt portfolio on the basis of the economic and financial shocks to which the government—and the country more generally—are potentially exposed. This assessment is often conducted using financial models ranging from simple scenario-based models to more complex models involving highly sophisticated statistical and simulation techniques.[31] When constructing such assessments, debt managers need to factor in the risk that the government will not be able to roll over its debt and will be forced to default—a risk whose costs are broader than their effect on the government's budget. Moreover, debt managers should consider the interactions between the government's financial situation and those of the financial and nonfinancial sectors in times of stress to ensure that the government's debt management activities do not exacerbate risks in the private sector.[32] In general, the models used should enable government debt managers to undertake the following types of risk analysis:

- Project future debt-servicing costs over a medium- to long-term horizon based on assumptions regarding factors that affect debt-servicing capability, such as new financing requirements, the maturity profile of the debt stock, interest rate and currency characteristics of new debt, projections for future interest rates and exchange rates, and the behavior of relevant nonfinancial variables (for example, commodity prices for some countries).
- Generate a debt profile, consisting of key risk indicators of the existing and projected debt portfolio over the projected horizon.[33]
- Calculate the risk of future debt-servicing costs in both financial and real terms by summarizing the results of stress tests that are formulated on the basis of the economic and financial shocks to which the government and the country more generally are potentially exposed. Risks are typically measured as the potential increase in debt-servicing costs under the risk scenarios relative to the expected cost.
- Summarize the costs and risks of alternative strategies for managing the government's debt portfolio as a basis for making informed decisions about future financing alternatives.

The appropriate strategy depends on the government's tolerance for risk. The degree of risk a government is willing to take may evolve over time, depending on the size of the government debt portfolio and the government's vulnerability to economic and financial shocks. In general, the larger the debt portfolio and the vulnerability of the country to economic shocks, the larger the potential risk of loss from financial crisis or government default—and the greater the emphasis should be on reducing risks rather than costs. Such strategies include selecting maturities, currencies, and interest rate terms to lower risk, as well as having fiscal authorities place more stringent limits on debt issuance. The latter approach may be the only option available to countries with limited access to market-based debt instruments, such as those that rely primarily on concessional financing from bilateral or multilateral creditors.

Debt managers in well-developed financial markets typically follow one of two courses: (a) periodically determine a desired debt structure to guide new debt issuance for the subsequent period, or (b) set strategic benchmarks to guide the day-to-day management of the government's debt portfolio. Such benchmarks typically are expressed as numerical targets for key portfolio risk indicators, such as the share of short-term to long-term debt and the desired currency composition and interest rate duration of the debt. The key distinction between these two approaches is the extent to which debt managers operate in financial markets on a regular basis to adhere to the benchmark. However, the use of a strategic benchmark may be less applicable for countries with less-developed markets for their debt, since a lack of market liquidity may limit their opportunities to issue debt with the desired characteristics on a regular basis. Many emerging countries have found it useful to establish somewhat less stringent guidelines for new debt in terms of the desired maturities, interest rate structure, and currency composition. These guidelines often incorporate the government's strategy for developing the domestic debt market.

For those governments that frequently adjust their debt stock, strategic portfolio benchmarks can be powerful management tools because they represent the portfolio structure that the government would prefer to have, based on its preferences with respect to expected cost and risk. As such, they can help guide sovereign debt managers in their portfolio and risk management decisions, for example, by requiring that debt management decisions move the actual portfolio closer to the strategic benchmark portfolio.[34] Governments should strive to ensure that the design of their strategic portfolio benchmarks is supported by a risk management framework that ensures the risks are well specified and managed, and that the overall risk of their debt portfolios is within acceptable tolerances. Where markets are well developed, debt managers should try to ensure that their desired debt structures or strategic benchmarks are clear, consistent with the objectives for debt management, and publicly disclosed and explained.

Scope for Active Management

Debt managers who seek to actively manage the debt portfolio to profit from expectations of movements in interest rates and exchange rates that differ from those implicit in current market prices should be aware of the risks involved and accountable for their actions. These risks include possible financial losses, conflicts of interest, and adverse signaling with respect to monetary and fiscal policies. To be able to lower borrowing costs without increasing risk by taking market views, debt managers require information or judgement that is superior to that of other market participants and must also be able to transact in an efficient manner.

Debt managers may have better information on financial flows in the domestic market and on the financial condition of market participants because of the government's privileged role as supervisor or regulator of the financial system. However, most governments consider it unwise and unethical to try to capitalize on such inside information, especially in the domestic market. In particular, debt managers and policy makers should not engage in tactical trading on the basis of inside information with respect to future fiscal or monetary policy actions, because the government is usually the dominant issuer of debt in the domestic market and therefore risks being perceived as manipulating the market if it buys and sells its own securities or uses derivatives for the purpose of trying to generate additional income. Moreover, if the debt managers adopt interest rate or currency positions, their actions could also be interpreted as signaling a government view on the desired future direction of interest rates or the exchange rate, thereby making the central bank's task more difficult.

In foreign capital markets, debt managers generally have little or no information on the nature of financial flows beyond that available in the market generally. Even so, some governments actively manage their foreign currency debt in the hope of generating risk-adjusted returns or of enabling their portfolio managers to accumulate greater market knowledge, in an attempt to generate cost savings on major borrowings. Many governments do not consider it appropriate to undertake such tactical trading. In cases where such trading is permitted, it should be conducted under clearly defined portfolio guidelines with respect to position and loss limits, compliance procedures, and performance reporting. In countries where government debt managers undertake tactical trading, it normally constitutes only a small fraction of a government's portfolio management activities.

Contingent Liabilities

Debt managers should consider the impact that contingent liabilities have on the government's financial position, including its overall liquidity, when making borrowing decisions. Contingent liabilities represent potential financial claims against the government that have not yet materialized but that could trigger a firm financial obligation or liability under certain circumstances. They may be explicit (such as government guarantees on foreign exchange borrowings by certain domestic borrowers, government insurance schemes with respect to crop failures or natural disasters, and instruments such as put options on government securities) or implicit (where the government does not have a contractual obligation to provide assistance but decides to do so because it believes the cost of not intervening is unacceptable). Examples could include possible bailouts of the financial sector, state-owned enterprises, or subnational governments. Unlike most government financial obligations, however, contingent liabilities have a degree of uncertainty—they may be exercised only if certain events occur, and the size of the fiscal payout depends on the structure of the undertaking. Experience indicates that these contingent liabilities can be very large, particularly when they involve recapitalization of the banking system by the government or government obligations that arise from poorly designed programs for privatization of government assets. If structured without appropriate incentives or controls, contingent liabilities are often associated with moral hazard for the government, because making allowances for potential liabilities can increase the probability of these liabilities being realized. As a result, governments need to balance the benefits of disclosure with the moral hazard consequences that may arise with respect to contingent liabilities.

Governments should monitor the risk exposures they are entering into through their explicit contingent liabilities, and they should ensure that they are well informed of the associated risks of such liabilities. They should also be conscious of the conditions that could trigger implicit contingent liabilities, such as policy distortions that can lead to poor asset and liability management practices in the banking sector. Some governments have found it useful to centralize this monitoring function. In all cases, the debt managers should be aware of the contingent liabilities that the government has entered into.

The fiscal authorities should also consider making budget allowances for expected losses from explicit contingent liabilities. In cases where it is not possible to derive reliable cost estimates, the available information on the cost and risk of contingent liabilities or a liquidity drain can be summarized in the notes to the budget tables or the government's financial accounts, because contingent liabilities may represent a significant balance sheet risk for a government.

Governments can also do a great deal to reduce the risks associated with contingent liabilities by strengthening prudential supervision and regulation, introducing appropriate deposit insurance schemes, undertaking sound governance reforms of public sector enterprises, and improving the quality of their macroeconomic management and other regulatory policies.

Development and Maintenance of an Efficient Market for Government Securities

To minimize cost and risk over the medium to long run, debt managers should ensure that their policies and operations are consistent with the development of an efficient government securities market. An efficient market for securities provides the government with a mechanism to finance its expenditures in a way that alleviates the need to rely on the central bank to finance budget deficits. Moreover, by promoting the development of a deep and liquid market for its securities, debt managers—in tandem with supervisors and regulators of financial institutions—and market participants (see box 5.5) can achieve lower debt-servicing costs over the medium to long term as liquidity premiums embedded in the yields on government debt wane.[35] In addition, where they have low credit risks, the yields on government securities serve as a benchmark in pricing other financial assets, thereby serving as a catalyst for the development of deep and liquid money and bond markets generally. This helps buffer the effects of domestic and international shocks on the economy by providing borrowers with readily accessible domestic financing. It is especially valuable in times of global financial instability, when lower-quality credits may find it particularly difficult to obtain foreign funding. Governments should exercise particular care in borrowing in external markets.

Experience suggests there is no single optimal approach for developing an efficient market for government securities. Countries in the Organisation for Economic Co-operation and Development (OECD), for example, have established government securities markets using a wide range of approaches involving different sequencing of reforms and speed of deregulation. However, experiences in developing these markets in many countries demonstrate the importance of having a sound macroeconomic policy framework, well-designed reforms to adopt and develop market-based monetary policy instruments, and careful sequencing in removing regulations around the capital account.

Portfolio Diversification and Instruments

The government should strive to achieve a broad investor base for its domestic and foreign obligations, with due regard to cost and risk, and should treat investors equitably. Debt issuers can support this objective by diversifying the stock of debt across the yield curve or through a range of market instruments. Such actions could be particularly beneficial to emerging-market countries seeking to minimize rollover risk. At the same time, issuers need to be mindful of the cost of doing this and the market distortions that might arise, since investors may favor particular segments of the yield curve or specific types of instruments. And in less-developed markets, the nominal yield curve may extend only to relatively short-term securities. Attempting to extend the yield curve quickly beyond that point may be impractical or infeasible. This has led some emerging-market countries to issue large amounts of longer-term inflation-indexed debt and floating-rate debt, because such debt may be attractive to

BOX 5.5   Relevant Conditions for Developing an Efficient Government Securities Market

In most countries, the development of a government securities market has been pivotal in helping to create a liquid and efficient domestic debt market. Countries have adopted different approaches to the timing and sequencing of measures to develop these markets; the main elements of many of these programs are summarized below. One important prerequisite for building investor confidence is a track record of a sound macroeconomic environment. This includes implementing appropriate fiscal and monetary policies, coupled with a viable balance of payments position and exchange rate regime. In addition, developing a domestic securities market involves addressing, even in the nascent stages, securities market regulation, market infrastructure, the demand for securities, and the supply of securities.

Early steps in developing securities market regulation to support the issuance and trading of government securities include

- establishing a legal framework for securities issuance
- developing a regulatory environment to foster market development and enable sound supervisory practices to be enforced
- introducing appropriate accounting, auditing, and disclosure practices for financial sector reporting

Market infrastructure to help build market liquidity and reduce systemic risk can be developed over time by

- introducing trading arrangements suitable for the size of the market, which include efficient and safe custody, clearing, and settlement procedures
- encouraging the development of a system of market makers to enable buyers and sellers to transact efficiently at prices reflecting fair value
- removing any tax or other regulatory impediments that may hamper trading in government securities
- fostering, at a later stage, the scope for other money market and risk management instruments, such as repos and interest rate futures and swaps
- using central bank operations to manage market liquidity

Strengthening the demand for government securities involves acting on a broad front to build the potential investor base through measures such as

- removing regulatory and fiscal distortions, which inhibit the development of institutional investors (for example, pension reform)
- eliminating below-market-rate funding through captive investor sources
- implementing appropriate rules and an appropriate regulatory regime affecting participation by foreign investors in the domestic market

(continued)

BOX 5.5   Relevant Conditions for Developing an Efficient Government Securities Market *(continued)*

In developing the supply of government securities the key elements for establishing an efficient primary market include

- establishing clear objectives for security issuance and debt management
- developing basic projections of the government's liquidity needs
- creating safe and efficient channels for the distribution of securities (for example, auctions, syndication, and possible use of primary dealers) targeted to investor needs and thereby lowering transaction costs
- progressively extending the maturity of government securities
- consolidating the number of debt issues and creating standardized securities with conventional maturities with a view to eventually providing market benchmarks
- moving toward a predictable and transparent debt management operation, for example, with pre-announced issuance calendars and greater disclosure of funding needs and auction outcomes

The development of government securities markets is discussed in more detail in World Bank and IMF (forthcoming).

investors in countries where government indebtedness is high and the credibility of the monetary authorities is low.

As investors seek to diversify their risks by buying a range of securities and investments, debt managers should attempt to diversify the risks in their portfolios of liabilities by issuing securities at different points along the yield curve (different maturity dates), issuing securities at different points during the year (rather than issuing a large amount of securities in a single offering), offering securities with different cash flow characteristics (for example, fixed coupon or floating rate, nominal or indexed) and securities targeted at specific investors (for example, wholesale or retail investors, or in certain circumstances, domestic and foreign investors).[36] In so doing, debt managers should strive to treat investors equitably and, where possible, develop the overall liquidity of their debt instruments. This would increase their attractiveness to investors and reduce the liquidity premium that investors demand, as well as reduce the risk that the pricing of government securities could be significantly affected by the actions of a small number of market participants. A well-balanced approach aimed at broadening the investor base and spreading rollover risks, while recognizing the benefits of building liquid benchmark issues, should contribute to the objective of lowering debt costs over the long run.

Offering a range of debt management instruments with standardized features in the domestic market helps make financial markets more complete. This enables all participants to better hedge their financial commitments and exposures, thus contributing to reduced risk premiums and vulnerability in the economy more generally.

Where appropriate, issuing instruments with embedded options (such as savings bonds, which are redeemable by the bondholder on demand) may also contribute to instrument diversification. However, even where valid reasons exist for issuing such securities, debt managers should exercise considerable caution to ensure that the risks inherent in embedded options and other derivative instruments are integrated in the risk management framework, and that the instruments and risks are well understood by the issuer and other market participants.

Primary Market

Debt management operations in the primary market should be transparent and predictable. Regardless of the mechanism used to raise funds, experience suggests that borrowing costs are typically minimized and the market functions most efficiently when government operations are made transparent— for example, by publishing borrowing plans well in advance and acting consistently when issuing new securities—and when the issuer creates a level playing field for investors. The terms and conditions of new issues should be publicly disclosed and clearly understood by investors. The rules governing new issues should treat investors equitably. And, debt managers should maintain an ongoing dialogue with market participants and monitor market developments so that they are in a position to react quickly when circumstances require.

To the extent possible, debt issuance should use market-based mechanisms, including competitive auctions and syndications. In the primary market for government securities, best practice suggests that governments typically strive, where feasible, to use market-based mechanisms to raise funds. For domestic currency borrowings, this typically involves auctions of government securities, although syndications have been successfully used by borrowers that do not have a need to raise funds on a regular basis, or are introducing a new instrument to the market.[37] Governments should rarely cancel auctions because of market conditions or cut off the amounts awarded below the pre-announced tender amount to achieve short-run debt-servicing cost objectives. Experience has shown that such practices affect credibility and damage the integrity of the auction process, causing risk premiums to rise, hampering market development, and causing long-run debt-servicing costs to increase.

Secondary Market

Governments and central banks should promote the development of resilient secondary markets that can function effectively under a wide range of market conditions. In many countries, debt managers and central banks work closely with financial sector regulators and market participants in this regard. This includes supporting market participants in their efforts to develop codes of conduct for trading participants, and working with them to ensure that trading practices and systems continuously evolve and reflect best practices. It can also include promoting the development of an active repo market, in order to enhance liquidity in the underlying securities and minimize credit risk through collateralization (Bank for International Settlements 1999).

A government can promote the development and maintenance of an efficient secondary market for its securities by removing taxation and regulatory impediments that hinder investors' willingness to trade securities. This includes removing regulations that provide captive funding from financial intermediaries to the government at low interest rates, and modifying tax policies that distort investment in and trading of financial and nonfinancial assets. In addition, government approaches to regulating financial markets and market participants often include a wide range of disclosure and supervision requirements to reduce the risk of fraud and limit the risk that market participants may adopt imprudent ALM practices that could increase the risk of insolvency and systemic failure in the financial system.

Central banks play a crucial role in promoting the development and maintenance of efficient markets for government securities through the pursuit of sound monetary policies. By conducting monetary policy in a way that is consistent with their stated monetary policy objectives, central banks help increase the willingness of market participants to engage in transactions across the yield curve. Central banks are increasingly implementing monetary policy using indirect instruments that involve transactions in government securities. Proper design and use of such instruments have typically played important roles in contributing to deep and liquid markets for these securities. For example, day-to-day open market operations to implement monetary policy can foster adequate market liquidity, thereby contributing to well-functioning financial markets.

The systems used to settle and clear financial market transactions involving government securities should reflect sound practices.[38] Sound and efficient payments, settlement, and clearing systems help minimize transaction costs in government securities markets and contain system risk in the financial system, thereby contributing to lower financing costs for the government. Agencies responsible for the payments, settlement, and clearing systems for financial transactions normally work closely with market participants to ensure that these systems are able to function well under a wide range of trading conditions.

Notes

1. Excessive levels of debt that result in higher interest rates can have adverse effects on real output. See for example, Alesina and others (1992).
2. In addition to governments' concerns about the real costs of financial crises, governments' desire to avoid excessively risky debt structures reflects concern over the possible effects of losses on the country's fiscal position and access to capital and the fact that losses could ultimately lead to higher tax burdens and political risks.
3. These guidelines may also offer useful insights for other levels of government with debt management responsibilities.
4. For further information on coordination issues, see Sundararajan, Dattels, and Blomestein (1997).
5. Various analytic frameworks have been developed to guide member countries on the sustainability of their public debt. For example, those used by the International Monetary Fund (IMF) in its surveillance activities can be found on its Web site: "Assessing Sustainability," http://www.imf.org/external/np/pdr/sus/2002/eng/052802.htm; "Debt Sustainability in Low-Income Countries—Towards a Forward-Looking Strategy," http://www.imf.org/external/np/pdr/sustain/2003/052303.htm; and "Sustainability Assessments—Review of Application and Methodological Refinements," http://www.imf.org/external/np/pdr/sustain/2003/061003.htm.
6. Further information on the analysis of the cost and risk of the debt portfolio can be found in the sections of these guidelines on "Debt Management Strategy" and "Risk Management Framework."
7. This section draws on aspects of the IMF (2001) *Code of Good Practices on Fiscal Transparency—Declaration of Principles* (henceforth the FT Code), and the IMF (1999a) *Code of Good Practices on Transparency in Monetary and Financial Policies: Declaration of Principles* (henceforth the MFP Transparency Code) that pertain to debt management operations. Subsections in this chapter follow the section headings of the MFP Transparency Code.
8. See MFP Transparency Code 1.2, 1.3, and 5.2 (IMF 1999a).
9. See MFP Transparency Code 1.3 and 5.1 (IMF 1999a).
10. See MFP Transparency Code 6.1.3 (IMF 1999a).
11. See MFP Transparency Code 1.3 (IMF 1999a).
12. See FT Code Section II (IMF 2001) and MFP Transparency Code Section VII (IMF 1999a).
13. See FT Code 2.2 (IMF 2001).
14. See the (IMF 2000b) *Government Finance Statistics Manual* for details on how to present such information. In addition, the Inter-Agency Task Force on Finance Statistics (TFFS) is developing a framework for the presentation of external debt statistics (see IMF 2003a).
15. The disclosure of contingent liabilities is discussed further in the section of this chapter on "Risk Management Framework."
16. See MFP Transparency Code Introduction (IMF 1999a).
17. See MFP Transparency Code 1.2, 1.3, Sections IV and VIII (IMF 1999a).

18. The audit process may differ depending on the institutional structure of debt management operations.

19. See also FT Code 1.2 (IMF 2001).

20. See also the section of this chapter on "Transparency and Accountability," subsection on "Clarity of Roles, Responsibilities, and Objectives of Financial Agencies Responsible for Debt Management" and MFP Transparency Code 5.2 (IMF 1999a).

21. A few countries have privatized elements of debt management within clearly defined limits including, for example, some back-office functions and the management of the foreign currency debt stock.

22. If the central bank is charged with the primary responsibility for debt management, the clarity of and separation between debt management and monetary policy objectives especially needs to be maintained.

23. The IMF is committed to promoting the use of CACs in sovereign bonds governed by foreign laws, and monitors their use in its surveillance activities.

24. In some countries, debt managers also have responsibility for the management of some foreign exchange reserve assets.

25. Financial derivatives most commonly used by debt managers include interest rate swaps and cross-currency swaps. Interest rate swaps allow debt managers to adjust the debt portfolio's exposure to interest rates—for example, by synthetically converting a fixed-rate obligation into a floating-rate one. Similarly, a cross-currency swap can be used to synthetically change the currency exposure of a debt obligation. In addition, some countries have issued debt with embedded call or put options.

26. While rollover risk can be reduced through such longer maturity instruments, the short duration of floating-rate and indexed debt still exposes the issuer to potential variability in debt-servicing costs.

27. Payment arrears are one common example of poor cash management. See box 5.2.

28. See section on "Debt Management Objectives and Coordination," subsection on "Coordination with Monetary and Fiscal Policies."

29. Additional information on the motivations for holding foreign exchange reserves and factors influencing the adequacy of reserves under different exchange rate regimes can be found in IMF (2000a).

30. Most countries measure the financial cost and risk of government debt over the medium to long run in terms of the future stream of nominal debt-servicing costs. However, for countries that actively manage their debt portfolios to profit from expected movements in interest rates and exchange rates, which differ from those implicit in current market prices, the net returns on their trading positions are often measured in terms of changes in the market value of the trading portfolio, while risk is often measured in terms of the variance of these changes.

31. Complex simulation models should be used with caution. Data constraints may significantly impair the usefulness of these models, and the results obtained may be strongly model dependent and sensitive to the parameters used. For example, some parameters may behave differently in extreme situations or be influenced by policy responses.

32. Of course, governments should also take corrective measures, such as eliminating policy biases that may encourage excessive risk taking by the private sector.

33. A typical profile will include such indicators as the share of short-term to long-term debt, the share of foreign currency to domestic debt, the currency composition of the foreign currency debt, the average maturity of the debt, and the profile of maturing debts.

34. However, debt managers should be mindful of the transaction costs associated with continuously rebalancing the debt portfolio to mirror the benchmark, as well as the costs associated with making a major shift in the structure of the portfolio over a short period of time. Common practice is ,therefore, to express the benchmark characteristics as a range for currency composition, interest rate duration, and level of refinancing.

35. Some governments are finding that declining government financing requirements have led to reduced liquidity in their government debt markets. This has triggered a debate regarding the benefits of rapidly paying down the debt stock. Partly as an alternative to extensive debt buybacks, a few governments are considering continuing to issue some debt to build or to maintain liquid financial markets. Similarly, the absence of sustained fiscal deficits in some countries has prevented the natural development of a government debt market. Some of these governments have nevertheless decided to issue debt to stimulate the development of a domestic fixed-income market.

36. Some countries are considering attaching renegotiation clauses or CACs to their debt instruments, such as majority voting rules.

37. Some governments have found that introducing a network of market makers can be a useful mechanism for distributing securities and fostering deep and liquid markets. Some countries have used primary dealers for this role, while others have sought to encourage a more open financial marketplace. Where primary dealers operate, the incentives and obligations, as well as the eligibility criteria for becoming a primary dealer, need to be defined and disclosed.

38. Relevant work in this area includes the Group of 30 (1989) recommendations on clearance and settlement of securities transactions, which cover nine general principles, including such aspects as central depositories, netting schemes, delivery versus payment systems, settlement conventions, and securities lending. See also Bank for International Settlements (1997, 2001a, b).

References

Alesina, Alberto, Mark de Broeck, Alessandro Prati, and Guido Tabellini. 1992. "Default Risk on Government Debt in OECD Countries." *Economic Policy: A European Forum* October: 428–63.

Bank for International Settlements. 1997. "Disclosure Framework for Securities Settlement Systems." CPSS Publication 20, Committee on Payment and Settlement Systems and the International Organization of Securities Commissions, Bank for International Settlements, Basel, Switzerland.

———. 1999. "How Should We Design Deep and Liquid Markets? The Case of Government Securities." CGFS Working Group Report 13, Committee on the Global Financial System, Bank for International Settlements, Basel, Switzerland.

———. 2000. "Core Principles for Systemically Important Payment Systems: Consultative Report." CPSS Publication 34, Committee on Payment and Settlement Systems, Bank for International Settlements, Basel, Switzerland.

———. 2001a. "Core Principles for Systemically Important Payment Systems." CPSS Publication 43, Committee on Payment and Settlement Systems, Bank for International Settlements, Basel Switzerland.

———. 2001b. "Recommendations for Securities Settlement Systems." CPSS Publication 46, Committee on Payment and Settlement Systems and Technical Committee of the International Organization of Securities Commissions, Bank for International Settlements, Basel, Switzerland.

Financial Stability Forum. 2000. "Report of the Working Group on Capital Flows." Paper presented at the meeting of the Financial Stability Forum, Singapore, March 25–26.

Greenspan, Alan. 1999. "Remarks before the World Bank Group and the International Monetary Fund." Paper presented at the 1999 Annual Meetings Program of Seminars, Washington, DC, September 25–28.

Group of 10. 2002. "Report of the G-10 Working Group on Contractual Clauses." OECD, Paris. http://www.bis.org/publ/gten08.htm#pgtop.

Group of 30. 1989. *Clearance and Settlement Systems in the World's Security Markets.* Washington, DC: Group of 30.

IMF (International Monetary Fund). 1993. *Balance of Payments Manual,* Fifth edition. Washington, DC: IMF.

———. 1999a. *Code of Good Practices on Transparency in Monetary and Financial Policies: Declaration of Principles.* Washington, DC: Interim Committee of the Board of Governors of the International Monetary Fund.

———. 1999b. "Communiqué of the Interim Committee of the Board of Governors of the International Monetary Fund." IMF, Washington, DC. http://www.imf.org/external/np/cm/1999/092699A.HTM.

———. 2000a. "Debt- and Reserve-Related Indicators of External Vulnerability." SM/00/65. IMF, Washington, DC.

———. 2000b. *Government Finance Statistics Manual.* 2nd edition, draft. Washington, DC: IMF.

———. 2000c. "Joint Ministerial Committee of the Boards of Governors of the Bank and the Fund on the Transfer of Real Resources to Developing Countries Communiqué." IMF, Washington, DC. http://www.imf.org/external/np/cm/2000/041700.htm.

———. 2001. *Code of Good Practices on Fiscal Transparency—Declaration of Principles.* Washington, DC: IMF http://www.imf.org/external/np/fad/trans/code.htm.

———. 2003a. *External Debt Statistics: Guide for Compilers and Users.* Washington, DC: Inter-Agency Task Force on Finance Statistics, IMF. http://www.imf.org/external/pubs/ft/eds/Eng/Guide/index.htm.

———. 2003b. *Collective Action Clauses: Recent Developments and Issues.* Washington, DC: International Capital Markets, Legal, and Policy Development and Review Departments, IMF. http://www.imf.org/external/np/psi/2003/032503.htm.

———. 2002a. *The Design and Effectiveness of Collective Action Clauses.* Washington, DC: Legal Department, IMF. http://www.imf.org/external/np/psi/2002/eng/060602.htm.

———. 2002b. *Collective Action Clauses in Sovereign Bond Contracts—Encouraging Greater Use.* Washington, DC: Policy Development and Review, International Capital Markets, and Legal Departments, IMF. http://www.imf.org/external/np/psi/2002/eng/060602a.htm.

Kester, Anne. 2001. *International Reserves and Foreign Currency Liquidity: Guidelines for a Data Template.* Washington, DC: IMF.

Sundararajan, V., Peter Dattels, and Hans J. Blomestein, eds. 1997. *Coordinating Public Debt and Monetary Management.* Washington, DC: IMF.

Wheeler, Graeme, and Fred Jensen. Forthcoming. *Sound Practice in Sovereign Debt Management.* Washington, DC: World Bank.

World Bank and IMF. Forthcoming. *Developing Domestic Debt Markets—A Practitioner's Manual.* Washington, DC: World Bank and IMF.

6

Looking Beyond the
Budget Deficit

HOMI KHARAS AND DEEPAK MISHRA

M any economists and policy makers view the budget deficit as
a summary measure of the fiscal position of the government. It is calculated as the difference between revenue on the one
hand, and expenditure and lending minus repayments on the other.
Although it seems straightforward to compute, given alternative
methodologies, various measurement issues, different valuation
techniques, and other complexities, the computation of the budget
deficit in practice can be a complicated exercise. While most of us
pay a lot of attention to the reported budget deficit number, few care
much about the accounting procedure used to derive this number.
The general impression is that, in terms of magnitude, the methodology and measurement issues are of minor importance.

But keen observers of budgetary accounting practices would
argue otherwise. For example, Blejer and Cheasty (1991) note
that conventional measures of the fiscal deficit miscalculate the
public sector's true budget constraint and give a misleading picture of the economy's fiscal stance (see also Eisner 1984; Eisner
and Pieper 1984). Daniel, Davis, and Wolfe (1997), who focus on
the fiscal accounting of bank restructuring, find that in many countries noncash operations are excluded from the budget and these
exclusions are significant. Easterly (1998) notes that countries have

managed to meet the budget deficit target of the International Monetary Fund (IMF) without a proportionate decline in their total indebtedness, either by drawing down their assets or by shifting expenses to the outside bounds of the budget. Brixi, Ghanem, and Islam (1999) find that in some Eastern European countries a significant amount of government activity, including expenditure on programs geared toward bank revitalization, are financed outside the budgetary system. Kharas and Mishra (2000a) show that off-budget expenses, including debt stock adjustments reflecting valuation changes and the assumption of contingent liabilities by the government, have been quantitatively much more significant in debt accumulation than reported budget deficits in many developing countries.

Despite such obvious limitations of the budget deficit—as it is being conventionally estimated—why does it continue to remain the leading indicator of the fiscal health of a government? The simple reason is that there has not been any systematic attempt to find out how large are the deficits that are not captured in the reported budget deficit numbers but affect the total liabilities of the government.

In this chapter, we show that the budget deficit can grossly underestimate, and in few rare instances overestimate, the true fiscal indebtedness of a government. The difference between the actual indebtedness and the reported deficit, which we call the *hidden deficit*, is found to be significantly higher in developing countries than in developed ones. For many developing countries, hidden deficits are found to be as high as the reported deficit. It is also noted that hidden deficits are large immediately preceding and following financial crises, indicating that hidden deficits are not randomly generated but are part of a strategic budgetary exercise to report a lower than actual deficit during periods of economic distress.

A number of factors are identified that have contributed to the emergence of the hidden deficits. Primary among them are noninclusion or partial inclusion of corporate and bank restructuring expenses, treatment of present and expected future costs of entitlements and contingent liabilities, exclusion of capital gains and losses from the budget, use of different valuation methods, and use of grants and aids to finance budget deficit.

The real issue here is the current budgetary accounting practices and guidelines, which leave room for discretion and encourage financial engineering. Such practices may help a country avoid underlying real fiscal adjustment in the short run, but in the long run it is counterproductive, as the country pays dearly in the form of fiscal or financial crises. So it is important to put in place appropriate accounting practices and guidelines, and to set up an independent central budget office to remove discretion in measurement of the budget deficit.

In the next section, we show that there are many factors other than conventional deficit that contribute to the total indebtedness of a government. In the following section, we estimate the size of hidden deficits and show that they are significantly large for developing countries. Then we examine the various sources of hidden deficits, such as restructuring of the financial system and corporations following a financial crisis, capital gains and losses from currency movements, and so on. The last section concludes with a discussion of the need to reform the current budgetary accounting practices and guidelines in many developing countries.

Debt and Deficit: Some Simple Algebra

In this section, we summarize some basic algebra to show that the conventional budget deficit is only one of the many components affecting the total indebtedness of the government. The government budget can be written as

$$E_t(B_t^e - B_{t-1}^e) + (B_t^d - B_{t-1}^d) + (H_t - H_{t-1}) = D_t + X_t \qquad (6.1)$$

where B_t^e is the total foreign currency debt (expressed in U.S. dollars), B_t^d is the total domestic debt in the local currency unit, H_t is the base money in the local currency unit, E_t is the nominal exchange rate relative to the U.S. dollar, D_t is the conventional (reported) budget deficit in the local currency unit, and X_t is the expenditures in the local currency unit incurred outside the bounds of the budget.

Dividing by P_tY_t (where P_t is the price index, and Y_t is the real gross domestic product [GDP]) throughout, after making few manipulations one gets

$$\left(\frac{E_tB_t^e}{P_tY_t} - \frac{P_{t-1}Y_{t-1}}{P_tY_t}\frac{E_t}{E_{t-1}}\frac{E_{t-1}B_{t-1}^e}{P_{t-1}Y_{t-1}}\right) + \left(\frac{B_t^d}{P_tY_t} - \frac{P_{t-1}Y_{t-1}}{P_tY_t}\frac{B_{t-1}^d}{P_{t-1}Y_{t-1}}\right)$$

$$+ \left(\frac{H_i - H_{t-1}}{P_tY_t}\right) = \frac{Dt}{P_tY_t} + \frac{Xt}{P_tY_t} \qquad (6.2)$$

Using lowercase letters to denote the corresponding uppercase letters as a percentage of GDP, namely, $b_t^e = E_tB_t^e/P_tY_t$, $b_t^d = B_t^d/P_tY_t$, $d_t = D_t/P_tY_t$, $x_t = X_t/P_tY_t$, $s_t = (H_t - H_{t-1}/P_tY_t)$, and denoting the growth rate of nominal

GDP as g, inflation rate as π, and nominal depreciation rate as ϵ, after a few more manipulations, one can write the above equation as

$$(b_t - b_{t-1}) = \left(\frac{-g}{1 + g + \pi}\right)b_{t-1} + \left(\frac{\epsilon - \pi}{1 + g + \pi}\right)b_{t-1}^e$$

$$+ \left(\frac{-\pi}{1 + g + \pi}\right)b_{t-1}^e - s_t + d_t + x_t \qquad (6.3)$$

where b_t denotes the total debt (foreign currency plus domestic currency) as a percentage of GDP. Thus the change in debt-GDP ratio can be decomposed into six components:

Change in debt-GDP ratio = Contribution of growth (A)

+ Movement of real exchange rate (B)

+ Domestic inflation (C)

+ Conventional deficit (D)

+ Seignorage revenue (E)

+ Expenditures outside the
purview of the budget (F)

This decomposition shows that, theoretically, conventional deficit is only one of six components contributing to the accumulation of government debt. The important question is, what is the contribution of conventional deficit to debt accumulation relative to these other components? To answer this, we introduce a new measure—hidden deficit—which measures the change in indebtedness of the government, outside conventional budget deficit and seignorage revenue. Thus, hidden deficit is measured as the sum of three components: B + C + F.

Size of Hidden Deficits

To estimate hidden deficit as defined above, we conduct a simple exercise. We estimate a hypothetical level of debt that the government would have accumulated had there been no capital gains and losses to government's liabilities (because of inflation, depreciation of the currency, etc.), and had it not incurred any expense outside the purview of the budget. So we set $\pi = 0$, $\epsilon = 0$, and $x_t = 0$, and rewrite equation (6.3) as

$$b_t^h = \left(\frac{1}{1+g}\right)b_{t-1}^h - s_t + d_t$$

where b_t^h is the hypothetical debt-GDP ratio that the government would have had, if past budget deficits and seignorage were the only two sources financing it. Noting that g is the growth rate of nominal GDP, one can express the above equation in levels, eliminate the output term for the equation, and then iterate backward to express b_t^h as the sum of past deficits, change in base money overtime, and initial level of debt, all deflated by current output:

$$b_t^h = \frac{1}{Y}\left[B_0 + \sum_{i=1}^{i=t} D_i - \sum_{i=1}^{i=t}(H_t - H_{t-1})\right] \tag{6.4}$$

Using data for 29 developing and developed countries for the 1980–97 period, we compare the actual debt-output ratio as reported in the World Development Indicator table, with the hypothetical debt-output ratio as obtained from equation (6.4).[1] The difference between the two ratios shows the accumulated hidden deficits of the government.

Table 6.1 shows the actual and hypothetical debt-output ratio and the accumulated hidden deficits in seven developed countries at the end of the sample period. The difference between the actual and hypothetical debt-output ratios at the end of the 15- to 18-year period is found to vary between 22 percent (Finland) and –2 percent (Sweden). The difference between the two series for other countries is found to be 6 percent in Spain and the United States, 8 percent in Australia, 13 percent in Norway, and 15 percent in Austria. If one divides the total accumulated hidden deficits by the number of years in the sample, the average hidden deficit per year for developed countries is found to be only 0.3 percent.

In developed countries, the conventional budget deficit and seignorage are the biggest contributors to the total government debt. This is illustrated in the last column of table 6.1. These two sources together contributed to more than 65 percent of all the accumulated debt in six of the seven developed countries (excluding Norway).

The story is, however, quite different for developing countries, whose ratios are reported in table 6.2. The divergence between the actual and hypothetical debt-output ratios at the end of the sample period is found to be 79 percent in the Philippines, 77 percent in Brazil (at the end of 1991), 74 percent in Indonesia, 48 percent in Jordan, 34 percent in Chile, 33 percent in Malaysia, 26 percent in Korea and Thailand, and so on. For three countries—Chile, the Philippines, and Thailand—the hypothetical debt-output ratio is negative

TABLE 6.1   Accumulated Hidden Deficits in Selected Developed
Countries

Country (sample period)	Actual debt-output at the end of the period	Hypothetical debt-output at the end of the period	Accumulated hidden deficits during the period	Contribution of budget deficit + seignorage to total debt
	(1)	(2)	(3) = (1) − (2)	(4) = (2)/(1), in %
Australia (1979–96)	22.53	14.78	7.75	65.60
Austria (1979–95)	58.38	43.23	15.15	74.05
Finland (1979–95)	66.10	43.85	22.25	66.34
Norway (1979–96)	28.07	14.78	13.29	52.65
Spain (1979–94)	52.84	46.75	6.09	88.47
Sweden (1979–96)	70.89	72.97	−2.08	102.9
United States (1979–97)	48.93	43.30	5.63	88.49

Source: World Development Indicators database.

at the end of the sample, implying that these countries were running such large budget surpluses (or collected so much seignorage revenues) that they should not only have retired all their debt but accumulated large foreign assets as well. But their actual debt-output ratios were positive at the end of the sample period, so they must have accumulated large hidden liabilities as well, which they had to repay.

If one divides the total accumulated hidden deficits by the number of years in the sample, the average hidden deficit per year for developing countries is found to be as much as 2.6 percent (excluding countries that had hidden surpluses). Unlike in the developed countries, the conventional budget deficit and seignorage are not the biggest contributors to total government debt in developing countries. This is illustrated in the last column of table 6.2. These two sources together contributed less than 50 percent of all the accumulated debt in seven of the eleven countries (excluding countries that had hidden surpluses).

A notable difference among the developing and developed countries is that in the former group, some of the countries, such as Mexico, South Africa, Turkey, and the República Bolivariana de Venezuela, have actual debt-output ratios substantially less than their implied debt-output ratios during certain

TABLE 6.2   Accumulated Hidden Deficits in Selected Developing
Countries

Country (sample period)	Actual debt-output at the end of the period	Hypothetical debt-output at the end of the period	Accumulated hidden deficits during the period	Contribution of budget deficit + seignorage to total debt
	(1)	(2)	(3) = (1) − (2)	(4) = (2)/(1), in %
Argentina (1981–98)	31.41	10.80	20.58	34.48
Brazil (1981–91)	149.27	72.47	76.80	48.55
Chile (1988–98)	11.24	−23.08	34.32	−205.3
Indonesia (1979–98)	82.11	7.84	74.27	9.55
Jordan (1979–95)	90.16	42.61	47.55	47.26
Korea, Rep. of (1979–98)	27.83	2.10	25.73	7.55
Malaysia (1979–98)	35.33	1.61	33.72	4.56
Mexico (1979–98)	41.21	32.33	−8.98	127.9
Philippines (1979–98)	65.84	−13.62	79.46	−20.68
South Africa (1979–95)	57.42	72.93	−15.51	127.0
Thailand (1979–98)	12.55	−13.62	26.17	−108.5
Turkey (1979–98)	38.69	61.97	−23.28	160.2
Uruguay (1979–94)	26.33	10.21	16.12	38.78
Venezuela, R.B. de (1979–98)	31.10	38.77	−7.67	124.66

Source: World Development Indicators database.

years of the sample period. There can be many reasons for this counterintuitive observation. First, the country may have received generous debt forgiveness. It may have used its privatization revenue to retire debt or may have obtained large amount of aids and grants from multilateral and bilateral donors to finance its budget. The gains in its capital accounts due to favorable change in prices (high inflation or large appreciation of the real exchange rate) may have more than offset its off-budgetary expenses.

Sources of Hidden Deficits

A number of factors or events could contribute to the build-up of the hidden deficits in developing countries. Primary among them are noninclusion of corporate and bank restructuring expenses; treatment of present and expected future costs of entitlements and contingent liabilities; exclusion of capital gains and losses from the budget; use of different valuation methods; and use of grants, aids, and privatization receipts as financing items. We discuss two of these sources below.

Restructuring Failed Financial Institutions and Corporations

It has been repeatedly observed that policy makers in both developed and developing countries have been unable to credibly commit themselves to letting large financial institutions and domestic firms fail during financial crises. The problem of bailing out failed institutions is more serious in developing and transition countries—where financial crises are more frequent and more severe, and where regulatory mechanisms to minimize governmental interventions are lacking. These restructuring expenses contribute toward increasing the indebtedness of the government, but are they included in the reported budget deficit?

Studies have shown that current guidelines and practices for classifying government-assisted operations for bailing out or restructuring banks and firms are inadequately captured in the fiscal balance. Daniel, Davis, and Wolfe (1997) show that governments that do not want to assist financial institutions directly through the government budget often use quasi-fiscal operations, and exclude noncash operations from the budget.

In one of our previous studies, Kharas and Mishra (2000b), we find that the accounting practice for bank-assisted operations in transition countries suffers from the same criticism. For example, in the Czech Republic, the debt-output ratio increased from 25 percent in 1994 to 36 percent in 1998. During the same period the conventional deficit ranged from a minimum of −0.9 percent surplus in 1994 to a maximum of 1 percent deficit in 1998. While spending on quasi-public institutions such as the Konsolidacni Banka, Ceska Insasni, and Ceska Financni, which were established to revitalize the banking sector, and the National Property Fund led to an increase in the government's total liabilities, expenses incurred on them were almost excluded in the estimation of the budget deficit. Thus, the Czech authorities ran an average hidden deficit of approximately 4.98 percent during the 1994–98 period.

Using the Caprio and Klingebiel (1996) study, we examine in table 6.3 whether the fiscal costs of various banking crises have been properly reflected in the budget deficits of the respective governments. Argentina experienced a banking crisis during 1980–82, and during these three years, the reported budget deficits were 3.11, 5.43, and 4.22 percent of GDP, respectively. At the same time, the total central government debt increased by three times, from $9 billion to $25 billion. Using the actual debt-output ratio, we estimate the implied deficit during these years for Argentina. It is found to

T A B L E   6 . 3   Fiscal Cost of Banking Crises

Country	Year	Estimated cost of the banking crisis (% GDP)	How much the total debt increased during period	Budget deficit as reported during the period (%)	Implied deficit during the period (%)
Argentina	1980–82	55.3	From US$9 billion in 1980 to US$25 billion in 1982	1980 : 3.11 1981 : 5.43 1982 : 4.22	1980 : n.a 1981 : 14.38 1982 : 12.79
Chile	1981–83	41.2	Actual data unavailable, except that debt to GDP ratio was 118 % in 1982	1981 : −2.59 1982 : 0.98 1983 : 2.63	n.a. n.a. n.a
Finland	1991–93	8.0	From US$22 billion in 1991 to US$48 billion in 1993	1991 : 6.95 1992 : 14.74 1993 : 13.38	1991 : 6.05 1992 : 15.21 1993 : 8.99
Hungary	1992–95	10	From US$23 billion in 1992 to US$37 billion in 1995	1992 : 7.29 1993 : 5.72 1994 : 7.12 1995 : 6.39	1992 : n.a. 1993 : 20.75 1994 : 5.09 1995 : 11.78
Malaysia	1985–88	4.7	From US$24 billion in 1985 to US$32 billion in 1988	1985 : 5.68 1986 : 10.48 1987 : 7.73 1988 : 3.62	1985 : 3.15 1986 : 11.07 1987 : 14.28 1988 : 5.25
Indonesia	1993–94	1.8	From US$57 billion in 1993 to US$62 billion in 1994	1993 : −0.61 1994 : −0.94	1993 : 3.41 1994 : 4.18

Source: Caprio and Klingebiel 1996.
n.a.=not available.

be 14.38 and 12.79 percent of GDP during 1981 and 1982, respectively (because of missing data, the implied deficit for 1980 cannot be calculated). This indicates that hidden deficits of nearly 9 and 8.5 percent of GDP were used during the 1981–82 period to bail out the banking sector in Argentina, and these expenses were not reported in the budget deficit. The story is not too dissimilar in the other five countries shown in table 6.3, namely, in Chile, Finland, Hungary, Malaysia, and Indonesia. In most cases where implied deficits can be estimated, they are found to be higher than the reported budget deficits.

Exchange Rate Movements and Capital Gains and Losses

As our decomposition exercise showed, large-scale depreciation or appreciation of the nominal or real exchange rate can have significant impact on the real value of the total debt. Given that depreciation of the real exchange rate is more frequent than appreciation in most developing countries, governments incur more capital losses than gains from their exchange rate movements. Especially during currency crises, which are associated with sharp and significant real depreciation. The capital losses to the government can be enormous.

Another source of capital gains and losses to the real value of the government debt can arise from cross-currency movements, which are mostly excluded from budgetary accounts. According to Cassard and Folkerts-Landau (1997), in Indonesia one-third of the increase in the dollar value of the external debt between 1993 and 1995 was due to cross-currency movements, primarily the appreciation of the yen. In Malaysia, the sharp appreciation of the yen in 1994 is reported to have increased the dollar value of the external debt by 6 percent. In the Philippines, the appreciation of the yen accounted for about half of the increase in the dollar value of the external debt in 1995. The subsequent depreciation of the yen in 1996 did offset some of the losses incurred by these countries, and this may be why the extrabudgetary expenses suddenly declined in many of these countries in 1996.

Concluding Remarks

In developed countries, the accumulation of public surpluses and deficits gives a fairly accurate picture of how public debt evolves over time. In developing countries, this has not been true. For the past 20 years, the actual growth of debt has been much greater than the accumulated sum of conventional deficits. There are a variety of measurement and methodological reasons as to why this is the case, and why developing countries are more susceptible to suffering problems of hidden deficits than developed countries.

Note

1. The number of developing countries is limited by data availability. The countries are Argentina, Australia, Austria, Brazil, Chile, Indonesia, Finland, Jordan, the Republic of Korea, Malaysia, Mexico, Norway, the Philippines, Spain, South Africa, Sweden, Thailand, Turkey, the United States, Uruguay, and the República Bolivariana de Venezuela. The data were obtained from the World Development Indicator database of the World Bank and are for the central government only. The data on base money, H_t, are obtained from the International Financial Statistics database of the IMF.

References

Blejer, Mario I., and Adrienne Cheasty. 1991. "The Measurement of Fiscal Deficits: Analytical and Methodological Issues." *Journal of Economic Literature* 29 (4): 1644–78.

Brixi, Hana Polackova. 1998. "Contingent Liabilities: A Threat to Fiscal Stability." Prem-Notes Economic Policy 9, World Bank, Washington, DC.

Brixi, Hana Polackova, Hafez Ghanem, and Roumeen Islam. 1999. "Fiscal Adjustment and Contingent Government Liabilities: Case Studies of the Czech Republic and Macedonia." Policy Research Working Paper 2177, World Bank, Washington, DC.

Buiter, Willem H. 1985. "A Guide to Public Sector Debt and Deficits." *Economic Policy* 1 (November): 13–79.

Caprio, Gerard, Jr., and Daniela Klingebiel. 1996. "Bank Insolvencies: Cross-Country Experience." Unpublished paper, World Bank, Washington, DC.

Cassard, Marcel, and David Folkerts-Landau. 1997. "Risk Management and Sovereign Assets and Liabilities." IMF Working Paper 97/166, International Monetary Fund, Washington, DC.

Daniel, James A., Jeffery M. Davis, and Andrew M. Wolfe. 1997. *Fiscal Accounting of Bank Restructuring.* IMF Paper on Policy Analysis and Assessments PPAA/97/5, International Monetary Fund, Washington, DC.

Easterly, William. 1998. "When Is Fiscal Adjustment an Illusion?" Policy Research Working Paper 2109, World Bank, Washington, DC.

Eisner, Robert. 1984. "Which Budget Deficit? Some Issues of Measurement and Their Implications." *American Economic Review* 74 (2): 138–43.

Eisner, Robert, and Paul J. Pieper. 1984. "A New View of the Federal Debt and Budget Deficits." *American Economic Review* 74 (1): 11–29.

Kharas, Homi, and Deepak Mishra. 2000a. "Fiscal Policy, Hidden Deficits, and Currency Crises." In *Economists' Forum 1999,* ed. Shantayanan Devarajan, F. Halsey Rogers, and Lyn Squire. Washington, DC: World Bank.

———. 2000b. "Hidden Deficits and Contingent Liabilities." In *European Union Accession Opportunities and Risks in Central European Finances.* Washington, DC: World Bank.

7

Addressing Contingent Liabilities and Fiscal Risk

HANA POLACKOVA BRIXI

£62

H50 H70

P35 H61 O23

Experience has suggested that governments may be accumulating significant obligations in the form of contingent liabilities that are neither recorded nor analyzed in fiscal documents.[1] Only a few governments have the institutional frameworks and capacities to effectively control and manage contingent liabilities. Relatively few analysts have the information and tools needed to analyze the fiscal risk arising from contingent liabilities. Emerging-market economies have been among those most prone to the accumulation of contingent liabilities and related fiscal risk, for four reasons.

First, the high cost of transition and structural reforms has invited the creation of schemes that involve contingent liabilities (which are either explicit or implicit, as illustrated in table 7.1) for the government and shift part of the cost into the future.

Second, the privatization of state functions driven by fiscal constraint, as well as by efficiency reasons (for instance, in pensions and infrastructure), has demanded contingent government support—again either explicit or implicit—to entice private interest.

Third, as the experience of many developed and developing countries can attest, the pursuit of deficit targets generates incentives for governments to favor off-budget forms of government support that do not require immediate cash and that, at least for

TABLE 7.1   The Current Contingent Liabilities and Fiscal Risk in New Member States of the European Union

	Direct obligation in any event	Contingent obligation if a particular event occurs
Explicit		
Government liability created by a law or contract	Sovereign debt—loans contracted and securities issued by central government ■ Cyprus, Malta, and Poland (size and portfolio risk) ■ Hungary (maturity risk) ■ Czech Republic (interest rate risk) Future nondiscretionary budgetary spending, mainly social security and health ■ Czech Republic, Malta, and Slovenia (pension and health cost of aging population) ■ Poland (health cost of aging population) ■ Cyprus (pension cost of aging population) Transition cost of ongoing reforms ■ Poland (public administration, health care, and social security reforms) ■ Lithuania (pension and health care reforms) ■ Estonia, Hungary, Latvia, and Slovakia (pension reform) Arrears ■ Lithuania (arrears on VAT refunds) Tax expenditures like exemptions ■ Poland (tax exemptions for state-owned companies) Spending commitments vis-à-vis the EU and NATO	State guarantees for borrowing of enterprises ■ Czech Republic, Cyprus, Malta, Poland, and Slovenia (credit guarantees mainly to state-controlled companies) Statutory guarantees on liabilities and other obligations of various entities, including financial institutions (state-owned banks, pension funds, infrastructure development funds, etc.) ■ Czech Republic (Czech Consolidation Agency, Ceska Inkasni, Czech Land Fund, Railway Transport Infrastructure Administration, Agriculture Guarantee, and Credit Support Fund) ■ Hungary (State Development Bank, EXIM Bank, Export Credit Insurance Company, Pension Reserve Fund to cover private pension annuity, Deposit Insurance Fund, Credit Guarantee Fund, Rural Credit Guarantee Foundation, Office of Agricultural Market Regime, and environment guarantees of the Privatization Agency) ■ Estonia, Latvia, Lithuania, Poland, and Slovakia (Guarantee/Reserve Funds and the related minimum pension/relative rate of return guarantees, deposit guarantee, investor protection, and credit and export guarantees) State guarantees on service purchase contracts ■ Poland (possible obligations arising from the past power-purchase agreements)

(continued)

	Direct obligation in any event	Contingent obligation if a particular event occurs
		Other state guarantees issued to private investors and service providers
		■ Hungary (guarantees related to the privatization of Postabank)
		State guarantees on debt and other obligations of local governments
		State insurance programs
		Litigation
		■ Poland (legal claims against the government with respect to weak copyright protection and 1944–62 property losses)
		■ Lithuania (legal claims for savings compensation and real estate restitution)
		■ Slovakia (legal claims by CSOB bank and the Slovak Gas Company)
Implicit		
A "political" obligation of government that reflects public and interest-group pressures	Future recurrent costs of public investment projects	Claims by public sector entities to assist in covering their losses, arrears, deferred maintenance, debt and guarantees
		■ Poland (obligations of state-owned companies—some arising during the restructuring of railways and mines; obligations of hospitals and state agencies)
		■ Hungary and Malta (obligations of state-owned companies and the related cost of restructuring)
		■ Czech Republic (environment guarantees issued by the National Property Fund; losses, arrears, and debt of the Czech Railways)
		Claims by local governments to assist in covering their own debt, guarantees, arrears, letters of comfort, and similar
		■ Poland (local government debt and guarantees related to regional development)

(*continued*)

TABLE 7.1   The Current Contingent Liabilities and Fiscal Risk in New Member States of the European Union (*continued*)

Direct obligation in any event	Contingent obligation if a particular event occurs
	■ Lithuania (municipal budget arrears)
	■ Czech Republic (bail-outs related to hospital arrears)
	Claims by financial institutions, such as state-owned banks, social security funds, and credit and guarantee funds
	■ Latvia (pension and social security funds)
	■ Slovenia (Small Business Development Fund, regional guarantee schemes)
	Noncontractual claims arising from private investment, for instance, in infrastructure
	■ Hungary (possible claims arising from motorway construction concessions—partly implemented through the Road Construction Corporation of the State Development Bank)
	■ Poland (claims arising from expressway construction concessions)
	Other possible obligations, such as environment commitments for still unknown damages and nuclear and toxic waste
	■ Lithuania (decommissioning of the Ignalina nuclear power plant)
	■ Cyprus (reunification cost)

Source: Various sources. The framework is based on Polackova 1998.
CSOB
VAT=value added tax; EU=European Union; NATO=North Atlantic Treaty Organization.
Note: This matrix presents fiscal risks that face the central government (the fiscal authority rather than the consolidated public sector). Countries listed are among those in which the respective source of risk has been significant. Not all entries in the table are, however, up to date and an update is forthcoming.

some time, hide the underlying fiscal cost—while creating contingent liabilities. Similarly, as the pursuit of fiscal adjustment and deficit targets complicates structural reforms, it may elevate long-term fiscal risks.

Finally, the growing developmental role and autonomy of local governments may be associated with the elevation of local government contingent liabilities and debt. Such local government obligations often represent either an explicit or an implicit contingent liability for the national government.

Insofar as domestic markets are still emerging, in the sense of being somewhat prone to failure, government contingent liabilities arise from explicit promises and implicit expectations of government help in case of a failure. Such expectations also give rise to moral hazard, which in turn exacerbates fiscal risk.

Whether a result of fiscal opportunism to conceal the true fiscal cost of government programs, or of an effort to find more efficient ways to achieve policy objectives, or of lenience toward moral hazard in the behavior of market agents, contingent liabilities have often turned out to be very costly. At some point, guarantees fall due, state insurance programs require subsidies, and banks involved in policy lending or exposed to excessive risk with the hope of a government bailout eventually file for such a bailout. International experience suggests that contingent liabilities tend to surface and require public resources, particularly in times of economic slowdown.

Therefore both explicit and implicit contingent liabilities need to be fully considered in fiscal analysis, fiscal management, and fiscal surveillance frameworks. A number of improvements in reporting, accounting, budgeting, and overall fiscal management have been achieved in countries in recent years, partly thanks to the initiatives led by international institutions such as the European Commission, Eurostat, the World Bank, the International Monetary Fund (IMF), the International Organization of Supreme Audit Institutions (INTOSAI), and the Organisation for Economic Co-operation and Development (OECD). Yet revealing, assessing, and addressing governments' contingent liabilities and associated fiscal risks is still far from easy. It is still the case—particularly in emerging-market economies—that a string of years of government-reported low budget deficit and debt levels suggests neither that the government has been fiscally prudent nor that it will enjoy fiscal stability in the near future.

The challenge is how best to capture contingent liabilities in the fiscal framework. The World Bank, along with the European Commission, IMF, and others, already has some experience in bringing contingent liabilities and related fiscal risk into the formal frameworks of fiscal analysis (European

Commission and World Bank 1998, 2000; European Commission 2004). A number of countries, including Canada, Colombia, the Czech Republic, the Netherlands, and the United States, have provided good examples of cap-turing at least selected contingent liabilities in the fiscal framework. In this context, several analytical and institutional concepts have been developed and applied in recent years, namely the fiscal risk matrix; the IMF Code of Fiscal Transparency; accounting, budgeting, and provisioning for risk; and the balance sheet approach to fiscal management (Cassard and Folkerts-Landau 1997; Brixi and Schick 2002; Irwin 2003a; IASB 2004). Moreover, some countries, including Chile, Turkey, and Sweden, have tried to deal with contingent liabilities with the help of sophisticated risk valuation method-ologies. This chapter draws lessons from this expanding range of experience.

Perhaps the main problem with fully including contingent liabilities in the fiscal framework is the willingness of governments to expose relevant information. Contingent liabilities may arise in many forms, may involve dif-ferent levels of government, and may not be detected until they fall due—and even then a bailout might be orchestrated through a financial institution rather than the government. Many contingent liabilities remain unknown unless the government exposes them at its own initiative. Some may not be known even to the government as a whole unless the government monitors all its possible sources of fiscal risk—including, for instance, contingent lia-bilities of local governments and state-owned utilities.

If the willingness of governments to reveal contingent liabilities is important, then incentives and enforcement matter. In effect the question becomes, are countries rewarded or punished for transparency?

Some country experience suggests that countries may be punished when they reveal contingent liabilities—rather than when those hidden contin-gent liabilities fall due. Take, for instance, the Czech Republic: In 1997, the Minister of Finance volunteered detailed information about previously unknown contingent liabilities arising from the so-called transformation institutions[2] and off-budget funds. Meanwhile, these entities have been either dismantled or scheduled for dismantling, and brought under the Maastricht fiscal framework. From the moment when the Czech Ministry of Finance opened a public discussion about contingent liabilities, however, many international institutions, sovereign credit rating agencies, and others have been expressing concern about contingent liabilities in the Czech Republic. Their focus has not been on the fact that the Czech Republic has finally become determined to bring its contingent liabilities under control. Rather than commending the formidable steps taken toward fiscal trans-parency and discipline, analysts have rung the bells of warning.

Current Risk Exposures: Examples from New EU Member States

Using examples from the new member states of the European Union (the Czech Republic, Cyprus, Estonia, Hungary, Latvia, Lithuania, Malta, Poland, Slovakia, and Slovenia), this section illustrates the types of government exposure to fiscal risk that commonly arise in emerging-market economies.

Currently, three main sources of contingent liabilities appear in the new EU member states. First, some countries have used contingent liabilities to deal with the cost of transition and restructuring of the financial and enterprise sectors and the cost of privatization. For instance, privatization funds, explicitly or implicitly guaranteed by governments, have issued their own guarantees in several countries, including the Czech Republic and Hungary. These mainly relate to possible environmental liabilities. In most new member states, economic restructuring continues. Ongoing economic restructuring and privatization, for instance, in the Polish mining and railway sectors or the Maltese shipyards, may generate contingent liabilities and fiscal risk for the state.

Second, more recently, new member states have found contingent liabilities a useful instrument for facilitating the change in the role of the state. All new member states that embarked on extensive pension reforms—namely Estonia, Hungary, Latvia, Poland, and Slovakia—provided guarantees with respect to minimum pension benefit or minimum returns of pension funds as part of the reform package. Although such guarantees may have been justified on both efficiency and equity grounds, they give rise to fiscal risk.

Many new member states have been considering expanding the use of public-private partnerships as a way of bridging the infrastructure gap. Public-private partnerships, however, tend to require government support through disguised subsidies, often in the form of explicit government guarantees or legally less binding "letters of comfort" issued by either the central or the local government. Experience so far, both around the world and in several new member states (for instance, in Hungary's road sector and Poland's power sector), indicates that public-private partnerships give rise to significant government contingent liabilities and fiscal risk. This problem will be large mainly if the government agrees to bear any risk other than risk directly associated with its own policies.

Third, contingent liabilities may appear as part of the involvement of local governments in promoting regional and local development. To fulfill their growing responsibilities, local governments need to reach beyond their budgets—by borrowing and accumulating contingent liabilities. Local government borrowing is well captured in consolidated government accounts, and most new member states have established strict monitoring systems with respect to local government borrowing. Contingent liabilities assumed by local governments, however, often remain outside the government accounts and outside the fiscal monitoring systems—exposing local governments, and ultimately also the central government, to fiscal risk.

Table 7.1 provides a snapshot of the current sources of fiscal risk. It illustrates the explicit and implicit contingent and direct liabilities in new member states. Many of these are mentioned, and some even assessed, by the European Commission (2004) based on the countries' convergence programs.

Although not explicitly captured by the European System of Integrated Accounts (ESA95), some contingent liabilities in the new member states have entered the government fiscal framework under the Maastricht criteria, as the countries have expanded their definition of general government. Bringing off-budget agencies in charge of financing quasi-fiscal activities into the general government has in essence redefined such agencies' liabilities from being contingent to being direct for the government.[3]

The Czech Republic and Slovakia have been the leaders in this respect, bringing most of their government risk exposures through state agencies, as well as state guarantees, under the formal fiscal framework. These two countries have assessed most of their outstanding government guarantees as risky and started to report their full values as government debt. Although this action negatively affected their reported deficit and debt in the short term, it prevents most old contingent liabilities from complicating future fiscal adjustment. This comes in contrast to the situation in other countries that have large portfolios of government guarantees, namely Cyprus, Malta, and Poland.

Fiscal adjustment and the associated focus of policy makers on reducing their deficits and debts in the short term have been known for making contingent forms of support attractive. In infrastructure, for instance, when government is concentrating on short-term control of the budget deficit and debt, it is more willing to encourage state-controlled financial institutions and nonstate parties to finance or operate facilities. Hence, private participation in infrastructure, rather than being a result of an effort to enhance efficiency, is sometimes associated with an effort to switch from explicit subsidies and capital expenditures (government direct obligations) to explicit or implicit guarantees (government contingent obligations). Many of the new member states (specifically Cyprus, the Czech Republic, Hungary,

Malta, Poland, and Slovakia) face the need to undertake fiscal adjustment in the future that, perhaps with the exception of Slovakia, is complicated by the sharply rising fiscal cost of their aging populations. They may thus be tempted to alleviate the immediate budgetary pressures by switching to contingent forms of government support.

Keeping fiscal opportunism in check will be mainly a task for the domestic fiscal institutions. By fully covering contingent liabilities in their analysis and surveillance, the European Commission, IMF, and World Bank, among others, may be able to motivate the correct use of contingent government support and deter excessive accumulation of contingent liabilities.

The following two sections discuss government fiscal risk arising from public-private partnerships in infrastructure and from local governments. The last section tackles domestic fiscal institutions and the possible roles of international institutions and civil society with respect to contingent liabilities.

Public Risk in Private Infrastructure

Many developed and developing countries seek to reach beyond their available financial resources to boost investment and service delivery across sectors. A number of countries in Latin America, Asia, and Central and Eastern Europe have approached the limits of their domestic financial sector and official development assistance. They have explored the options of handing over parts of the physical and social infrastructure to private finance. This chapter considers only the public (fiscal) aspects of this experience—mainly related to the fact that governments are under pressure because too little public support may dissuade private investors and adversely affect the government's aims of attracting investment in the sector.

Experience suggests that fiscal savings in private infrastructure are to be found in improvements in the efficiency with which businesses are run or in the quality of public policy—not in transforming subsidies into contingent liabilities. Private investors frequently seek some form of financial support from host governments—to increase a project's expected net cash flows or to reduce the variability of those cash flows (that is, to reduce risk). Up-front grants (in cash or in kind), ongoing subsidies, and subsidized credit increase project cash flows without necessarily altering risk. Other forms of fiscal support also reduce investors' or lenders' risk exposure, including loans subordinated to other debt, minimum revenue guarantees, credit guarantees, and foreign exchange guarantees. It is these risk-reducing instruments of contingent government support that in due time generate unforeseen fiscal cost.

It is not certain whether, when, and in what amount the fiscal cost of government contingent support to infrastructure will surface. The probability of the contingency occurring and the magnitude of the government outlay required to settle the ensuing obligation are typically difficult to forecast. Probability and magnitude may depend on some exogenous conditions (such as low demand for the services of a particular infrastructure project), including the occurrence of a particular event (for example, a natural disaster or debtor's default). They may also depend on some endogenous conditions, such as government policies (an example being tariff policy and exchange rate policy) and the design of government programs (an example being the distribution of risks under guarantee contracts to private providers of infrastructure), as well as on the quality and enforcement of regulations and supervision.

To complicate matters, the boundary between explicit and implicit government obligations in infrastructure is not always sharp. Because the provision of infrastructure services is often a politically sensitive issue, governments face pressure to ensure certain outcomes in service delivery and hence, if necessary, bear costs even when not legally obliged to do so. In the extreme, governments bail out infrastructure providers. Many countries around the world have seen large bailouts of parties involved in infrastructure, including state-controlled banks and financial institutions, local governments, and state-controlled nonfinancial corporations (with respect to their debt, arrears, and other obligations, as well as deferred maintenance and backlog of investment needs for asset renewal).

Contingent fiscal support to infrastructure often comes in various forms. The state may issue various types of guarantees for private participation in infrastructure. Guarantees and other commitments are sometimes also issued by other parts of the government and public sector, and as nonsovereign obligations these commitments constitute an implicit rather than explicit obligation for the central government. Local governments and state-controlled corporations issue guarantees, letters of comfort, and other commitments to absorb credit risk or other types of risk. Although the legal implications of such nonsovereign obligations may not be clear, they ultimately may create fiscal costs for the state. Nonsovereign obligations are generally not monitored and often not properly understood by their issuers.

Aside from the problem of ultimate fiscal cost, the effect of disguised subsidies on future development in infrastructure sectors may actually be negative. Disguised fiscal support that makes financing for infrastructure easy and cheap may mask the need for structural reforms in the infrastructure sectors. For projects that are commercially viable, such support may crowd out the private sector. Efficiency in infrastructure provision suffers in consequence.

Private infrastructure projects introduce new hidden fiscal costs and risks in three main cases: First, when the government bears policy risks relating to the project; second, when the government bears other (nonpolicy) risks; and third, when the government is the purchaser of the services under a long-term take-or-pay contract.

Policy risk is unpredictable variation in the value of a project that results from the unpredictability of government policy, where *policy* means all the rules the government imposes—in laws, regulations, and contracts—and all the ways the government chooses to implement those rules in practice. Uncertainty about the prices the government will allow is usually a major cause of policy risk in most infrastructure projects. Other sources of policy risk are rules governing taxes, the quality or quantity of the output the firm must produce, and whether other firms may compete.[4]

Governments bear policy risk as way of protecting a firm from risks to which it is vulnerable and that the government can control but the firm cannot. Exposing the firm to some policy risks greatly increases the risk premium demanded by the firm and has relatively little benefit. Exposing the government to risk, however, may encourage the government to maintain good policies.[5] Overall, it can reduce the costs of the project.

Yet bearing policy risk does have a fiscal cost. There is always a chance that the government will want to change the policy to which it has committed itself and will have to pay the firm if it does so. For example, the government may grant a monopoly to a private infrastructure firm and then decide that competition would be better.

Nonpolicy risks are those over which the government has little or no influence. Examples include risk arising from uncertainty about the costs of construction, future demand for the infrastructure project's services, the value of a freely floating local currency, and whether (for reasons unrelated to changes in policy) the firm will repay its debt. Governments can bear these risks by giving the firm construction cost, revenue, exchange rate, and debt repayment guarantees, respectively.

Protecting the firm from nonpolicy risk reduces the price the firm needs to charge to be willing to undertake the project. Guarantees such as those just mentioned reduce investors' exposure to risk and lower the expected returns they demand. They also allow the firm to borrow more or at lower interest rates. But bearing nonpolicy risk has a cost to government. And, in contrast to policy risk, the cost of bearing nonpolicy risk is likely to be as high to the government as it is to the firm.

In this context, the key question is whether the risk bearing really addresses a significant market failure without creating a bigger problem than it solves. The fact that the costs are opaque exacerbates the severity of the potential problems. It also raises a question: Is support being given because it is a well-targeted response to a market failure or because of this very opacity?

Under pressure not to provide cash subsidies or borrow, governments sometimes enter into long-term purchase contracts signed by the utility and sometimes guaranteed by the state—a form of disguised borrowing. Under such a contract, the government agrees in advance to purchase a given output of a private infrastructure project for an agreed price. It might agree, for instance, to make fixed "capacity" payments to an independent power producer every month for 20 years so long as the power plant is capable of producing power—the discounted sum of the payments equaling the cost of building and maintaining the plant. Similar deals are done in the water sector, in which governments sometimes ask a firm to build a water or wastewater treatment plant, agreeing in advance to purchase the output on a take-or-pay basis.

These obligations can be analyzed as the government's agreeing to bear policy and nonpolicy risks in the project. In contrast to the typical case in which the government agrees simply to bear certain project risks, the (gross) cost of the government's obligation is likely to be roughly equal to the total cost of the project. Although the projects are usually described as private, they are in substance similar to public projects, in which the government contracts out construction and operation to a single firm.

Often governments do not enter into such agreements directly; instead, the contracts are signed by the electricity or water utilities that the government owns, often with a guarantee from the government that the utility will honor its purchase obligations. In estimating the total cost of obligations incurred in this way, the government might choose to "see through" the legal distinction between the government and the utility and consolidate the utility in its accounts at least, for analytical purposes, if not in its financial statements. In this case, the government can treat the utility's purchase obligations as a government liability and not count the cost of the guarantee separately. Alternatively, it may choose not to consolidate the utility and to consider its own obligation to be the purchase guarantee alone.

Either directly or through a public utility, the government may expose itself to significant fiscal risk (a) by signing a contract with an infrastructure firm giving it the right to charge certain prices; (b) by covering the risks related to the construction cost, exchange rate, or the firm's future revenue and debt repayment; and (c) by entering long-term purchase contracts.

The pressures on governments to incur fiscal obligations in infrastructure industries are affected by government policy toward competition and ownership in these industries. The preservation of state-owned monopolies in infrastructure industries makes it hard, or impossible, for governments to avoid providing fiscal support for infrastructure. Progress on competition and ownership can facilitate progress on the fiscal side. At the same time, changes in fiscal policy toward infrastructure can facilitate progress on competition and privatization. Although the problems occur in other industries as well, they are starkest in the electrical industry. (Figure 7.1 illustrates the extent of competition in telecommunications across countries.)

In seeking any reductions in the fiscal cost of infrastructure, offering contingent support should come as the last option. The government first needs to explore nonfiscal options, such as improving policies on ownership, competition, and regulation in infrastructure and improving the investment climate for all firms in the relevant localities and in the country as a whole. The government also needs to explore the option of not providing any fiscal support, or at least no fiscal support specific to infrastructure services. Finally, the transparency and simplicity of providing an explicit cash subsidy to the infrastructure firm or its customers, or capital in the form of equity or debt, need to be weighed against the opacity and fiscal risks of contingent government support.[6]

Local Government Risk

Growing experience indicates that the central government and the country's public finances are at risk when local governments expose themselves to excessive fiscal risk. Local fiscal risk can be defined as a source of financial stress that could face a local government in the future. Similarly to central government, local governments can accumulate direct and contingent liabilities. The fiscal risk matrix in table 7.2 gives a list of examples relevant for local governments.

The fiscal hedge matrix (table 7.3) complements the fiscal risk matrix to illustrate the different financial sources that can be used to cover local government obligations. Sources of local government financial safety can also be divided into direct and contingent liabilities, either explicit or implicit. Direct explicit sources reflect the local government's legal power to raise income from its existing, tangible assets. Direct implicit sources are also based on existing assets, but they are not under the local government's direct control and, thus, may offset fiscal risks to a limited degree only. Contingent explicit sources relate to the local government's legal power to raise money in the future from sources other than its own assets. Finally, contingent implicit

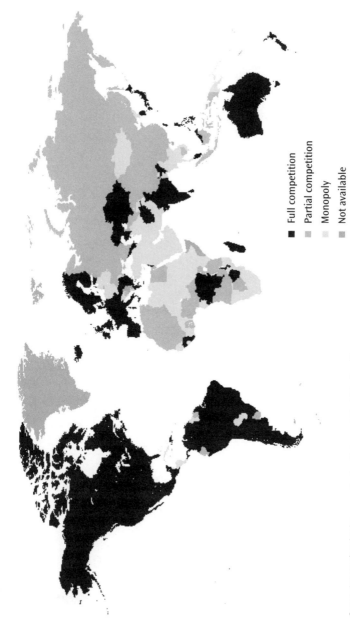

Source: International Telecommunication Union and World Bank staff.

FIGURE 7.1 The Risk of Low Competition: Telecommunications

Full competition
Partial competition
Monopoly
Not available

TABLE 7.2   Fiscal Risk Matrix—Local Government Exposures

Sources of risk	Direct obligation in any event	Contingent obligation only if a particular event occurs
Explicit Government liability as recognized by a law or contract	▪ Local government debt (loans contracted and securities issued by the local government) ▪ Arrears in wage and benefit payments (if legal responsibility of the local government) ▪ Nondiscretionary budgetary spending ▪ Expenditures legally binding in the long term (civil service salaries and pensions)	▪ Local government guarantees for debt and other obligations of public sector entities ▪ Local government guarantees for debt and other obligations of nonpublic sector entities ▪ Local government guarantees on private investments (infrastructure) ▪ Local government insurance (crop insurance)
Implicit A moral obligation of the government that reflects public and interest-group pressures	▪ Remaining capital and future recurrent costs of public investment projects ▪ The Cost of future benefits under the local social security schemes ▪ Future spending on public health and disease control and on goods and services that the local government is expected to deliver	▪ Claims related to local government letters of comfort ▪ Claims by failing financial institutions ▪ Claims by various entities to assist on their nonguaranteed debt and their own guarantees, arrears, letters of comfort, and other possible obligations ▪ Claims related to enterprise restructuring and privatization ▪ Claims by beneficiaries of failed local pension fund, employment fund, or social security fund—beyond any guaranteed limits ▪ Claims related to local crisis management (public health, environment, disaster relief, and so on)

Source: The author. Based on a framework presented in Polackova 1998.
Note: This matrix presents fiscal risks from the perspective of local (provincial, county, township, or other local) government.

TABLE 7.3   Fiscal Hedge Matrix—Local Government Sources of
Financial Safety

Sources of financial safety	Direct based on existing assets	Contingent dependent on future events
Explicit Sources directly (legally) under local government control	■ Local government-owned assets available for possible sale or lease (own enterprises, land, other local public resources)	■ Local tax revenues less tax expenditures ■ Transfer income from the central government ■ Recovery of loans made by the local government (on-lending)
Implicit Sources indirectly (not in legal terms) under local government control	■ Existing local funds—other than those under direct control of the local government (possibly local pension funds, local health funds)	■ Future profits of enterprises and agencies under some local government control ■ Contingent credit lines and financing commitments from official creditors to the local government

Source: The author. Based on a framework presented in Brixi and Schick (2002).
Note: This matrix presents sources of fiscal safety from the perspective of the local (provincial, county, township, or other local) government.

sources are not available to the local government until a particular situation occurs and even then, require the local government to make a special case for their utilization.

The two matrices outline the scope for local government fiscal analysis and fiscal management. The two matrices, in fact, represent an extended balance sheet of the local government. Compared with the standard balance sheet, the extended balance sheet provides invaluable information about contingent and direct implicit items that may affect the future net worth of local government.

Although one cannot always measure all items in the extended balance sheet, the approach is a useful way to consider which local government actions imply progress or regress toward the long-term fiscal stability of local government. Analyzing this broader notion of fiscal stability requires making many assumptions to calculate concepts such as the local implicit pension debt and the value of local land. This kind of analysis illustrates how the local government's long-term finances will evolve if certain assumptions hold.

In most countries, local governments are playing an increasing role in delivering public services and in promoting development. Related to this role, they increasingly need to take risks. To finance investments, local governments may need to borrow. In some instances, local government support in the form of contingent liabilities may also be justified. With respect to local enterprises under privatization, for example, it may be acceptable that the local government protects the new enterprise owners against any environmental liabilities incurred before the time of privatization but discovered only after that time.

Compared with the central government, however, fiscal discipline at the local level is undermined by the perception that the central government will ultimately bail out local governments should they become insolvent.[7] This perception influences the behavior of both local government officials (who may tend to overborrow, issue too many guarantees and letters of comfort, establish and provide backing to extensive local insurance programs, and take on financial risk through commercial activity) and creditors (who may expose themselves to excessive credit risk relative to local governments either by lending to local governments or by recognizing local government guarantees, letters of comfort, and perceived backing).

Local policy makers also tend to build up government contingent liabilities to avoid difficult adjustment and painful structural reforms in their localities, and to escape fiscal discipline and control mechanisms (such as fiscal deficit targets and debt ceilings). In this process, raising funds through local government-controlled corporations substitutes for direct government borrowing. Credit guarantees issued by various entities under local government control replace local budgetary subsidies. Take-or-pay contracts come in lieu of investing public resources; liberalizing prices; and restructuring the energy, water, and other vital sectors. Letters of comfort signed by local government officials allow insolvent enterprises and banks to access new credit and avoid bankruptcies.

The consequences may be costly. These mechanisms work for a limited period of time, longer in periods of economic prosperity and growth. But, ultimately, off-budget support may affect the local government budget, and it can do so to an extent that requires financial intervention from the central government. The following section tackles this problem, as well as the problem of other contingent liabilities, from the angle of domestic fiscal institutions and civil society.

Implications for Fiscal Management

This section discusses domestic fiscal institutions and the possible role of civil society with respect to contingent liabilities. It suggests measures to promote appropriate incentives and capacities in dealing with contingent liabilities.

Promote Risk Awareness

An open discussion of risks and possible government risk exposures enhances government understanding and handling of contingent liabilities. Similarly, at the level of local governments, introducing an open discussion and acknowledgment of risks and their sources, types, and possible fiscal implications may deliver significant benefits in terms of the soundness of local government policies, as well as local governments' overall fiscal performance. Many countries have been trying to collect, analyze, and discuss information about the risk exposure emerging from state guarantees. Few have initiated a discussion about the whole portfolio of contingent liabilities and fiscal risk.

Civil society, along with international institutions, sovereign credit rating agencies, and others, could further encourage fiscal risk analysis and discussions with government officials that go beyond the government's official statements. It may be valuable to develop a survey of the risk exposures of local governments, the risks arising in the infrastructure sectors, and the risk exposures of state-controlled and strategically important companies, especially major suppliers of vital services and various risk-prone financial institutions, such as credit and guarantee funds. Such a survey may promote the government's understanding of its contingent liabilities and related fiscal risk.

Reward Disclosure, Punish Opacity and Excess

Disclosure benefits scrutiny, fiscal discipline, and contestability of resources. Information that is disclosed invites scrutiny by people outside the government and by the government itself. When disclosure rules have broad coverage, they enable the government at its different levels to improve its monitoring of lower-level governments and public sector units, and expand the share of government activities open to public scrutiny. Scrutiny is likely to generate pressure for greater discipline—applied by, as well as on, the local governments.

Modern financial reporting standards require the disclosure of commitments, contingent liabilities, and certain other sources of financial risk. So adopting such a standard automatically creates a requirement to disclose information about hidden borrowing and hidden subsidies. And it automatically creates a mechanism for enforcing disclosure, since the government's auditor must express an opinion on the accuracy of the disclosures.

Disclosure should not be constrained by the weaknesses in the existing financial reporting standards or by slow progress in their improvement. Improvements in standards governing government financial reporting and accounting may deliver many benefits, including improvements in disclosure. But promoting disclosure should not be held hostage to improvements of these standards. Statements of risk, for instance, can complement any financial statement or report.

At the level of central government, Australia, Canada, the Czech Republic, the Netherlands, New Zealand, the United Kingdom, and the United States offer some good practices to consider. In these countries, the government publishes a list of the sources of its risk exposures, with statements on the nature, sensitivities, and possible financial and allocative implications of the risks. The statement can provide an estimate of the possible future fiscal cost associated with an item on the list. Such information sometimes comes in a separate statement of contingent liabilities, a statement of commitments (including long-term purchase or subsidy contracts), or an analytical report on fiscal risk disseminated as one of the budgetary documents.

In infrastructure and other government-sponsored projects, both explicit and implicit contingent government support associated with non-policy risk deserve attention. In this regard, country practices, as well as fiscal policy surveillance, need to go beyond existing regulation.[8]

Local government statements of risk can complement their existing reports that are made public or submitted to a higher level of government. These statements can discuss local government guarantees, letters of comfort and other explicit contingent liabilities, local government commitments, the limits of local government responsibility relative to its implicit contingent liabilities, and activities of local government–controlled financial and nonfinancial enterprises. Among local governments, Australia's state of Victoria, Canada's province of Ontario, India's state of Tripura, and the United Kingdom's England and Wales offer aspects of good practice.

There are several prerequisites for disclosure, as well as for adequate risk awareness, at both the central and the local government levels. They include a database of the respective government's direct and contingent obligations, to form a basis for analysis; adequate institutional capacity, including the capacity to gather and analyze relevant information and evaluate risk exposures; and for internal disclosure, an adequate enforcement mechanism, including a supportive political and legal environment (for instance, with respect to local government reporting on direct and contingent obligations to the central government), to ensure compliance. For public disclosure, local governments may agree (or the central government may need to issue rules) regarding the format in which to make the information public. Local grassroots agencies, investors, and local public pressure may be effective in monitoring local government performance, including risk exposure and disclosure.

In addition to disclosing their own risk exposure, the central and local governments need to promote disclosure in the public sector and the economy at large. Again, these efforts should relate to but not be constrained by the status and progress of financial reporting standards in the public sector and in the domestic market.

The most vital contribution that the international and other influential organizations could make to promoting disclosure in countries is to reward it. Countries that voluntarily expose the full scale of their contingent liabilities and fiscal risk, for instance, should be, first of all, publicly commended. In such instances, the positive value of transparency should be weighed carefully against the negative value of the revealed risks. That is to say that perhaps a country deserves an "upgrade" for efforts at transparency rather than a "downgrade" for additional risks that have been revealed. Furthermore, international organizations can be instrumental in arranging for further assistance in building countries' capacities for disclosure, as discussed above.

International and other organizations, within their areas of influence, also need to punish opacity and excessive risk taking. For instance, countries could be punished if explicit contingent liabilities that had not been admitted earlier by the government surfaced by way of falling due, or if implicit contingent liabilities that had been known to exist but not admitted by the government were realized. A punishment in the form of a public statement of disappointment would be easy to implement. Another more difficult but more effective option would be for international organizations such as the European Commission, IMF, and World Bank to require the government to build a contingent liability fund. (Issues associated with contingent liability funds are discussed below.) This would be particularly important for countries that are exposed to excessive fiscal risk and have high levels of government debt, limited access to borrowing, and limited ability to cut spending under the government budget. Alternatively, international organizations could require countries exposed to excessive fiscal risk to maintain low debt to create a cushion for the future realization of contingent liabilities. In this regard, international organizations could seek to set rules on government risk exposure and establish a set of fiscal risk warning indicators.

Enhance Accounting and Budgeting

Accounting and budgeting rules influence the allocation of resources. They affect the timing and recognition of transactions, and they may provide opportunities and incentives to shift costs and risks from one period to another and from one part of a government (or of the public sector) to another. Cash flow budgeting, which is implemented in most countries, makes guarantees, take-or-pay contracts, and purchase of infrastructure services from private providers look more attractive than cash subsidies and publicly financed projects. It treats subsidies and publicly financed projects as outlays but does not recognize contingent liabilities until default occurs, at which point the government has little choice but to make good on past commitments. Publicly financed projects and subsidies thus appear expensive, and contingent forms of support appear cheap. To make matters worse, in cash flow accounting and budgeting, any income earned from origination fees on guarantees is booked as current revenue, making it appear that government is profiting by taking these risks—irrespective of the cost.

An accrual-based accounting and budgeting system requires many noncash costs to be included in budgets and thus made visible from the moment the government decides to incur them. As for contingent liabilities, accrual-based budgeting and financial reporting can help reveal and confront policy makers with the costs of guarantees and long-term purchase contracts. As discussed in the section on disclosure, accrual-based standards can require the disclosure of information about contingent liabilities created by guarantees and commitments created by long-term purchase contracts. How well accrual-based budgets and financial reports reflect costs, however, depends on the particular standards that are applied and how well they are enforced.

Accrual-based standards are helpful but neither sufficient nor necessary for solving all the problems. Accrual-based accounting standards do not cause all costs and all liabilities to be revealed. They do not necessarily require the costs of guarantees to be included in calculations of budget deficits. And they do not necessarily require the liabilities created by long-term purchase agreements to be recognized alongside ordinary debts on the balance sheet. The leading international standards appear to be improving: The International Financial Reporting Standards, International Public Sector Accounting Standards (which modify the International Financial Reporting Standards for use by governments), and Generally Accepted Accounting Principles in the United States, for example, appear to be converging toward more accurate accounting for such instruments. According to each of these three sets of standards, many guarantees would be recognized at their fair value, while the value of most other guarantees would at least be disclosed. It will likely be some time, however, before the standards require a fully satisfactory approach (Irwin 2003b).[9] Moreover, although adopting accrual standards can help address the problems, the problems can also be addressed without adopting such standards.

In government budgeting, contemporary approaches reflect two important principles for budgeting for fiscal risk (Brixi and Schick 2002):

1. Apply a joint ceiling to the cost of budgetary and off-budget support for each sector in a fiscal year. Off-budget support is considered a form of subsidy and thus subject to the same scrutiny and limits as any spending program. The size of the hidden subsidy is calculated as the present value of the future expected fiscal cost.
2. Have the budget immediately reflect the full likely fiscal cost of contingent support when a contingent support scheme is approved.

Another, possibly complementary, option is to create a contingent-liability fund. Some governments have created a special fund (a new bank account, in other words) that is used to meet calls on guarantees and other liabilities. When guarantees are issued, the sector ministry can be required to transfer to the fund an amount equal to the estimated value of the guarantee. In Canada and the Netherlands, which follow the two principles above as well as use a special fund, the finance ministry computes the expected annual payout on contingent liabilities undertaken on behalf of the programs of each line ministry. The finance ministry then deducts these expected payouts from the annual budgetary allocation for the ministry concerned. Similar arrangements, including mechanisms to provide reimbursement to the line ministry for such provisions if a payout on the contingent liability does not occur ex post, have also been tried in Colombia.

These principles have several important implications for government fiscal performance. Budgeting for risk may or may not affect cash-based estimates of the government's fiscal deficit. It depends on whether the effect on the deficit is recorded when money is transferred from the budget to a contingency fund (then no effect is recorded when a guarantee is called and paid for from the contingency fund) or only when actual cash payments are disbursed from the program account. But budgeting for risk makes policy makers more cash neutral—that is, neutral between alternative forms of providing government support in terms of deficit measurement, budget ceilings, or medium-term fiscal outlook. And most importantly, perhaps, budgeting for risk promotes risk awareness among policy makers.

Experience suggests that the benefits of greater scrutiny, cash neutrality, and risk awareness can be achieved with or without a comprehensive transition of the accounting and budgeting systems to the accrual basis. Countries that have successfully combined reporting of contingent liabilities (and wider disclosure of risk) with cash accounting include the Czech Republic and South Africa, and those budgeting for risk within a cash-based budgeting system include Canada, Colombia, the Netherlands, and the United States. Similarly, fiscal risk can be brought into the government's medium-term budgetary framework. Setting the government budget and risk exposures in the context of a publicly announced medium-term budgetary framework later makes any departures from the original risk analysis apparent. It has already strengthened the accountability of policy makers and the quality of fiscal policy in many countries, including Australia (including New South Wales at the local level), Canada (including British Columbia and Ontario at the local level), Hungary, and South Africa.

The inclusion of contingent liabilities in the areas of concern of international organizations and investors is likely to encourage further accounting and budgeting reforms. International organizations could also assist in broadening the scope of the annual budget process to involve any major questions related to government risk exposures, so that the process provides an effective platform for an open discussion of policy choices.

Build Fiscal Risk Management Capacity

The experience of governments trying to actively manage their risk exposures shows that fiscal risk management is very demanding. Governments find that to manage their risk exposures they need (a) adequate information, hence a comprehensive database of all major risk exposures, the capacity to gather relevant information, and the opportunity for open discussion; (b) the ability to understand, which may be assisted by useful analytical frameworks; and (c) incentives to act correctly—incentives that are supported by disclosure and adequate accounting and budgeting rules, as discussed above.

Proper incentives in dealing with local government risk are supported by appropriate accountability structures. Policy makers need to be accountable for the adequacy of their risk analysis, assumptions, and decisions that involve fiscal risks and for managing the overall risk exposure of the government. Therefore, the role of the supreme audit institution (and the local audit bureaus) is to audit all aspects of government risk analysis and risk management.

Practice has shown the importance of three additional features of risk management: a clear risk management strategy (to specify to what extent is the government is prepared to take on fiscal risk), centralized risk-taking authority (possibly in the budget office of the ministry of finance), and risk monitoring that is separate from risk taking (possibly the debt management office and the supreme audit institution could be responsible for monitoring risk internally and externally, respectively). The division of responsibilities and functions in risk management and the underlying reporting arrangements need to be very clear to provide a basis for adequate accountability structures.

For fiscal risk monitoring to be effective it needs to be comprehensive. Specifically, it needs to cover the whole range of channels through which governments at the local, as well as the central, level generate fiscal risks, including letters of comfort, credit and guarantee funds, development corporations, local government–controlled enterprises, and so on.

Among government agencies and departments, the debt management office is often most able to analyze and manage government risk exposures. Specifically, the debt management office is often best equipped to gather and analyze information about government contingent liabilities, evaluate government risk exposure and future possible implications of contingent liabilities on government debt, reflect on the analysis of contingent liabilities in borrowing and debt management strategy, and advise the government on the future possible fiscal cost of newly proposed programs and on how to structure these programs to reduce government risk exposure. Debt management agencies are likely also to be in a good position to understand off–balance sheet debt in the form of long-term purchase agreements. Debt management offices have been placed in charge of risk analysis and management in a number of countries, most notably in Sweden.

Take Measures to Reduce Government Risk Exposure

Reducing government risk exposure entails three complementary tasks: involving the private sector, transferring the risk to parties better able to bear the risk, and managing any residual risk that cannot be mitigated or transferred.

Involving the private sector mainly implies mitigating the risk at the source and developing the financial markets. Ultimately, risk mitigation with private sector involvement is the most desirable long-run strategy. It not only reduces the government's exposure to fiscal risks, but also reduces the vulnerability of the economy to shocks.[10]

Risk transfer mainly implies creating risk-sharing arrangements. Creating a good risk-sharing mechanism requires clear policy objectives and understanding of all underlying risks in a project. For both central and local governments, so far the primary method of transferring risk has been through risk-sharing provisions in guarantee and insurance contracts. In private infrastructure, recent practice has suggested that carving out commercial risk from the coverage of government guarantees reduces moral hazard under the project as well as limiting government risk exposure.

Residual risk can sometimes be hedged. The private sector and, for some risks, international financial institutions offer useful risk mitigation tools. Governments and public sector entities, for instance, sometime use currency swaps and commodity futures to hedge their foreign exchange and commodity price risks. They have also purchased reinsurance for disaster risk and weather risk from large international reinsurers. Increasing integration and liberalization in the market for insurance has made it easier to pool risk across countries and, increasingly, to insure risks that were until recently considered uninsurable. Governments might use some of these tools to hedge their exposure to risks in infrastructure projects. For the largest projects exposed to catastrophic risk, governments might also be able to issue catastrophe bonds, which offer lower yields when a catastrophe occurs. Given the still nascent stages of the international catastrophe bond market and weaknesses in the derivatives market, however, it is likely that governments will be able to reduce their risk exposure more effectively by first focusing on policies to mitigate the risk at the source and develop the domestic financial markets discussed above.

Risks that cannot be avoided or hedged must be absorbed, requiring the government to manage its financial assets so that it has cash when it needs it. If the government cannot avoid bearing a risk and cannot hedge the risk, it has no choice but to absorb the risk—that is, to bear any losses and, depending on the nature of the contracts it has written, reap any gains. It must therefore have sufficient cash on hand to enable it to make payments when they fall due. It can aim to do this in three ways:

1. Put cash in a contingent liability fund (as discussed above) and hope the funds are sufficient to meet future payments.
2. Use the cash to reduce debt and hope it can use tax revenues or additional borrowing if and when it needs to make payments.
3. Enter into a standby credit agreement with a bank that will allow it to borrow if it needs to make payments.

Each option has advantages and disadvantages. Having cash in a fund may give the government stronger assurance that cash will be available when needed. But it also has a cost, because the cash could otherwise be used to repay debt or invest in public services. Using the cash to repay debt may be cheaper, but leaves open the question of whether the government will be able to borrow or raise taxes when liabilities fall due—possibly at a time of crisis.

A standby credit agreement, if available, solves the last problem, but at a cost that may be high.

The options are not mutually exclusive. A government can, and may indeed have to, use more than one option. The contingent liability fund, for example, cannot cover all contingencies. Even if the fund has the limited purpose of meeting calls on guarantees, it will be large enough to meet the worst possible losses only if the contributions are set according to the face value of the guarantees, not according to their expected costs. If contributions are smaller, the fund may need to be combined with reliance on taxing and borrowing or on a standby credit agreement.

The existence of cash in a fund may also tempt the government to use the money for other purposes. One option is to contract out management to a reputable foreign entity. The contract could specify permissible reasons for withdrawing cash from the fund without penalty and make other claims subject to a penalty and to prior public disclosure.

This discussion has indicated that reducing government risk exposures, as well as its overall dealing with contingent liabilities and fiscal risk, is relatively complex and difficult for policy makers to address. Therefore, many countries would benefit from having access to relevant technical assistance in these areas.

Concluding Remarks

Fiscal analysis and management frameworks need to cover contingent liabilities to promote appropriate disclosure and to deal with contingent liabilities. This chapter suggests that the growing role of local governments and of the private sector in the delivery of public services raises the possibility that government contingent liabilities may grow in the future.

Policy makers, encouraged and supported by international and other relevant institutions, need to promote risk awareness and reforms that would further strengthen government capacity to deal with contingent liabilities and fiscal risk exposures. To strengthen the incentives toward disclosure and adequate management of contingent liabilities, countries need to be rewarded rather than punished at the time when they reveal contingent liabilities; they need to be punished rather than forgiven at the time when hidden contingent liabilities fall due.

Notes

1. Contingent liabilities are obligations triggered by a discrete event that may or may not occur. International financial reporting standards define a contingent liability as (a) a possible obligation that arises from past events and whose existence will be

confirmed only by the occurrence or nonoccurrence of one or more uncertain future events not wholly within the control of the enterprise; or (b) a present obligation that arises from past events but is not recognized because (i) it is not probable that an outflow of resources embodying economic benefits will be required to settle the obligation; or (ii) the amount of the obligation cannot be measured with sufficient reliability (IASB 2004). This chapter draws on Brixi and Irwin (2004) and Brixi (forthcoming).

2. Transformation institutions had been created as off-budget agencies to borrow, issue guarantees, and finance government support programs for banks, enterprises, and other entities. Some transformation agencies were covered by an explicit government guarantee and others were not. Brixi and Schick (2002) provide a brief analysis.

3. Separately, however, there remains the question of the agencies' own guarantees and other contingent liabilities.

4. In most private infrastructure projects in developing countries, governments bear at least some policy risks. The mechanism is usually a contract with the firm that gives the firm certain rights (as well as obligations). The contract may, for example, give the firm the right to charge prices determined by a formula. If the government subsequently prevents the firm from charging the price permitted by the contract, the government will, all else being equal, have to compensate the firm.

5. More precisely, it encourages the government to maintain the policies offered to the investor unless the benefits of changing the policy exceed the costs that the change imposes on the investor.

6. Giving the infrastructure firm or its customers an explicit cash subsidy is perhaps the simplest type of support. The practice is widespread in Latin America, where many governments have awarded concessions to the bidder seeking the lowest cash subsidy or provided voucher-like subsidies to selected customers.

7. Rodden, Eskeland, and Litvack (2003) provide a set of country examples describing the issues related to the soft budget constraint of local governments.

8. With respect to public-private partnerships, Eurostat (2004) recommends that the assets and associated liabilities in a public-private partnership should be classified as not belonging to the government and therefore kept off the government's balance sheet, only if (a) the private partner bears the construction risk, and (b) the private partner bears either the availability or the demand risk. If the construction risk is borne by government, or if the private partner bears only the construction risk, the assets and liabilities are considered the government's.

9. In addition, there are various rules that can be helpful in regard to government risk exposure. For instance, according to the IMF (2004), nonfinancial public enterprises that are not commercially run should be included in fiscal statistics.

10. In infrastructure, policy makers may need to ask how to reduce the dependence of private providers and investors on government guarantees and other kinds of support. Countrywide legal, regulatory, and administrative changes and proper debt management strategies can facilitate the establishment of an efficient domestic bond market, which in turn will smooth the progress of private infrastructure, as well as improve the government's capacity to absorb risk. Private investors and providers in infrastructure may also be more willing to forgo government guarantees when the investment climate in the country improves. Regulatory changes can encourage large international insurers to access the local market and pool risks, such as weather risk,

that are uninsurable in a small economy. New financial instruments, such as asset-backed securities or catastrophe bonds, may help domestic financial institutions manage risk better, thus reducing their demand for government guarantees. Strategies to promote risk mitigation and financial market development, however, often hinge on fundamental sectoral reforms, such as reforms in energy pricing, production, and distribution systems.

References

Brixi, Hana Polackova. Forthcoming. "Contingent Liabilities in New Member States." In *Fiscal Surveillance in EMU: New Issues and Challenges.* Cheltenham, U.K.: Edward Elgar.

Brixi, Hana Polackova, and Timothy Irwin. 2004. "Fiscal Support for Infrastructure: Toward a More Effective and Transparent Approach." Background paper for EAP Infrastructure Flagship report, "Connection Matters: A New Framework for Infrastructure in East Asia and the Pacific," World Bank, Washington, DC.

Brixi, Hana Polackova, and Allen Schick. 2002. *Governments at Risk: Contingent Liabilities and Fiscal Risk.* Washington, DC: World Bank and Oxford University Press.

Cassard, Marcel, and David Folkerts-Landau. 1997. "Risk Management of Sovereign Assets and Liabilities." IMF Working Paper 97/166, International Monetary Fund, Washington, DC.

European Commission. 2004. "Public Finances in EMU 2004." *European Economy* 3.

European Commission and World Bank. 1998. *European Union Accession: The Challenges for Public Liability Management in Central Europe.* Washington, DC: European Commission and World Bank.

———. 2000. *Opportunities and Risks in Central European Finances.* Washington, DC: European Commission and World Bank.

Eurostat. 2004. "New Decision of Eurostat on Deficit and Debt: Treatment of Public-Private Partnerships." News release, February 11.

IASB (International Accounting Standards Board). 2004. *International Financial Reporting Standards (IFRSs)—Including International Accounting Standards (IASs) and Interpretations as at 31 March 2004.* London: IASB.

IMF (International Monetary Fund). 2004. "Public Investment and Fiscal Policy." IMF, Washington, DC. http://www.imf.org/external/np/fad/2004/pifp/eng/.

Irwin, Timothy. 2003a. "Public Money for Private Infrastructure: Deciding When to Offer Guarantees, Output-Based Subsidies, and Other Fiscal Support." Working Paper 10, World Bank, Washington, DC.

———. 2003b. "Accounting for Public-Private Partnerships: How Should Governments Report Guarantees and Long-Term Purchase Contracts?" World Bank, Washington, DC.

Polackova, Hana. 1998. "Contingent Government Liabilities: A Hidden Risk for Fiscal Stability." Policy Research Working Paper 1989, World Bank, Washington, DC.

Rodden, Jonathan, Gunnar Eskeland, and Jennie Litvack. 2003. *Fiscal Decentralization and the Challenge of Hard Budget Constraints.* Cambridge, MA: MIT Press.

8

On Measuring the Net Worth of a Government

MATTHEW ANDREWS AND ANWAR SHAH

H60 H11
H61 H62

In many ways one sees the public asking, "What is government worth?" or "What is government's value?" In attempting to answer such questions, citizens usually have access to limited financial reports—like the one in Table 8.1. What kind of information do such reports typically convey regarding government worth or value?

The answer is very little. Government financial reporting is notoriously limited to short-term activities, as represented in line-item reports that detail money spent on inputs. From such reports it is possible to work out the size of the civil service (at least roughly) and how much government has overspent in the current period (the deficit). Accompanying documents sometimes provide detail about longer-term capital and debt positions, but this information is usually selective and difficult to locate. One is thus left asking typical questions households ask of their own net worth or value: "Apart from my short-term position, how am I faring over the long run—do my assets exceed my liabilities, especially those that could be called contingent liabilities?" "How valuable are my long-term assets, are they holding their value, and am I using them efficiently?" "How much value do I add on an annual basis —what kind of performance do I achieve with my short-term cash outlays?"

191

TABLE 8.1   Financial Statement of Government *X* for Year *Y*

Revenue	
Levied through the government's power	
Direct taxation	21,260
Indirect taxation	11,722
Compulsory fees, fines, penalties and levies	258
Subtotal	33,240
Earned through the government's operations	
Investment income	1,154
Unrealized gains(losses) arising from changes in the value of commercial forests	78
Other operational revenue	420
Sales of goods and services	689
Subtotal	2,341
Total revenue	**35,581**
Total revenue as a % of GDP	36.0%
Expenses (by line item)	
Salaries and other personnel	13,000
Service expenditures	10,000
General expenditures	8,000
Capital expenditures	2,000
Capital expenses	800
Working capital	100
Debt repayments	100
Other	211
Total expenses	**34,211**
Total expenses as a % of GDP	34.6%
Surplus: Revenue Less Expenses	**1,370**

These kinds of questions suggest the multiple dimensions of a household's or organization's worth or value: short-term solvency, long-term worth, and value added (or performance). These dimensions pertain to governments as well. Common financial management practices in the developing world, often influenced by reforms focused on deficit reduction, reflect a short-term value concentration and encourage the entrenchment of incentives associated with such a concentration. This narrow valuation approach ignores the other important value dimensions.

Reform literature argues that the long-term and performance dimensions can only be introduced once the basics of short-run financial management are in place (Schick 1998; World Bank 1998). This chapter argues differently—that a continued narrow evaluation approach yields potentially permanent organizational damage because of the narrow behavioral incentives it entrenches. If developing governments are allowed (and encouraged) to concentrate on short-term financial conditions alone, the importance of long-term financial management and public sector service performance will be undermined, and these government value dimensions will deteriorate. Governments need to move beyond a short-term focus, by adopting new tools and institutionalizing new reporting procedures and conventions, to ensure an effective and appropriate picture of net worth or value is constantly available.

The Three Dimensions of Government Value

Evaluation literature emphasizes that government evaluations should extend beyond short-run issues of control and liquidity (Osborne and Gaebler 1992; Shah 1998). Such evaluations, it is increasingly argued (at least in the Western world), should reflect short-term financial conditions, as well as long-term financial concerns and achievements in terms of service provision (Buschor and Schedler 1994; Mikesell 1995; Auerbach, Kotlikoff, and Leibfritz 1999). These three value dimensions are shown in table 8.2.

Short-term liquidity and financial accountability is an important focus in the public sector. It is important that governments, like any going concern, report on their in-period financial position, ensuring a constant view

TABLE 8.2 Government Value Dimensions

Value dimension	Focus	Bottom line
Short-term financial condition	Short-term liquidity	Ability of government to spend within cash resources, and not to burden society with excessive spending
Long-term financial condition	Short-, medium-, and long-term financial condition	Ability of government to manage resources effectively and efficiently over the long run, and to maximize the use of social resources
Service performance	Efficient provision of relevant services	Ability of government to respond to citizen needs effectively and efficiently, facilitating growth and development

of their liquidity and promoting accountability. Governments failing to maintain necessary balances, or to control funds reliably from budget to activity, are considered inefficient. A second value dimension emphasized in recent work is long-term financial condition. Concern for pervasive mismanagement of long-term finances in governments has led to a certain degree of what could be called "generational angst"—"the fear that we are bequeathing enormous fiscal bills to our children" (Kotlikoff and Leibfritz 1999, 73). This concern has stimulated a need for evaluations of government management of factors affecting organizational and social wealth—capital, liabilities, and so forth. Evaluating these aspects encourages governments to focus on the future, as well as on the present. Recent literature suggests that emphasizing short-term control and liquidity and long-term financial position is also insufficient to provide a complete view of government value, however. There is a growing interest in how governments affect society through their performance and a focus on making "government managers . . . accountable to ensure that their organizations are as productive as possible" (Dittenhofer 1994, 103). This focus yields an evaluation emphasis on government service performance. The measurement and evaluation of such performance is the driving thrust of the results movement.

The Deficit Concentration in Developing Country Reforms

Financial management in the developing world often involves a mix of deeply entrenched rules and as deeply entrenched disdain for rules (Schick 1998). Commentators suggest that the rules are applied to limit access to financial information, not to increase information-based accountability as they do elsewhere (Andrews 2002). Dominant reforms emphasize establishing basic enforceable controls and promoting a value orientation and evaluation mechanisms focused on improving short-term fiscal discipline (Schick 1998; World Bank 1998).

The Reform Argument: Short-Term Rules Now Facilitate Other Value Concerns Tomorrow

These reform perspectives argue that the multidimensional public value perspective, encapsulating concern for service performance and long-term wealth, is relevant only in governments in which the basics of financial management have been established. These voices support the introduction of reforms focused on improving short-term financial management and controls, aimed at achieving short-run fiscal discipline in public financial management systems before attempting to develop a performance orientation and long-run planning and budgeting capacity. As such, these commentators believe that a narrow value orientation in the short run could be expanded once such an orientation is reliably established.

The Reform Argument: Reforms with a Short-Run Concentration Lead to a Neglect of Other Value Dimensions

South Africa is a good example of these reforms in action, where rule-bound cash accounting and incrementalism characterized traditional practices and deficits dominated financial reports. Reforms in the late 1990s were specifically directed at lowering the deficit, reflecting the state macroeconomic strategy (Abedian 1998; Wray 2004). These reforms involved direct applications of legislation to control spending in subnational governments, the imposition of hard budget constraints on government departments, and the development of medium-term expenditure frameworks to improve short-run allocative efficiency and to provide a basis for longer-run planning.

In an analysis of the status of financial management and budgeting in South Africa between 1997 and 2001, a focus on short-term value emerges. The country enjoyed success in reducing deficits as a percentage of the total budget, for which it received significant praise. Departments and subnational governments appeared more disciplined in their short-run fiscal management, which brought them praise. Unfortunately, however, even with these positive achievements, other dimensions of government performance suffered:

- Long-run concerns such as investment in new capital and management of long-term liabilities were neglected in the budget for a period of years (Cameron and Tapscott 2000–3). National and provincial capital spending decreased as a percentage of the budget, and the budgeting focus was placed squarely on control of short-term activities, even though the government emphasized its own long-run developmental role in principle.[1] Increases in capital allocations in the 2001–3 period have not led to increased spending, because many departments were found to lack the ability to program and implement capital projects. Wray (2004) wrote, "Capital spending, seen by many as the lynchpin of future economic growth, was budgeted to increase 26 percent—a welcome shift in emphasis, although cynicism about the state's ability to deliver was later proved valid."
- Government service performance has come under increasing criticism and is not effectively reported on in budgets or financial reports. Government entities at all levels are argued to lack the capacity to perform

even basic services well, and they are criticized for concentrating on managing their inflated personnel bills instead of their service performance.

The Burning Questions

Observers of financial management reforms in countries such as South Africa are left asking the following questions:

- Do good short-term evaluations in terms of deficit figures outweigh bad evaluations in terms of service performance and long-term financial condition?
- Will the neglect of two dimensions of government value—long-run financial position and service performance—hurt countries in the long run, or will the achievement of short-run value facilitate a multidimensional perspective in the future?
- How can government finances be managed (and reported on) to facilitate a multidimensional reflection of government value?

Incentives Associated with Short-Run Evaluations and Concern for Government Value

All evaluation methods have an impact on incentives. The old performance adage is that what gets measured gets done. This established, the argument of this chapter is that focusing on one aspect of government value (the short-run fiscal discipline), when government value consists of three aspects, leads to incentives that make a more comprehensive valuation perspective difficult to establish in the future. In governments where entrenched practice and conventional reforms both foster a short-run discipline concentration, it is typical to find managers behaving in certain ways, responding to short-term incentives. These incentives become entrenched in public sector budgeting and financial exchanges, leading to a concentration on inputs instead of results, capital neglect, and intergenerational money shifting.

Concentration on Inputs, Not Results, of Government Action

The short-run discipline emphasis communicates that government value is all about government controlling what it does, rather than government doing what it does well and ensuring that what it does is relevant. This message helps create an incentive for managers to concentrate on inputs and rules rather than on results. This incentive is manifest internationally where government financial systems have public managers accounting for their input expenditures, and reporting on their ability to abide by rules of process and procedure instead of the results they produce. Reforms concentrating on these factors entrench this incentive and will reduce the potential for government managers and policy makers to embrace a more comprehensive value perspective in the future.

Capital Neglect

Another incentive of the short-run bias manifests in poor management of long-term assets. The influence of traditional valuation methods on capital management is quite complex, and in every way negative. On the one hand, managers neglect infrastructure maintenance and the purchase of new infrastructure in the current period because short-term cash drains to pay for maintenance in the current period are not visibly offset by long-term gains in added capital value. On the other hand, because the value of existing capital is not included in regular evaluations, it is considered a free good for public service managers. This discourages the responsible use of assets and results in managers holding onto (but neither using effectively nor maintaining) old infrastructure that could generate value in other hands. Managers also neglect the development of new capital required to generate value and services in the future, failing to build the capacity to develop new infrastructure (because management concerns are focused on the present, not the future). South Africa is an example, with decreases in capital expenditure between 1997 and 2001 (in absolute terms and as a percentage of total expenditure), tracking both the short-term policy orientation and the short-term value gains (the reduced deficits) (Andrews 2002). Positive evaluation, measured in terms of a reduced deficit, comes at a high price when managers are simultaneously encouraged to neglect future investment. The argument is potentially countered when increased capital allocations in the 2003–05 period are considered. However, increased allocations have not led to increased expenditures on capital, partly because the deemphasis of this kind of expenditure has limited departmental abilities to deliver new projects (Wray 2004).

Intergenerational Money Shifting

A final incentive manifests in the temptation to move money gained from past savings or due for future commitments into current funds to bolster the picture of current value, because shifting future income to the present can reduce current deficits and boost current evaluation results. There are many examples of governments' spending reserves without citizen permission or knowledge and showing current period surpluses, when in fact dwindling reserves are not reported or are hidden in the details of financial reports reflecting a current period bias. Governments also use money meant for future commitments to account for current shortfalls (the future commitments could be either explicit future liabilities, contingent liabilities, or intergenerational items such as social security or pensions). This kind of behavior leaves governments open to significant financial shock when the future commitments fall due. It is entrenched whenever the short-run value perspective is allowed to consolidate the already short-run personal interests of individual budgeters.

Choosing Tools That Measure and Report on Net Worth in All Its Dimensions

The obvious argument here is that governments need to go beyond the short-run fiscal discipline emphasis if they are to truly facilitate evaluations of government net worth, and to create incentives for managers to develop all three dimensions of such worth. The concentration of government evaluations is dependent on the facts and figures on which the evaluation is based, however. The quality and scope of these facts and figures is strongly related to the tools used (and the focus they reveal) in the accounting process from which such figures emanate. This is shown in figure 8.1.

The challenge for government accountants and financial managers is to adopt accounting tools that are both strong and multidimensional, so that they yield financial accounts that reflect all three aspects of government value. Consider, for example, the challenge of refocusing deficit figures. Governments in the developing world (and the developed world) are often evaluated on the basis of their deficit performance, although it is accepted in

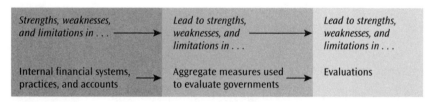

FIGURE 8.1 Financial Systems, National Income Accounts, and Deficit Evaluations

some arenas that "the deficit is an arbitrary accounting concept whose value depends on how the government chooses to label its receipts and payments" (Kotlikoff and Leibfritz 1999, 73). Consider, for example, that in developed countries such as the United States the deficit statistic is developed without recognition of some important long-term liabilities and public commitments, while in countries in the developing world the deficit statistic is drawn from an accounting process in which cash-based accounts fail to reflect even medium-term commitments made in a given period. In no country does the deficit incorporate accounts that reflect the effectiveness or efficiency of spending, largely because of the inherent limitations of the measure and various political interests that systematically oppose its adjustment (for example, political re-election interests focus on short-term, not long-term, expenditure effects).

To ensure that a government is evaluated in a multidimensional sense, government financial managers need to reconsider how it labels its receipts and payments, what it measures, and how it reports. To do this, governments around the world are being forced beyond using traditional accounting tools, which focus on short-term value. Countries such as Malaysia, New Zealand, and the United Kingdom have built on traditional accounting approaches to provide more complete measures of the three dimensions of government value. The main accountability dimension emphasized in the new financial management practices in these countries is the performance focus. The particular tools that have been adopted to improve internal and external evaluation in these governments include accrual accounting, explicit valuation of contingent liabilities, intergenerational accounting, and capital charging, activity-based costing.

Accrual Accounting

A number of countries, including Australia, Iceland, New Zealand, Singapore, the United Kingdom, and the United States, have adopted accrual-based accounting for their financial statements and budgets covering the whole of the government. Accrual accounting has several implications for the incorporation of longer-term issues into the budget process and into aggregate figures used to evaluate governments. First, expenses are recognized when they are incurred rather than when they are paid. As a result, expenditures that are building up over time but are not payable until later are nonetheless reported as expenses, showing total resource costs of commitments. Second, all assets, including infrastructure, are valued and reported in the balance sheet to draw attention to their management, as well as to the maintenance of their values. Third, all liabilities are recorded in the balance sheet. For example, unfunded public service pension plans are recognized as liabilities in the balance sheet and, correspondingly, the full increase in this liability in any period is recorded as an expense in the budget operating statement.

Explicit Valuation of Contingent Liabilities

Most public accounts processes do not report on or attach an explicit value to contingent liabilities. This problem is being addressed through a two-pronged process of reporting on such liabilities, and valuing them through a *marketizing process*. In New Zealand, a Statement of Contingent Liabilities is presented with other financial statements, facilitating an evaluation of the details of contingent liabilities. Contingent liabilities are also shown in Australian government financial statements. Since 1996 such information has appeared in the public sector account and as separate lists to facilitate a partial evaluation of the statistics within the aggregate deficit figures and a more complete analysis supplementing such statistics (providing detail of the liabilities). In both countries, the contingent liabilities are being explicitly valued through a marketizing process. There are several ways of marketizing contingent liabilities, including purchasing insurance to cover expenses arising from a potential liability, selling the rights over the yield of pending debt, and reflecting that sale in the deficit.

Intergenerational Accounting

One of the big questions of government accounts is this: How does today's spending affect tomorrow's fiscal condition? One way of valuing this intergenerational effect is through intergenerational accounting, a tool first used in the 1993 budget in the United States and later in other countries, including Germany, Italy, New Zealand, Norway, and Sweden.[2] It was developed to estimate what different generations would pay in taxes and receive in benefits over their lifetimes given existing policies, thus focusing on questions of intergenerational equity. Although some authors are skeptical of intergenerational accounting, its recent popularity speaks to its potential, especially in providing a clear assessment of the impact of long-term commitments on society and on government value (Haveman 1994).

Activity-Based Costing

Good cost accounting is central to collecting accurate data for evaluation. There is a need "to evaluate the costs of producing outputs and outcomes on a continuing basis in order to evaluate performance and allocate resources" (Rodriguez 1995, 32). Governments generally lack an accepted methodology of cost measurement and evaluation, however, particularly one that allows for cost comparisons of outputs (Tierney 1994). Activity-based costing is the most common device in results-oriented governments in the developed world (Simpson and Williams 1996). It has been used widely, especially in local governments. It has proved particularly popular in entities attempting to compare their performance with private sector standards and to evaluate the full costs of production (including overhead and capital costs) (Andrews and Moynihan 2002). Activity-based costing involves relating input costs to activities within organizations and then relating the activities to the factors that drive costs—generally the output objectives of the organization.

Capital Charging

Full costing not only provides a more accurate picture of relative production efficiency, but it also plays an important role in developing incentives for efficient results production. If administrators are not required to measure their overhead and capital costs accurately, they lack the incentive to manage these resources efficiently and effectively. When these costs are included in their management decisions, managers have an incentive to actively manage how much capital they use and to strategize about latent capacity. The cost of asset usage may also be incorporated in the operating statement by a capital charge, which is a charge against a department's or agency's appropriation to cover the cost of the assets it uses in delivering its programs. This encourages attention to asset management; for example, by reducing or restraining its asset levels, a department can reduce the amount of the capital charge against its appropriation. The experience in countries such as New Zealand suggests that capital charging, when applied in conjunction with accrual accounting, increases the focus on longer-term issues.

Capital charging requires the valuation of capital assets, another important element of determining government net worth. Many governments are being called to value assets and report on and account for their use (as evidenced, for example, in the Governmental Accounting Standards Board [GASB] 34 requirements in the United States). Governments have not traditionally valued assets, however, and often have many questions regarding how this should be done (questions that are also convenient to hide behind). Conventional accounting practices in the private sector require that assets be valued according to their depreciated historical costs, but governments generally have very little information about the historical cost of assets, especially those dating back decades (Patton and Bean 2001). Because of this kind of problem, GASB 34 allows time for retroactive reporting and requires reporting only of major assets in the United States. Approaches taken to evaluate assets include using historical records that exist for some assets (recently built) as the basis of evaluation for all, and using a deflated current replacement cost approach whereby a current replacement cost is calculated and then deflated, given the age of the asset in question. These approaches allow governments to provide some detail as to the worth of their physical infrastructure—a key aspect of their net worth and social value.

Multidimensional Reporting

The various mechanisms discussed briefly here all point to a financial management approach that reflects value or worth in terms of more than a short-term perspective. It is important that, once these tools are in place, managers also report on worth or value along different perspectives. In New Zealand this is achieved by providing three reports, the Operating Statement, the Statement of Financial Position, and the Statement of Service Performance (countries like South Africa are progressively moving to this multidimensional reporting method as well. All three are provided as tables 8.3, 8.4, and 8.5, respectively, reflecting details from the same government whose financial statement opened the chapter in table 8.1. Consider the improved reporting detail, especially as it pertains to the way in which government net worth (on all three dimensions) is portrayed.

Table 8.3 reports on the short-term financial condition in a subtly different way than table 8.1. Expenditures are listed by functional department, all of which are accountable for performance in terms of set contracts. This allows citizens to see exactly where money is going (by department, each of which is a performance entity and independent cost center). There are also expenditure items facilitating allocations to future projects and to contingencies.

Table 8.4 allows observers to view the long-term worth of a government, detailing its assets (which have all notably been valued) and its liabilities (including such contingent liabilities as pensions). Observers can assess exactly which kinds of assets the government owns and can compare the government's asset wealth with its liabilities to investigate its long-term net worth (calculated as the difference between total assets and total liabilities).

As in the example in table 8.5, departments in countries such as New Zealand and the United Kingdom produce a version of a Statement of Service

TABLE 8.3 Reporting on Short-Term Fiscal Position Related to Value or Worth—Operating Statement

Revenue	
Levied through the government's power	
Direct taxation	21,260
Indirect taxation	11,722
Compulsory fees, fines, penalties, and levies	258
Subtotal	33,240
Earned through the government's operations	
Investment income	1,154
Unrealized gains/(losses) arising from changes in the value of commercial forests	78
Other operational revenue	420
Sales of goods and services	689
Subtotal	2,341
Total revenue	**35,581**
Total revenue as a % of GDP	36.0%
Expenses (by functional department, entity, all of which are accountable for performance in terms of set contracts)	
Securities commission	423
Education	5,714
Social security and welfare	13,003
Health	6,001
Core government services	1,562
Law and order	1,345
Defense	1,065
Transport and communications	948
Economic and industrial services	840
Heritage, culture, and recreation	297
Housing and community development	29
Other	167
Finance costs	2,804
Net foreign-exchange losses/gains	13
Provision for future initiatives	—
Contingency expenses	—
Total expenses	**34,211**
Total expenses as a % of GDP	34.6%
Surplus: Revenue less expenses	**1,370**

Note: Information in tables 8.1 and 8.3 are based on the Statements of Financial Performance in New Zealand (shown in New Zealand dollars).
— denotes not available.

TABLE 8.4   Reporting on Long-Term Fiscal Value or Worth

Assets	
Cash and bank balances	196
Marketable securities and deposits	7,581
Advances	2,871
Receivables	5091
Inventories	295
State-owned enterprises	18,483
Other investments	214
Physical assets	14,502
Commercial forests	505
State highways	8,210
Intangible assets	20
Total assets	**57,968**
Liabilities	
Payables and provisions	4,457
Currency issued	1,741
Borrowings	35,972
Pension liabilities	8,328
Total liabilities	**50,498**
Net worth: Total Assets less total liabilities	**7,470**

Performance, outlining the outputs produced against the benchmarked production goals (Ball 1994). Because statements are uniform, requiring information about outputs, outcomes, and results (in terms of quantity, quality, timeliness, and costs), the government can sum them up to provide holistic financial statements about the in-period results of government entities. In these countries the performance data are presented and published in conjunction with other financial statements, providing a source of evaluation of the social impact of government, as well as a device to help governments allocate resources strategically. The kind of information found in such statements provides insight into the results produced by specific parts of government and, when summed up, sheds light on the performance (or value added) of government as a whole.

Conclusion: Accounting and Reporting for Government Net Value

This chapter has looked at the link between financial evaluations and the way government conceptualizes (and reports on) its net worth or value. It has shown that, although three dimensions of government value are reflected in

TABLE 8.5 Reporting on Value Added or Performance—Statement of Service Performance

Department/ agency/ other entity	Output and related outcome goal	Results: quantity (activities), quality, timeliness, and costs
Securities Commission	*Output:* To promote public understanding of securities law through publications, communications, and such (as detailed in service contract). *Outcome:* To strengthen public and institutional confidence in securities markets.	*Quantity:* The Commission published four issues of *The Bulletin* (as was targeted in the Commission's Performance Targets). The Commission satisfied 1,607 miscellaneous inquiries from members of the public (target for the year: 1,200). The Commission issued 22 statements to the news media (target for the year: 25). The Commission published 51 exemption notes on the Web site (no target for the year). *Quality:* The Commission based its work on observed market practice and on sensible interpretations of securities law. It aimed to simplify the expression and content of the law. Material in *The Bulletin* and on the Web site was current, relevant, and useful (as determined by the National Bar Association review, and the results of the National Securities Association member survey). *Timeliness: The Bulletin* and other public understanding projects were completed on time. Public inquiries were all actioned within five working days of receipt (as targeted). *Costs:* The Commission allocated 11.7% of its expenditure to this output (budget for the year 11%).

(continued)

TABLE 8.5 Reporting on Value Added or Performance—Statements of Service Performance *(continued)*

Department/agency/other entity	Output and related outcome goal	Results: quantity (activities), quality, timeliness, and costs
	Output: To review securities law and make recommendations for reform. *Outcome:* To strengthen securities markets.	*Quantity:* The Commission worked, often with the Ministry of Economic Development, on a number of projects and reviews, including work on the Securities Regulations 1991, the Securities Act, administration and efficiency, surveillance and detection powers, insider trading law, and retirement village schemes. *Quality:* The Commission complied with its obligations under the Securities Act and with other relevant legislation. It based its work on accurate research into, and analysis of, the existing law and practice. Any recommendations set out and applied the relevant values and principles, including, where appropriate, the costs and benefits of the Commission's proposals according to the best available information and method of analysis. The Commission aimed to simplify the expression and content of the law. The process was based on wide and open consultation with all affected interests, including the general public or organizations representing sections of the general public. The Commission acted independently. *Timeliness:* The Commission aimed to meet the timetables of all those to whom its communications were addressed (as required

by its performance agreement). The Commission met agreed timetables when working on specific projects with other agencies.

Costs: The Commission allocated 15.2% of its expenditure to this output (budget for the year 14%).

Quantity: The Department completed building on 20 high schools to house between 100 and 200 children in district X, which is 80% of the target. Five schools previously planned were not completed but are in various stages of construction. Plans for five other primary schools were completed in the period, to be built in the coming year (this planning activity matches targeted performance).

Quality: The 20 completed schools were built according to the highest industry standards in the area, with at least 20% of the worker-hours coming from local contractors. The plans are of the highest standard (as verified by the National Institute of Architects) and the building processes meet all standards of the National Building Federation.

Timeliness: The 20 completed schools were generally completed on time, as specified in the performance targets. The two schools in District Y were completed one month after target.

Costs: The Department allocated 30% of its allocation to building schools in this District. In the year the Department spent 22% of its allocation on building schools in the District (underspending)

Education Department

Output: To build new schools in District Y.
Outcome: To increase citizen access to schooling facilities.

the literature, most developing countries emphasize only one dimension in their financial management approaches and reforms. Dominant reform voices argue that this narrow value orientation is appropriate for reforms in the short run, and that it can be expanded once such an orientation is reliably established. The authors of this chapter disagree, suggesting that incentives associated with the narrow-value orientation, and entrenched through current short-run focused reforms, constitute a barrier to financial evaluation based on all three dimensions.

The broad picture of government value is a central tenet of recent public reform successes in countries such as Australia and New Zealand. These reforms emphasize establishing a government culture and government evaluations that emphasize all three value dimensions. This emphasis is credited with the successful outcomes of those reforms, and perhaps more importantly, with encouraging incentives for public accountability in terms of the funds governments use in the short run, the services they provide to their constituents, and the plans they enact for future development. One can contrast this comprehensive evaluation approach with the short-run concentration in many developing countries. Such countries can also be contrasted with these successes in terms of the kinds of incentives that characterize their organizations. Emphasizing one value aspect to the exclusion of the others is harming the ability of these governments to truly achieve multidimensional value. The only way to achieve such value is by expanding their scope and adopting reforms in which practices are introduced that focus attention on cash flows, outcomes, and investments—moving from one-dimensional financial management to three-dimensional financial management.

There are a number of practices that governments are being encouraged to adopt to provide a more holistic picture of government worth or value, facilitating more effective reporting on service performance and long-term financial position—two dimensions of government accountability emphasized in recent literature and policy. Practices such as accrual-based accounting do not make all the difference on their own, however, because each individual new practice reflects individual aspects of government value. This is shown in table 8.6, where each practice is generally linked with only one or two aspects of government accountability.

It is when new practices are combined (with each other as well as with old cash management approaches) that they help provide a larger picture of government worth and value, through bolstering deficit figures and supplementing them with other information that is as important, if not more important, in the current report card public accounts environment. New Zealand provides an example.

TABLE 8.6   Putting the Practices Together to Fill Evaluation Gaps

Value aspect	Focus	Practice
Short-term financial condition	Short-term liquidity	Cash accounting, accrual accounting, marketizing contingent liabilities, activity-based costing
Long-term financial condition	Short-, medium-, and long-term financial condition	Accrual accounting, marketizing contingent liabilities, intergenerational accounting, capital charging
Service performance	Efficient provision of relevant services	Activity-based costing, performance reporting

On the basis of accrual accounting, incorporating a capital charge, and activity-based costing, government departments in New Zealand provide a full set of financial statements to the executive and the treasury each month. This full set of statements facilitates the development of more complete aggregate financial statistics, and because statements are uniform, they can be summed to provide holistic financial statements. Government accounts thus show the net worth of government. They are also supplemented with a Statement of Service Performance, outlining the outputs produced and the outputs agreed upon, and giving information about purchase performance much as a private firm would. All these practices combined provide information about the government's short-term fiscal accountability and position, its long-term financial health and asset worth, and its short-term value added (or performance).

Notes

1. National spending on fixed assets accounted for about 3 percent of the budget in 1990 and now accounts for 1.3 percent, according to South African Reserve Bank statistics. Provincial expenditure on capital was less than 6 percent of the budget in all nine provinces, with KwaZulu-Natal reporting zero capital spending in 1999 (Cameron and Tapscott 2000; Andrews 2002).

2. A list of countries is found in Auerbach, Kotlikoff, and Leibfritz (1999).

References

Abedian, Iraj. 1998. "Economic Globalisation: The Consequences for Fiscal Management." In *Economic Globalisation and Fiscal Policy,* ed. Iraj Abedian and Michael Biggs, 3–26. Cape Town, South Africa: Oxford University Press.

Andrews, Matthew. 2002. "A Theory-Based Approach to Evaluating Budget Reforms." *International Public Management Journal* 5 (2): 1–21.

Andrews, Matthew, and Don Moynihan. 2002. "Why Reforms Don't Always Have to 'Work' to Succeed: A Tale of Two Managed Competition Initiatives." *Public Performance and Management Review* 25 (3): 282–97.

Auerbach, Alan, Laurence J. Kotlikoff, and Willi Leibfritz, eds. 1999. *Generational Accounting Across the World*. Chicago: University of Chicago Press.

Ball, Ian. 1994. "Reinventing Government: Lessons Learned from the New Zealand Treasury." *Government Accountants Journal* 43 (3): 19–28.

Buschor, Ernst, and Kuno Schedler, eds. 1994. *Perspectives on Performance Measurement and Public Sector Accounting*. Bern, Switzerland: Paul Haupt Publishers.

Cameron, Robert, and Chris Tapscott. 2000. "The Challenges of State Transformation in South Africa." *Public Administration and Development* 20 (2): 81–86.

Dittenhofer, Mort. 1994. "Auditing to Improve Government Performance in Government Support Functions." In *Perspectives on Performance Measurement and Public Sector Accounting*, ed. Ernst Buschor and Kuno Schedler. Bern, Switzerland: Paul Haupt Publishers.

Haveman, Robert. 1994. "Should Generational Accounts Replace Public Budgets and Deficits?" *Journal of Economic Perspectives* 8 (1): 95–111.

Kotlikoff, Laurence J., and Willi Leibfritz. 1999. "An International Comparison of Generational Accounts." In *Generational Accounting Across the World*, ed. Alan Auerbach, Laurence J. Kotlikoff, and Willi Leibfritz, 73–102. Chicago: University of Chicago Press.

Mikesell, John L. 1995. *Fiscal Administration*, 4th ed. New York: Wadsworth.

Osborne, David, and Ted Gaebler. 1992. *Reinventing Government*. Reading, MA: Addison-Wesley.

Patton, Terry K., and David R. Bean. 2001. "The Why and How of New Capital Asset Reporting Requirements." *Public Budgeting and Finance* 21 (3): 31–46.

Rodriguez, Justine Farr. 1995. "The Usefulness of Cost Accounting in the Federal Government." *Government Accountants Journal* 44 (1): 31–35.

Schick, Alan. 1998. "Why Most Developing Countries Should Not Try New Zealand Reforms." *World Bank Research Observer* 13 (1): 123–131.

Shah, Anwar. 1998. "Balance, Accountability, and Responsiveness." Policy Research Working Paper 2021, World Bank, Washington, DC.

Simpson, Wayne K., and Michael J. Williams. 1996. "Activity-Based Costing, Management, and Budgeting." *Government Accountants Journal* 45 (1): 26.

Tierney, Cornelius, E. 1994. "Cost for Government: What Costs: How Much Accounting?" *Government Accountants Journal* 43 (1): 5–9.

World Bank. 1998. *Public Expenditure Management Handbook*. Washington, DC: World Bank.

Wray, Quentin. 2004. "From Fiscal Restraint in 1997 to Spending with Confidence in 2004." Business report. http://www.businessreport.co.za/index.php?fArticleId=352379&fSectionId=1036&fSetId=304

9

[US, Canada, Malaysia, New Zealand]

On Getting the Giant to Kneel

Approaches to a Change in the Bureaucratic Culture

ANWAR SHAH

D73

H83

O17

Introduction

The public sector continues to face a crisis of public confidence in both industrial and developing countries. Examples of government inefficiency and waste abound in most countries. For example in the United States, the Federal Aviation Administration until recently relied on dinosaur computers with green screens that ran on vacuum tubes. These computers were estimated to impose $3 billion annually in wasted aircraft fuel, delays, missed connections, and labor costs. The U.S. Defense Department has in the past paid $89 each for screwdrivers worth $1 each, and the U.S. Department of Agriculture until recently had a 2,700-word specification for french fries (see Gore 1995 for examples of obsolete regulations and pointless paperwork in the U.S. government). Of course, these examples pale in comparison to the grand theft carried out by "roving political and bureaucratic bandits"—to use Mancur Olsen's typology—in some developing countries. In industrial countries, citizens are expecting their governments to do more with less. In developing countries, the fairly fundamental dysfunctionality of public governance remains an area of major concern. In a few of these countries, a government is seen as predatory or even criminal. In some countries, the concept of citizenship or civic responsibility does not exist, and effective management of the state in this context means that the ruling elite doles out benefits to its personalized client networks. Perceptions of some governments as—in Nietzsche's words— "the coldest of all cold monsters . . . whatever it says, it lies—and whatever it has, it has stolen" and as institutions that exist simply to extract rents may not be very far from the truth.

A major difficulty in these countries is that public theft by these roving bandits encourages capital and skilled labor flight, leading the economy to a state of collapse so that not much is left for either the roving bandit or his victims unless external help is available. But external help aggravates the temptations of such a bandit because he has a short time horizon. It helps if such a bandit makes the country a home and becomes Olsen's *stationary bandit.* In such circumstances, the time horizon of the ruler expands and the ruler's fortune gets tied to the fortune of the nation. This explains why, in countries ruled by roving bandits, people show a great deal of tolerance for military coups d'état that impose the rule of stationary bandits. Such transformations typically lead to a short period of tranquility but little improvement in the quality of life in the long run.

Why the Road to Reforms Remains a Field of Dreams in Developing Countries

A simple way to see why the public sector is dysfunctional and does not deliver much in developing countries yet is difficult to reform is to have a closer look at the mission and values of the public sector, its authorizing environment, and its operational capacity.

■ *Public sector mission and values:* Societal values and norms, such as those embodied in the constitution or in annual budget policy statements, may be useful points of reference for public sector mandates and the values inherent in these mandates. Unwritten societal norms that are widely shared or acknowledged should also be taken into consideration. In industrial countries, the mission and values of the public sector are spelled out in terms of a medium-term policy framework. For example, there is a formal requirement in New Zealand that a policy statement of this type be tabled in the Parliament by March 31 (about two to three months in advance of the budget statement). Public sector values in developing countries are rarely addressed. This is because the orientation of the public sector remains toward "command and control" rather than to serve the citizenry. For an official trained in command and control, the need to develop a code of conduct with a client orientation may appear frivolous.

- *Authorizing environment:* This includes formal (budgetary processes and institutions) and informal institutions of participation and accountability. Do these institutions and processes work as intended in providing an enabling environment for the public sector to meet its goals? Do various levels of government act in the spirit of the constitution in exercising their responsibilities? What are the checks and balances against deviant behavior? In industrial countries, institutional norms are strictly adhered to, and there are severe moral, legal, voter, and market sanctions against noncompliance. In developing countries, noncompliance is often neither monitored nor subject to any sanctions.

- *Operational capacity and constraints:* What is authorized is not necessarily what will get done, as the available operational capacity may not be consistent with the task at hand. Furthermore, even the operational capacity that is available may be circumvented by the bureaucratic culture or incentives that reward rent seeking, command and control, and corruption and patronage, with little concern for responsiveness to citizen preferences in service delivery and almost total lack of accountability to citizen-voters. Some key questions, the answers to which will give a better understanding of operational capacity, include the following: Do the agencies with responsibility for various tasks have the capacity to undertake them? Do they have the right skills mix, as well as the incentive to do the right things and to do them correctly? Is the bureaucratic culture consistent with the attainment of societal objectives? Are there binding contracts on public managers for output performance? Does participation by civil society help alleviate some of these constraints? To what extent can these constraints be overcome by government reorganization and reform? Whereas in industrial countries answers to most of the above questions are expected to be affirmative, that is not true in the case of developing countries.

Figure 9.1 shows that discordance among mission, authorizing environment, and operational capacity contributes to a dismal public sector performance in the delivery of public services. Furthermore, what is delivered in terms of outputs and outcomes is typically inconsistent with citizens' preferences. The challenge of public sector reform, therefore, in any developing country is to harmonize the mission and values of the public sector, its authorizing environment, and its operational capacity so that there is a close, if not perfect, correspondence among these three aspects of governance

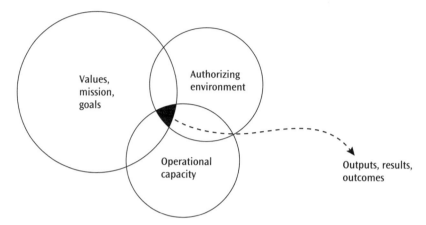

FIGURE 9.1   Public Sector Institutional Environment in Developing Countries

(see figure 9.1). Such a task is daunting for many developing countries because they often have lofty goals but lack an authorizing environment that is capable of translating these goals into a policy framework. This problem is often compounded further by bureaucratic incentives that make any available operational capacity to implement such a framework completely dysfunctional.

Table 9.1 presents a stylized comparison of the institutional environment in a traditional society, a developing country, and an industrial country. It is interesting to note that, although technical capacity in the modern sense was nonexistent in a traditional society, public sector outcomes were consistent with member preferences because of harmonization of the society's goals, its authorizing environment, and its operational capacity. The cultures of such societies more often than not focused on accountability for results. The system of rewards and punishment was credible and swift, and many of the business relations were based on informality and trust. Thus, although per capita gross domestic product (GDP) in such societies was quite low, member satisfaction with collective action was observed to be high and quite possibly not too far behind the degree of satisfaction with public sector experienced in today's industrial societies.

This picture contrasts with that for a typical developing country. In such a country, there is discordance in the society's goals, authorizing environment, and operational capacity. As a consequence of this dishar-

TABLE 9.1 Public Sector Institutional Environment—Stylized Facts

	Traditional society	Developing country	Industrial country
Goals	Clear and realistic	Vague and grandiose	Clear and realistic
Authorizing environment	Strong	Weak	Strong
Operational capacity	Consistent and functional	Dysfunctional	Consistent and functional
Evaluation capacity	Strong	Weak	Strong
Public sector orientation	Output	Input controls, and command and control	Input, output, and outcome monitoring
Public sector decision making	Decentralized	Centralized	Decentralized
Private sector environment	Informality and trust	Semiformality but lack of trust and disregard for rule of law	Formal and legal
Evaluation culture	Snakes and ladders	"Gotcha"	Learning and improving

mony, not much gets accomplished, and citizens' expectations are belied. Lack of accountability and focus of the evaluation culture on frying a big fish occasionally but doing nothing with the systemic malaise mean that any self-correcting mechanisms that may exist are blunted. Semiformality imposes additional costs on doing business but does not lead to any benefits in business relations because of disrespect for law. Contracts may not be honored and, therefore, carry little value. In view of this completely dysfunctional nature of public sector in many developing countries, it is important for these countries to leapfrog forward (or even backward) to a public sector culture that puts a premium on client orientation and accountability for results. This is, however, unlikely to happen soon for reasons to be discussed later.

In the following section, we look at the experience of industrial countries to draw some lessons of interest to developing countries in harmonizing the mission and values of the public sector, its authorizing environment, and its operational capacity.

The Genesis of Experiences of Industrial Countries

The experience of industrial countries shows that institutions of participation and accountability in governance, including a management paradigm that placed premium on governing for results, played a major role in creating responsive and accountable public sector governance. The record of industrial countries shows that democratic participation is the only form of government with a consistent record in ensuring good governance. This is because only the democratic form of government ensures property rights and enforcement of contracts. Democratic governance, however, cannot simply be mandated from above. Putnam (1993), in *Making Democracy Work,* argues that "democratic institutions cannot be built from top down. They must be built in the everyday traditions of trust and civic virtue among its citizens" (172). Localization and accountability for results helps in building such trust and virtue.

Over the years, industrial countries have shown a remarkable change in the performance of their public sectors. It is interesting to note that this change was brought about not through a system of hierarchical controls as is the focus in most developing countries, but more through strengthened accountability to citizens at large. The elected representatives made a commitment along the lines of the oath required of the members of the city of Athens, Georgia, which stated, "We will strive increasingly to quicken the public sense of public duty; that thus . . . we will transmit this city not only not less, but greater, better, and more beautiful than it was transmitted to us." (Athenian oath inscribed on the base of the statue of Athena, located in the front of the Athens Classic Center, Athens, Georgia.)

This accountability for results was further strengthened by accountability of the executive to the legislative branch. Overall, the emphasis of these systems of accountability has been to bring about a change in both bureaucratic culture and the incentives that public employees face. This cultural change during the 1990s has been brought about by strengthening the results orientation of the public sector. This has been done by steering attention away from internal bureaucratic processes and input controls (hard controls) toward accountability for results (soft controls). Various countries have followed diverse policies to achieve this transformation. The underlying framework driving these reforms is approximately uniform and firmly grounded in the results-oriented management and evaluation (ROME) framework. Under ROME, a results-based chain provides a framework for measuring public sector performance. Figure 9.2 provides an illustration of this results-based chain that suggests that, to enforce a culture of accountability for

Program objectives →	Inputs →	Intermediate inputs →	Outputs →	Outcomes →	Impact →	Reach
Improve quantity, quality, and access to education services	Educational spending by age, sex, urban/rural; spending by grade level, teachers, staff, facilities, tools, books, regulations	Enrollments, student-teacher ratio, class size	Achievement scores, graduation rates, drop-out rates	Literacy rates, supply of skilled professionals	Informed citizenry, civic engagement, enhanced international competitiveness	Winners and losers from government programs

FIGURE 9.2 Results-Oriented Management and Evaluation Results Chain with an Application to Education Services

results, one needs to monitor *program activities* and *inputs* (resources used to produce outputs), including *intermediate inputs* and *outputs* (quantity and quality of goods and services produced), *outcomes* (progress in achieving program objectives), *impacts* (program goals), and *reach* (people who benefit or are hurt by a program). Such a focus in management dialogue reinforces joint ownership and accountability of the principal and the agent in achieving shared goals by highlighting terms of mutual trust.

Results-Oriented Management and Evaluation Chain

Most ROME-related approaches have the following common elements:

- contracts or work program agreements based on prespecified outputs and performance targets and budgetary allocations
- managerial flexibility but accountability for results
- subsidiarity principle (that is, public sector decision making at the government closest to the people, unless a convincing case can be made for higher-level or -order assignment)
- incentives for cost efficiency

ROME provides a coherent framework for strategic planning and management based on learning and accountability in a decentralized environment. The key to successful implementation of ROME is the transparency achieved by the public commitment to a few but vital expected results, which are based in turn on the agency's outcome-related strategic goals. Thus internal and external reporting shifts from the traditional focus on inputs to a focus on outputs, reach, and outcomes—in particular, outputs that lead to results. Furthermore, these results are themselves now stated in terms of development achievements. Programs, activities, processes, and resources are thus aligned with the strategic goals of the agency. Flexibility in project definition and implementation is achieved through a shift in emphasis from strict monitoring of inputs to monitoring of performance results and their measurements. Tracking progress toward expected results is done through indicators, which are negotiated between the provider and the financing agency. This joint goal setting and reporting helps ensure client satisfaction on an ongoing basis while building partnership and ownership into projects.

ROME reforms within an institution are underpinned by devolution and delegation of authority. This requires a two-way flow of information, which is achieved through a strengthened accountability mechanism in the form of performance reporting, greater emphasis on monitoring and evaluation of results, and individual performance agreements that focus on results. Thus under ROME accountability becomes positive and forward looking, based on continuous and systematic feedback and learning.— that is, each unit provides information on results achieved against the agency's strategic goals, allowing for benchmark comparisons and learning across organizational boundaries. ROME also provides senior management with concrete evidence on which to base allocation decisions. Thus devolution, participation, and accountability are all important aspects of this process.

Under ROME, budget allocations support contracts and work program agreements, which are based on prespecified outputs and performance targets. Managerial flexibility in input selection—including hiring and firing of personnel and program execution—is fully respected, but at the same time managers are held accountable for achieving results. The subsidiarity principle (assigning the responsibility to the lowest level of government unless a case can be made for assignment to a higher level of government) strengthens accountability for results while enhancing the consistency of public service provision with local preferences. Finally, under a ROME framework cost efficiency is rewarded through retention of savings. Costing is activity based—that is, the full cost of each activity, including charges for capital and asset use, is required for calculation of costs. Because the focus of the approach is on learning, failure to meet commitments may be tolerated, but failure to share values invites severe sanctions.

Implications of ROME for Civil Service Reform

Civil servants in developing countries are typically poorly paid for the work rendered, but they receive a lot of perks, and a significant number of these employees further enrich themselves through graft and corruption. They have lifelong tenures. Innovation and risk taking are not tolerated. In an attempt to limit graft, strong input controls and top-down accountability is enforced. In addition, senior civil servants are rotated periodically from one position to another. But such practices weaken accountability further. A ROME framework, in contrast, provides a new vision for public management in the 21st century (see table 9.2). It calls for competitive wages and task specialization (a "stay with it" culture), and lack of formal tenures. Public providers are given the freedom to fail or succeed. Instead public employees hold their jobs so long as they are able to fulfill the terms of their contracts. Only persistent failures initiate the exit process.

TABLE 9.2 On Getting the Giant to Kneel: Public Management
Paradigm for the 21st Century

20th century	21st century
Centralized	Globalized and localized
Center manages	Center leads
Command and control	Responsive and accountable governance
Bureaucratic	Participatory
Internally dependent	Competitive
Government as the sole provider	Government as a purchaser and competitive provider of public services
Input controls	Results matter
Focus on rules and procedures	Managerial flexibility but accountability for results
Top-down accountability	Bottom-up accountability
Low wages but many perks	Competitive wages but little else
Lifelong appointments in civil service	Contractual appointments
Rotating jack-of-all trades appointments	Task specialization ("stay with it" culture) but exit with persistent failures
Closed and slow	Open and quick
Intolerance for risk and innovation	Freedom to fail or succeed
Citizens as passive receivers of public services	Citizens empowered to demand accountability for government performance
Focus on government	Focus on citizen-centered governance

Responsiveness to citizenry and accountability for results together form
the cornerstone of this approach. The ROME framework offers a great
potential in developing countries to improve public sector governance by
nurturing responsive and accountable governance. It may also prove to
be one of the most potent weapons against bureaucratic corruption and
malfeasance (see Shah and Schacter 2004). A recent empirical study on the
determinants of corruption by Gurgur and Shah (2005) supports this view,
showing that political and bureaucratic culture and centralization of authority represented the most significant determinants of corruption in a sample
of 30 countries. They further find that an anticorruption strategy based sim-

ply on raising public sector wages without fundamental institutional reforms is not likely to yield any significant reduction in corruption.

Experience with ROME

Several countries have experimented with various versions of ROME. The experiences of New Zealand, Canada, and Malaysia offer interesting insights, as discussed below.

The State under Contract: The New Zealand Model

New Zealand represents one of the boldest experiences in transforming the public sector by using a private sector management and measurement approach to core government functions. To introduce a cultural change from input control to output accountability in the public sector, New Zealand, during the past decade, revamped a tenured civil service and made all public positions contractual, based on an agreed set of results. Even the central bank governor was required to enter into a contract with the parliament. Under the terms of this contract, the tenure of the central bank governor was linked to inflation staying within a band of 3 percent per annum. The policy development and implementation, financing, purchasing, and providing functions were separated. This enabled the government to focus on policy and financing and bringing the private sector in partnership with the public sector in the provision function. Program management was decentralized at delivery points, and managers were given flexibility and autonomy in budgetary allocations and program implementation within the policy framework and the defined budget. Capital charging and accrual accounting (expenditures are deemed to have been made when commitments are done) were introduced, to provide a complete picture on the resource cost of each public sector activity. Nonpublic functions were either commercialized or privatized. Responsible fiscal management was encouraged by requiring the maintenance of a positive net worth of the government, as part of the contract for the Minister of Finance.

The *new contractualism* version of ROME introduced by New Zealand led to a remarkable transformation of the economy. It was transformed from a highly protected and regulated economy with an expansive range of intrusive and expensive interventions, to an open and deregulated economy with a lean and efficient public sector (see Boston 1995, Walker 1996, Kettl 2000). The central government deficits were eliminated, debt was reduced, and the government net worth became positive while improving the quantity and quality of public services. Even more remarkable results were achieved at the local level. For example, in the early 1990s, the mayor of Papakura, by introducing new contractualism, brought an astonishing turnaround to the fortunes of the town by eliminating debt and reducing taxes while improving the quality and quantity of public services provided.

To be sure, there were limited social policy fallouts with this approach. Social service provision to minority communities experienced some difficulties as cost-cutting pressures under commercialization occasionally led to curtailed access for minority communities. In isolated cases, the new contractualism failed because bureaucratic incompetence failed to ensure strict safety standards, as witnessed in the collapse of a newly constructed viewing platform at Cave Creek that resulted in the deaths of scores of tourists.

Getting Government Right: The Canadian Approach

In 1994, Canada adopted its own version of ROME to deal with persistent public sector deficits, a large overhang of debt, and growing citizen dissatisfaction with the public sector. Canada rejected new contractualism and instead opted for the *alternative service delivery* framework for public sector reforms using the *new managerialism* approach. The alternative service delivery framework represents a dynamic consultative and participatory process of public sector restructuring that improves the delivery of services to clients by sharing governance functions with individuals, community groups, the private sector, and other government entities.

As part of the program review process under this framework, departments and agencies were required to review their activities and programs against the following six guidelines:

1. *Public Interest Test:* Does the program area or activity continue to serve a public interest?
2. *Role of Government Test:* Is there a legitimate and necessary role for the government in this program area or activity?
3. *Federalism Test:* Is the current role of the federal government appropriate, or is the program a candidate for realignment with the provinces?
4. *Partnership Test:* What activities or programs should or could be transferred in whole or in part to the private or voluntary sector?
5. *Efficiency Test:* If the program or activity continues, how could its efficiency be improved?
6. *Affordability Test:* Is the resultant package of programs and activities affordable within the fiscal constraints? If not, what programs or activities should be abandoned?

The Canadian experience with the alternative service delivery framework has shown remarkable results. The federal deficit was cut from 7.5 percent of GDP in 1993 to reach a balanced budget in 1998 and surplus budgets thereafter. The number of federal departments was reduced from 38 to 25, and the civil service roll was reduced from 220,000 to 178,000. Allocations to social services, justice, and science and technology were increased, while the remaining services saw a reduction in the budgetary allocations. Citizen-centered service delivery enhancements were achieved by clustering services around the needs of citizens, enacting regulatory reform to encourage competition and innovation, recovering costs from services that benefited special segments, and continuing to reevaluate programs to support alternative service delivery mechanisms. The overall impact of these reforms was an improvement in service delivery and citizen satisfaction.

From Government- to Citizen-Centered Governance in Malaysia

ROME was not built in a day, and there is now abundant literature on the ROME-type innovations pioneered by Australia, Canada, and New Zealand, among other countries. Interestingly enough, this literature has not fully recognized the contribution of Malaysia, where some of the innovations predate the experience in industrial countries. The Malaysian experience is of special relevance to developing countries, because the Malaysian public sector suffered at least some of the dysfunctionality of the public sector that was experienced in other developing countries in the late 1980s. Since the early 1990s, Malaysia, has gradually and successfully put in place aspects of results-oriented management to create a responsive and accountable public sector governance structure. Noteworthy elements of this reform approach were as follows:

- *Missions and values:* All public agencies are required to specify their mission and values with a view to justifying their roles and to inculcating positive values in public administration.
- *Strengthening client orientation and citizen-centered governance:* A "clients' charter" was established in 1993 that required specification of standards of services to form the basis of public accountability of government agencies and departments. This charter requires all agencies and departments to identify their customers and establish their needs. Agencies are further required to notify clients about the standards of services available. Public agencies are required to report and publish (in print and on the Web) annually on both service improvements and compliance failures. Corrective

action is required to deal with compliance failures. Clients also have a right to redress through the Public Complaints Bureau.

■ *Managerial flexibility with strong accountability for results:* This is achieved through the implementation of an output-based budgeting system and an activity-based accounting system. It has further introduced capital charging and accrual accounting. The output budgeting system requires *program agreements* for delivery of outputs but permits managerial flexibility in achieving agreed-upon results. Performance indicators for government agencies and other public service providers are maintained and widely disseminated.

■ *Decentralized decision making:* Malaysia has over time sought to strengthen decentralized decision making by strengthening local governments by both decentralizing and deconcentrating federal government functions.

■ *Strengthening the integrity of the Malaysian civil service:* Malaysia has one of the strongest anticorruption laws and devotes significant resources to implementing this law.

■ *Partnership approach to service delivery:* A partnership approach to service delivery is attempted by ensuring contestable policy advice, deregulation, and active promotion of public-private collaboration in public services.

■ *Ensuring financial integrity:* This is achieved through internal and external audit. The auditor general provides the Parliament with a financial integrity audit. This report is widely disseminated.

In sum, Malaysia is at the cutting edge of public sector institutional development, innovation, and performance in developing countries. It has followed innovative approaches to improve public sector performance. Its challenge is to strengthen the new culture of governance that it has attempted to create, by dealing with implementation issues through training and corrective action.

Beyond ROME: Measuring Performance When There Is No Bottom Line

The whole of government performance monitoring is of interest to get an overall measure of public sector performance and accountability of the political regime to citizens. Such measurement is becoming increasingly popular in industrial countries. The U.S. state of Oregon set up an independent board to develop and monitor measures of social well-being (158 such measures in 1991, reduced to 20 in 1999) of state residents. The U.S. state of Florida initially established 268 indicators dealing with progress in families and communities, safety, learning, health, economy, environment, and government; it has more recently abandoned this effort. The Canadian province of Alberta has established 27 "measuring up" quality of life indicators. New Zealand reports on the net worth of the government. The United Nations publishes human development indicators. Huther and Shah (1998) developed comprehensive indicators of the quality of governance, incorporating citizen participation, government orientation, social development, and economic management for a sample of 80 countries.

The experience with government performance measurement has shown mixed results, partly due to a lack of interest by the media and legislatures. In general, in the absence of major crises, the politics of budgetary decision making reduces the usefulness of these performance indicators. A major difficulty with aggregate performance indicators arises from the "looking for keys under the lamppost reflex," meaning that what may be measurable and what is measured may not be relevant for policy or accountability purposes. Outcome measures at the conceptual level offer diffused accountability. Instead, the focus on outputs and reach as practiced in New Zealand and Malaysia offers greater potential for accountability for results.

Epilogue: ROME—A Road Map to Wrecks and Ruins or to a Better Tomorrow?

The success of ROME in practice in a few selected countries has invited heated controversy and debate among public sector management practitioners, with a fairly vocal group (Schick [1998] is the leading exponent) arguing against application of such principles in developing countries. A plethora of arguments are put forward to support this view. It has been argued that the real issue of civil service reform is not its efficiency but its underdevelopment. Input control systems are not well developed. There is no sense of public responsibility, and as a result managerial discretion will enhance opportunities for the abuse of public office for private gain. Because of political interference, the potential for contract enforcement is quite weak. The use of ROME will further weaken top-down accountability as the focus changes to results rather than inputs, rules, and procedures. It is further argued that the use of this approach will not work for craft (research and development) and coping (for example, disaster relief) organizations because the focus on outputs will discourage innovation, risk taking, and timely response. In social services, it is argued that access to the needy and the poor may not be assured under a system that places a high premium on operational efficiency. Finally, others have argued that

ROME is a fad and developing countries should simply wait it out, until a new fad emerges.

Although there is some merit in the arguments advanced against the use of ROME, on balance, the case for application of ROME in developing countries is further strengthened in view of the institutional weaknesses highlighted above. The underdeveloped bureaucracy and input controls argument suggests that modern accounting systems that trace the flows of inputs have not proved helpful. This is because experience shows that performance improvement gains from the implementation of such systems have been minimal; instead, these systems provide a cover for the abuse of public funds under the guise of "getting the books in order." Because outputs for a large majority of public services are readily observable and their reach can be measured, ROME provides a much better handle on accountability in governance in weak institutional environments.

Hierarchical input-based accountability has typically failed to deliver public sector mandates. Indeed, craft and coping organizations require care in how their results-based chain is evaluated. Similarly, in social services the design of incentives is critical to forestall any fallout and instead encourage access to all through competition and innovation. For example, a grant structure that treats all providers—public and private—on an equal basis, with continuation of funding eligibility tied to success in meeting conditions for the standards of services and access to such services, rather than spending levels, can overcome the moral hazard (see box 9.1).

BOX 9.1   Education Grant to Encourage Competition and Innovation

- *Basis for allocation among local governments:* Equal per capita, based on school-age population (say, ages 5–17 years)

- *Distribution to providers:* Equal per pupil to both government and private schools, based on school enrollments

- *Conditions:* Private school admissions on merit and fees consistent with parents' ability to pay; improvements in school retention rates, achievement scores on standardized tests, and graduation rates; no conditions on the use of grant funds

- *Penalties:* Public censure and reduction of grant funds

- *Incentives:* Retention and use of savings consistent with school priorities

Source: Shah 1999, 408.

ROME is of course not a fad either. It was practiced with great success in traditional societies long before modern bureaucracy was invented. Even in personal and family decision making, ROME is the only approach typically taken by most individuals (for example, in building and fixing a home or in seeking other services). Many developing countries facing large fiscal crises, in the absence of external help, would simply have no choice but to adopt ROME to overcome these crises and set their houses in order. In general, bottom-up accountability is the key to the success of ROME, and such accountability requires decentralized decision making. In conclusion, globalization, localization, and ROME offer strong potential for improving public sector performance in developing countries.

References

Boston, Jonathan, ed. 1995. *The State under Contract.* Wellington, New Zealand: Bridget Williams Books.

Gore, Albert. 1995. *Common Sense Government: Works Better and Costs Less.* New York: Random House.

Gurgur, Tugrul, and Anwar Shah. 2005. "Localization and Corruption: Panacea or Pandora's Box?" Policy Research Working Paper 3486, World Bank, Washington, DC.

Huther, Jeff, and Anwar Shah. 1998. "A Simple Measure of Good Governance and Its Application to the Debate on the Appropriate Level of Fiscal Decentralization." Policy Research Working Paper Series 1894, World Bank, Washington, DC.

Kettl, Donald F. 2000. *The Global Public Management Revolution.* Washington, DC: Brookings Institution.

Putnam, Robert D. 1993. *Making Democracy Work: Civic Tradition in Modern Italy.* Princeton, NJ: Princeton University Press.

Shah, Anwar. 1999. "Governing for Results in a Globalised and Localised World." *Pakistan Development Review* 38: 4 (part 1, winter): 385–431.

Shah, Anwar, and Mark Schacter. 2004. "Combating Corruption: Look before You Leap." *Finance and Development* 41 (4): 40–43.

Schick, Allen. 1998. "Why Most Developing Countries Should Not Try New Zealand Reforms." *World Bank Research Observer* 13 (1): 123–31.

Walker, Basil. 1996. "Reforming the Public Sector for Leaner Government and Improved Performance: The New Zealand Experience." *Public Administration and Development* 16: 353–76.

10

A Framework for Evaluating Institutions of Accountability

MARK SCHACTER

H83

D73

Why Institutions of Accountability Matter

> If men were angels, no government would be necessary. If angels were to govern men, neither external nor internal controls on government would be necessary. In framing a government which is to be administered by men over men, the great difficulty lies in this: you must first enable the government to control the governed; and in the next place oblige it to control itself. A dependence on the people is, no doubt, the primary control on the government; but experience has taught mankind the necessity of auxiliary precautions. (James Madison or Alexander Hamilton, *The Federalist No. 51,* in Rossiter 1961)

In politics as in government, first comes power and then comes the need to control it (Schedler 1999a). The concept of accountability, together with the institutions through which the concept is articulated and implemented, is perhaps the single most important factor that controls holders of political and public administrative power. As Thomas (1998) has observed, "Accountability is at the heart of governance within democratic societies" (348).

Citizens grant sweeping powers to the political executive. They entrust it with the authority to raise and spend public funds, and the responsibility to decide on the design and implementation of public policy. At the same time, citizens want to guard against abuse of these powers by the executive. On a more operational level, they also want to ensure that the executive uses its power wisely, effectively, and efficiently, and that it will be responsive to demands by citizens to change the ways in which it carries out its functions. They expect, therefore, that the executive will be held accountable to them for its actions.

Accountability has a particular urgency in the developing world, where many countries are groping their way through transition to democracy or are seeking to consolidate a democratic order. Though the formal trappings of democracy may have been installed, states may still find themselves "haunted by old demons that they had hoped to exorcise with democratic rule: violations of human rights, corruption, clientelism, patrimonialism, and the arbitrary exercise of power" (Schedler, Diamond, and Plattner 1999, 1).

To an unacceptable extent in many democratic states, rulers remain free to act as they please, unfettered by an infrastructure of checks and balances. This indicates that direct accountability to citizens through the ballot box is not sufficient to ensure a healthy relationship between the governors and the governed. As the quotation at the head of this chapter suggests, there is an additional requirement for the state to restrain itself by creating and sustaining independent public institutions that are empowered to oversee its actions, demand explanations, and, when circumstances warrant, impose penalties on it for improper or illegal activity.

Horizontal versus Vertical Accountability

There is a distinction to be made between the accountability imposed on a government by its citizens, and the accountability that a government imposes on itself through the creation of public institutions whose mandate is precisely to act as a restraint on government (see figure 10.1). This distinction is referred to by some theorists as vertical accountability (to citizens directly) versus horizontal accountability (to public institutions of accountability [IAs]) (see O'Donnell 1999; Stevens undated).

Vertical accountability may include citizens acting directly through the electoral process, or indirectly through civic organizations ("civil society") or the news media (Schedler, Diamond, and Plattner 1999). Horizontal accountability, because it refers to the range of public entities that check abuses by the executive branch of government, may be exercised by institutions and organizations as diverse as

- the legislature
- the judiciary

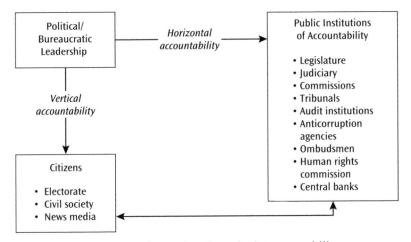

FIGURE 10.1 Horizontal and Vertical Accountability

- electoral commissions and tribunals
- auditing agencies
- anticorruption bodies
- ombudsmen
- human rights commissions
- central banks

Some of these bodies may have a constitutional basis, while others may be founded in statute. Some may have a purely watchdog function, while others may have quasi-judicial or punitive powers (see Diamond 1999; Schedler, Diamond, and Plattner 1999; Stevens undated). Institutions of horizontal accountability, carrying the formal stature and legitimacy that goes with having been created and empowered by the state itself, play the dominant role in restraining executive power. As the World Bank (1997) has observed, "Sustainable development generally calls for formal mechanisms of restraint that hold the state and its officials accountable for their actions. To be enduring and credible, these mechanisms must be anchored in core state institutions" (99).

Even so, institutions of horizontal accountability on their own are not enough. It has been plausibly argued that institutions of horizontal and vertical accountability are fundamentally interconnected, in that the former are not likely to exist in a meaningful fashion without the latter. Horizontal accountability, being the work of public institutions, amounts to a restraint that the government consents to impose upon itself. This begs the question:

> Who is eager to respond to nasty questions in public? Who yearns for punishment for misbehavior? Governments usually do not. They understand that institutions of accountability limit their freedom of action and that they contain the potential to bring them into painful and embarrassing situations. So why should they be interested in establishing them? (Schedler 1999b, 334)

The response is that governments agree to bind themselves through institutions of accountability under circumstances in which citizens will punish them for failing to do so. In other words, horizontal accountability will only be effective and sustainable if governments see benefits in it, and it is the operation of vertical accountability, particularly the electoral process, that causes governments to perceive the benefits.[1]

There is good reason for arguing that an active and organized civil society is another important vertical factor compelling governments to bind themselves to horizontal accountability, especially when there is also a democratic electoral process in place. Tendler's recent work (1997) provides persuasive evidence on this point. This chapter focuses primarily, though not exclusively, on institutions of horizontal accountability.

Analytical Framework for Evaluating Institutions of Accountability—Working Model

This section proposes an analytical framework or model for understanding and evaluating the performance of IAs with respect to their impact on controlling public sector corruption.

Accountability problems in developing countries are numerous and diverse, as are their causes and eventual impacts. It is intended that the framework presented here will help the World Bank and its developing-country partners see the forest for the trees. It is hoped that it will expedite the analysis and prioritization of problems concerning IAs and corruption in developing countries. The framework should provide a sound basis on which the Bank and its partners may develop and implement strategies for strengthening accountability as a countervailing force to corrupt behavior by public officeholders.

The model presented here concentrates on the interaction between IAs and the executive branch of government, and on how the interaction is mediated by various factors. (Vertical accountability institutions such as civil society and the news media play an important role in affecting the performance of horizontal IAs. Thus, although this chapter focuses primarily on horizontal IAs, it will also address these key vertical IAs.) The chapter also takes initial steps in developing performance measures to evaluate the effectiveness of IAs with respect to controlling corruption (see annex 10.A).

In particular, the objective is to provide a simple but robust analytical tool that will facilitate the World Bank's anticorruption work by helping it and its partners to

- proceed on the basis of a succinct and robust working model of IAs and their relationship to corruption
- identify critical blockages to the effective operation of IAs with respect to corruption
- untangle IA problems that can effectively be addressed through external development assistance from those that are primarily dependent on local actors and local efforts
- identify the most relevant forms of development assistance for particular IA problems
- set priorities and strategies for dealing with IA problems

The Accountability Cycle

At the core of the analytical model is an *accountability cycle* set within contextual factors (see figures 10.2–10.4).

The accountability cycle (see figures 10.2 and 10.3) is an idealized model of the relationship between an IA and a unit of the executive branch. It describes in stylized form the internal logic of the IA-executive relationship. The cycle has three stages: information (or input), action (or output), and response (or outcome). The model assumes that the presence of a minimum level of information is a primary binding constraint on the effective operation of the cycle.

Analysis of contextual information is necessary to understand and explain the workings of the accountability cycle (see figure 10.4). In some cases, the degree to which the accountability cycle functions well or poorly may be explained by factors internal to the cycle itself. But often, the cycle will be profoundly affected by social, political, and economic factors that shape the environment within which the cycle operates. Attempting to understand the accountability cycle without reference to contextual information is likely to lead to misleading conclusions and inappropriate remedial interventions.

The accountability cycle is illustrated in figure 10.3. The model describes a relationship between the IA and the executive the ultimate purpose of

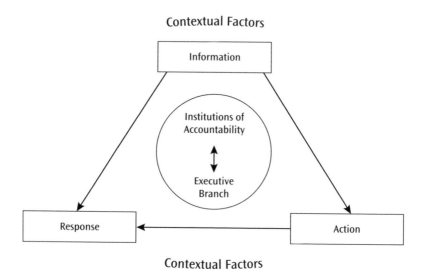

FIGURE 10.2   The Analytical Model: Accountability Cycle Embedded in Contextual Factors

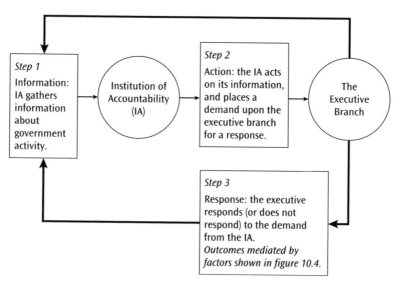

FIGURE 10.3 The Accountability Cycle: Model of the Relationship between an IA and the Executive Branch

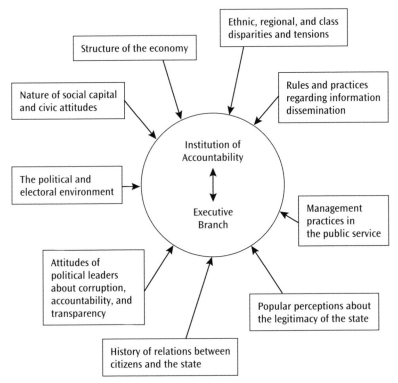

FIGURE 10.4 Some Contextual Factors Affecting the Accountability Cycle

which is to compel the executive to explain and justify its behavior, and, where appropriate, take corrective action.

The model has three steps, which may be described as information, action, and response[2] (or input, output, and outcome), as follows:

- *Information or input:* The framework proceeds from the assumption that information is the critical input into the IA. Effective performance of the IA depends on the degree to which it can obtain—either directly from the executive or indirectly from other sources—relevant, accurate, and timely information about the activities of the executive. Developments at this stage of the cycle depend on the amount of information made available by the executive, as well as the capacity of the IA to gather whatever information may be available.

- *Action or output:* On the basis of the information inputs, the IA should be able to act. It produces demands (explicit or implicit)[3] on the executive to explain and to justify the manner in which it is discharging its responsibilities. Developments at this stage of the cycle depend on what the IA is able and willing to do with the information—that is, the capacity and willingness of the IA first, to evaluate and analyze the information and, second, to use that information as a basis for making relevant and important demands on the executive for explanation and justification of its actions.

■ *Response or outcome:* The IA's outputs are intended to incite a response from the executive. For the purposes of the framework, an outcome is a response (which could take varying forms, such as explanation, justification, corrective action, etc.) by the executive to the demand placed on it by the IA. The IA's effectiveness is determined, ultimately, by the appropriateness and timeliness of the reaction that it is capable of eliciting from the executive. Developments at this ultimate stage of the cycle depend on the degree to which the executive feels compelled to respond to the IA.

The accountability cycle provides a template for understanding and evaluating the performance of any IA. The focus of the analysis and the kinds of performance indicators that might be used for a particular IA would depend on the characteristics and circumstances of that IA. But the logic of the accountability cycle suggests that in all cases, the evaluation would focus on three kinds of questions:

■ What information can the IA obtain, and how well does the information meet the criteria of relevance, accuracy, reliability, timeliness, and comprehensiveness?
■ What is the IA able to do with the information?
■ What kind of response is the IA able to generate from the executive?

The accountability cycle in its idealized form—that is, in the absence of contextual information—provides a hierarchy of priorities for crafting a program of action to build the capacity of IAs. The information-action-response sequence builds on an assumption that information is the most basic, necessary condition for the effective functioning of an IA. Every IA needs some minimal level of access to information related to the activities of the executive. We assume that no meaningful accountability relationship is possible in the absence of a certain minimum quantity and quality of information being available to an IA.[4]

Assuming that the fundamental information hurdle can be overcome, one proceeds to the next critical barrier to effective IA performance, which relates to the IA's capacity to use information to produce outputs—that is, actions in regard to the executive. To be effective, the IA must be capable of understanding and analyzing information about the executive, transforming the analysis into coherent demands on the executive for answers, and communicating those demands to the executive.

Finally, even if the IA has the minimum level of capacity required to place demands on the executive, it must have sufficient power, either formal or informal,[5] to elicit a meaningful response from the executive.

Therefore, if evaluation of IAs provides evidence of poor performance in more than one of the three areas, the prima facie rule of thumb (before contextual factors are added to the analytical mix) would be to concentrate remedial efforts on the lowest rung of the hierarchy—that is, address problems at the information stage before tackling those at the action stage, and address problems at the action stage before tackling problems at the response stage.

This is not to suggest that one could in fact operate in this strictly sequential manner, isolating problems at one level from problems at the other two and focusing on only one stage of the cycle at a time. Reality is too messy and complicated to permit such a surgical approach. Efforts to build capacity in IAs, as a practical matter, may well end up spilling across all three areas. But given the scarcity of resources and the need to concentrate them where they are likely to have the greatest effect, it is useful to have an analytical basis for concentrating efforts in one of the three areas. The model of the accountability cycle offers a basis for making the necessary choices.

Viewing IAs through the framework of the accountability cycle also helps to focus attention on appropriate kinds of interventions within priority areas. For example, if the binding constraint on effective performance of a given IA was found to be at the level of inputs, this would suggest a need to analyze and address questions related to some combination of the quantity, quality, timeliness, and relevance of information flowing to the IA.

If the binding constraint was found to be at the level of outputs, then a different approach would be indicated, one that focused on analyzing and understanding the capacity of the IA to receive and analyze information and to transform the analysis into coherent demands that are then placed on the executive.

If the binding constraint was found to be at the level of outcomes, then one would be compelled to focus on the nature of the relationship between the IA and the executive.

Contextual Factors

The findings and conclusions that emerge from an analysis of the account-ability cycle need to be refined by understanding the related contextual factors at the national level.

IAs do not operate in a vacuum. At every stage of the accountability cycle an IA's capacity to interact effectively with the executive is affected by social, political, and economic factors that are outside the IA's control (see figure 10.3) but that must be taken into account when formulating any strategy for building its capacity. Contextual factors form an integral part of the explanation of why an IA functions or fails to function, and they provide guideposts to effective remedial strategies.

Examples of key contextual factors include:

- attitudes of political leaders with respect to corruption, accountability, and transparency
- the nature of civil society and civic attitudes
- the perceived legitimacy of the state
- the history of relations between citizens and the state
- the political and electoral environments
- social tensions based on ethnic, regional, or class distinctions
- the structure of the economy
- rules and practices related to public information
- management practices in the public service

The critical operational message with respect to contextual factors surrounding IAs is twofold: First, IAs are only one part (albeit an important part) of the battle against corruption. It cannot be assumed that getting a country's IAs "right" will, alone, amount to a cure-all for public sector corruption. Second, the effort to get IAs right must look beyond the inner workings of the IA, and beyond the immediate relationship between the IA and the executive, to the broader environmental factors mediating the impact of IAs on the executive.[6]

A helpful model for understanding the relationship of accountability to corruption within a broader context of contextual factors is Robert Klitgaard's well-known heuristic formula (1988, 75):

Corruption = Monopoly + Discretion − Accountability

Public sector corruption, the formula suggests, can to a large extent be explained by two positive independent variables (monopoly and discretion) and one negative one (accountability).

Take the example of a government agency with a monopoly on the issuance of business licenses to entrepreneurs. Assume that there are few detailed regulations governing this activity, and that copies of whatever regulations may exist are not easily obtained. The government agency therefore not only has monopoly power, but is also free to exercise considerable discretion. The combination of monopoly and discretion puts the agency in a strong position with respect to license applicants. Applicants would be reluctant to resist demands for bribes in return for licenses because they have nowhere else to go and because they are unsure of their rights (given that licensing regulations are not well known).

Klitgaard's model implies three possible remedial approaches: (a) address the monopoly problem by empowering one or more other public agencies to issue the same licenses; (b) address the discretion problem by, for example, publishing the regulations widely, or by instituting automatic issuance of licenses upon completion of a simple form and payment of a fee; and (c) create accountability pressure on the agency by intensifying oversight of its activities.

The Klitgaard formula illustrates how the impact of an IA on corruption depends on three interrelated but distinct sets of circumstances (figure 10.5):

- the IA itself—its internal strengths and weaknesses and its immediate relationship with the executive
- the strength of contextual factors contributing to a lack of accountability and corruption, against which the IA is a counterweight
- the degree to which the contextual factors are subject to change

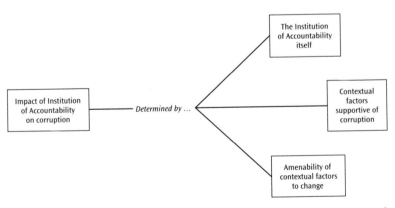

FIGURE 10.5 Multiple Factors Affecting Impact of an IA on Corruption

The accountability cycle provides a basis for inquiring into the first point, which describes my core concern. The second and third points must be addressed by understanding the contextual factors relevant to the IA. In the simple example cited here, the key contextual factors have to do with the structure of public service delivery (a monopoly over the provision of a service) and the management of the public service (rules and practices that allow relatively low-level officials a high degree of discretion, and that place a low value on transparency). The presence of these factors places limits on what an IA might be able to accomplish.

Apart from providing a sample list of contextual factors (figure 10.4), this chapter does not provide an explicit model for incorporating contextual factors into the analysis. The accountability cycle is the primary analytical tool in this model. It points the way to the kinds of contextual questions that need to be asked; the rest depends on the judgment, skill, and common sense of the researcher.

At this point in the discussion, it is useful to highlight two critical contextual factors that emerge from the literature and from lessons learned over the past 15 years or so of governance-related programming supported by development assistance agencies. These two factors are government attitudes toward accountability, corruption, and transparency; and the role played by civil society in creating demand for accountability.

Government Attitudes toward Accountability

Within the context of the accountability cycle, I argued that information was the primary binding constraint on the effective functioning of IAs. Within the broader contextual universe, I would argue that the absence of firm support and strong leadership from the bureaucratic and political elite on matters of accountability and corruption is a binding constraint on the effective functioning of IAs.

Horizontal accountability, by its very nature, will not and cannot happen unless the government allows it to happen:

> By legal necessity, all paths of institutional creation pass through the offices of top state officials and, in this sense, accountability-promoting reforms cannot come from anywhere else than "from above." There is no way to ignore or bypass the centers of state power. Unless they consent to institutionalize "self-restraint," the road to horizontal accountability is blocked. (Schedler 1999b, 339)

Numerous case studies and analyses of governance-related reforms supported by development agencies have arrived at similar conclusions.[7]

For the purposes of this chapter, the operationally oriented conclusion is that an absence of sufficient political and administrative commitment to accountability and insufficient availability of information regarding the activities of the executive are the two primary constraints on the effective operation of IAs.[8] Strategies that fail to address either of these factors will not produce effective IAs and will have no significant impact on corruption.

Civil Society

In situations in which IAs are highly dysfunctional, it is naive to think that the political or administrative elite can be counted upon to initiate reform. It is in such situations that the nexus of horizontal and vertical accountability becomes critical. As just suggested, if horizontal accountability relationships are not working, it is undoubtedly because those who hold power want it that way. "Somebody has to kick the status quo from its point of equilibrium" (Schedler 1999b, 347). In cases in which the political elite is unlikely to act and the influence of international actors is circumscribed, that "somebody" may well be civil society. The degree to which civil society is able to articulate demands related to accountability and honest government, mobilize support, and communicate its demands to government is likely to have an important impact on strengthening the position of IAs with respect to the executive.[9]

Performance Indicators

The preceding analytical framework attempted to provide an organized set of concepts to aid in understanding and evaluating the performance of IAs with respect to public sector corruption. The framework ought to provide a basis for developing an analysis of an IA that would include a reliable overview of its strengths and weaknesses, and of internal and external obstacles to improved performance. Such an analysis would in turn be the basis for a prioritized program of action for building the IA's capacity.

In addition to being asked to develop this framework, I was invited by the World Bank to go a step further and propose a set of qualitative and quantitative indicators for measuring the performance of IAs with respect to corruption. Lists of possible indicators, or areas in which indicators might be developed, appear in annex 10.A.

For the reasons presented below, I have developed this list of indicators with some hesitation. They are presented mainly as a basis for further thought and research, rather than as an attempt at a definitive list. The list borrows heavily from others who have already devoted effort to the development of various governance-related indicators.[10]

The analytical framework and the performance indicators are meant to be complementary. The analytical framework provides concepts around which to build an analytical story line for a set of IAs. These core concepts are sufficiently well defined to produce a consistent analytical approach across different IAs (and different countries) but still leave the requisite room for local context and the researcher's judgment.

The point of performance indicators, however, is to overlay a precise set of tools for measuring progress on a necessarily fuzzy analytical approach. In other words, having analyzed the problem and proposed a plan for addressing it, how would one know, exactly, when we had achieved success? How would one know (a prior question, and one that perhaps is more easily answered) when the conditions were in place that were likely to lead to eventual success?

Performance indicators are meant to help answer these kinds of questions. They are landmarks that tell either that one has reached one's destination, or (if that cannot be determined) that one is heading in the right direction, at a satisfactory speed. Unlike the components of the analytical framework, performance indicators are not, by their nature, meant to be fuzzy. One either reaches a landmark or misses it (and if one misses it, one wants to know by how much). Moreover, performance indicators, if they are to be useful, have to be useable. That means that the connection between them and the underlying issues should be clear, and that the data gathering required to support the indicators should not be administratively or financially onerous.

For this reason, developing performance indicators for IAs in relation to corruption is from the outset a hazardous (some would say foolhardy) task. On the one hand (referring back to the model of the accountability cycle), this is a clear picture of what successful performance looks like for an IA. Success is when an IA compels some part of the executive to respond appropriately to that IA by explaining and justifying its actions, and taking corrective actions where necessary.

But on the other hand, when one tries to reduce this picture of success to the language of meaningful, measurable, and useable performance indicators, serious problems arise. To begin with, the ultimate phenomenon being measured—the appropriate response by the executive to an IA—may be a contentious question of judgment. Suppose, for example, that the executive responds to findings of corruption by introducing laws or regulations covering certain behaviors or processes. Is that appropriate? What if the laws and regulations are not properly enforced? Should the government have fired people as well? Should it have launched criminal proceedings? These important questions are not easily handled in the context of an indicator-based performance framework.

Moreover, even if there was agreement on the description of an appropriate response, questions of attribution would arise. Given that the IA is only one among many factors affecting the behavior of the executive, to what extent can one attribute the executive's response to the IA's action—or conversely, to what extent can one attribute the executive's failure to respond to some failing on the part of the IA?

This is not to say that one should not make an attempt at performance measurement in this area. Imperfect information, opaque or complex causal relationships, and the inevitable need for subjective interpretation pose difficulties for virtually all forms of performance measurement in the public sector (Schacter 1999). The measurement task is feasible. However, it must be approached with the recognition that although performance indicators may complement one's understanding of IAs in relation to corruption, they will have meaning only when incorporated into a larger picture that allows for open-ended description, analysis, and judgment. Understanding the performance of IAs and their interaction with government is, to a large degree, a matter of history, local context, and the observer's experience and tacit knowledge. Albert Einstein is reputed to have said that "not everything that counts can be counted, and not everything that can be counted counts." This is as true of the performance of IAs as it is of any other phenomenon.

Notes

1. Schedler (1994b, 334) argues that certain conditions must apply to the electoral process for vertical accountability to be an incentive for the creation of horizontal accountability.
2. The model follows from a commonsense understanding of the relationship between IAs and the political executive. It also emerges from the accountability literature. Thomas (1998) observes that "the regular reporting of information, monitoring and periodic answerability are the procedural manifestations of the existence of an accountability relationship" (353). Schedler (1999a) maintains that accountability "involves the right to receive information and the corresponding obligation to release all necessary details. But it also implies the right to receive an explanation and the corresponding duty to justify one's conduct" (15).
3. Implicit demand would be, for example, when an IA produces a report suggesting unacceptable practices within the executive but does not explicitly demand an explanation. Under some circumstances, publication of such a report could generate a demand for a response, even if the demand does not come directly from the IA that produced the report.
4. This proposition is well grounded in common sense. It is also found in the scholarly and practical literature. Some examples include Dye and Stapenhurst (1998): "The

currency of accountability is information"; Caiden (1993): ". . . dealing with administrative corruption . . . [presupposes] freedom of information", and "The public cannot hold anyone responsible for things that they do not know about". See also Tendler (1997) and Stevens (undated).

5. The news media in advanced democratic societies is an example of an IA with fairly significant informal power relative to the executive. The executive has no particular formal responsibility to the news media and yet may feel compelled to answer to news stories about public sector misbehavior, and perhaps take corrective measures as a result.

6. A similar rationale is presented by Dye and Stapenhurst (1998), who describe efforts to combat corruption as being supported by eight "pillars of integrity".

7. See for example, Schacter (2000), which includes references to other studies.

8. The two are of course closely linked. Weak political commitment to accountability is often the reason why the executive refuses to disclose information about itself.

9. Tendler (1997) provides a recent compelling example of civil society's impact on a government's approach to accountability. She attributes to civil society activism a large part of the rapid reform of one of Brazil's most corrupt and unaccountable state administrations. See also World Bank (1998, 25 and 116).

10. Sources include Stevens (1990), Makanda (1994), World Bank (1997), Dye and Stapenhurst (1998), OECD (1998, 1999), and USAID (1998).

References

Caiden, Gerald. 1993. "Dealing with Administrative Corruption." In *Handbook of Administrative Ethics,* ed. Terry Cooper, 305–22. New York: Marcel Dekker.

Diamond, Larry. 1999. "Institutions of Accountability." *Hoover Digest* 3: 87–91.

Dye, Kenneth M., and Rick Stapenhurst. 1998. "Pillars of Integrity: The Importance of Supreme Audit Institutions in Curbing Corruption." Economic Development Institute of the World Bank, Washington, DC.

Klitgaard, Robert. 1988. *Controlling Corruption.* Berkeley and Los Angeles: University of California Press.

Makanda, Judy. 1994. "Financial Accountability and Economic Performance in Sub-Saharan Africa." Internal document, World Bank, Washington, DC.

O'Donnell, Guillermo. 1999. "Horizontal Accountability in New Democracies." In *The Self-Restraining State: Power and Accountability in New Democracies,* ed. Andreas Schedler, Larry Diamond, and Marc F. Plattner, 29–51. Boulder, CO, and London: Lynne Rienner.

OECD (Organisation for Economic Co-operation and Development). 1998. "The Budget Process Affects Economic Results." *Focus: Public Management Gazette* 10: 4.

———. 1999. "Shaping the Government of the Future." *Focus: Public Management Gazette* 14: 4.

Rossiter, Clinton, ed. 1961. *The Federalist Papers.* New York: New American Library.

Schacter, Mark. 1999. "Means . . . Ends . . . Indicators: Performance Measurement in the Public Sector." IOG Policy Brief 3, Institute on Governance, Ottawa.

———. 2000. "Monitoring and Evaluation Capacity Development in Sub-Saharan Africa: Lessons from Experience in Supporting Sound Governance." ECD Working Paper 7, Operations Evaluation Department, World Bank, Washington, DC.

Schedler, Andreas. 1999a. "Conceptualizing Accountability." In *The Self-Restraining State: Power and Accountability in New Democracies,* ed. Andreas Schedler, Larry Diamond, and Marc F. Plattner, 13–28. Boulder, CO, and London: Lynne Rienner.

———. 1999b. "Restraining the State: Conflicts and Agents of Accountability." In *The Self-Restraining State: Power and Accountability in New Democracies,* ed. Andreas Schedler, Larry Diamond, and Marc F. Plattner, 333–50. Boulder, CO, and London: Lynne Rienner.

Schedler, Andreas, Larry Diamond, and Marc F. Plattner, eds. 1999. *The Self-Restraining State: Power and Accountability in New Democracies.* Boulder, CO, and London: Lynne Rienner.

Stevens, Mike. 1990. "Assessing Public Expenditure Management Systems." Internal document, World Bank, Washington, DC.

———. Undated. "Institutions of Horizontal Accountability." Government Services Administration, Washington, DC. http://policyworks.gov/org/main/mg/intergov/letter6/Stevens.htm.

Tendler, Judith. 1997. *Good Government in the Tropics.* Baltimore and London: Johns Hopkins University Press.

Thomas, Paul G. 1998. "The Changing Nature of Accountability." In *Taking Stock. Assessing Public Sector Reforms,* ed. B. Guy Peters and Donald J. Savoie, 348–93. Ottawa: Canadian Centre for Management Development.

USAID (U.S. Agency for International Development). 1998. *Handbook of Democracy and Governance Program Indicators.* Technical Publications Series, Center for Democracy and Governance. Washington, DC: USAID.

World Bank. 1997. "The State in a Changing World." In *World Development Report 1997,.* New York: Oxford University Press.

———. 1998. *Assessing Aid: What Works, What Doesn't, and Why.* New York: Oxford University Press.

Annex 10.A: Performance Indicators Related to Institutions of Accountability

The following list of indicators is offered as a basis for further thought and research. It is not intended to be a definitive list. It provides an idea of the range of indicators, or measurement areas, from which one might choose in seeking to develop a reliable, practical, and reasonably comprehensive list of performance indicators. Final decisions would depend upon a diverse range of issues, including the IA in question, local circumstances, available resources, time constraints, and so on. Further research and analysis—beyond the resources available for this chapter—would be required to develop a more refined list of options.

The kind of data and data gathering required to support these indicators varies widely, as would the cost of establishing and maintaining the indicators. Some of the indicators involve answers to simple yes or no questions. Others involve simple, direct quantitative measures, while still others require the development of scale or index data. Some of the indicators are qualitative.

Data-gathering techniques may include survey questionnaires, open-ended interviews, key informant interviews, expert panel opinions, expert observation, desk research, or file reviews. Most of these indicators are drawn from the work of others.

Indicators Related to Information Made Available to IAs by the Executive Branch

- percentage of citizens who believe they have adequate access to public information
- percentage of journalists who believe government is providing them with adequate access to information
- percentage of nongovernmental organizations (NGOs) that say they can obtain needed information from key public agencies
- percentage of legislators and staff who say they are able to obtain information when they need it
- existence of laws and regulations requiring access to information
- percentage of public agencies providing full information to public about services they are required to deliver
- timely availability to the legislature, media, and public of government budgets
- timely availability to the legislature, media, and public of public expenditure reports

Indicators Related to Civil Society as an IA

- laws supporting freedom of speech and association
- number of NGOs advocating for accountability or against corruption
- number of NGOs that have specialized expertise and capacity in reporting on corruption
- number of NGOs showing improvement in their capacity to advocate for issues related to accountability, transparency, and corruption
- number of public policies changed consistent with NGO advocacy
- perception of NGOs and others of government's willingness to engage in dialogue on accountability, corruption, and other matters of public concern
- percentage of citizens who have civic knowledge
- percentage of citizens exhibiting democratic values
- examples of government decisions taken as a consequence of pressures from civic groups

Indicators Related to the News Media as an IA

- percentage of population that trusts available news sources
- number of legal actions against media organizations for criticizing government
- number of violent incidents targeting journalists
- content analysis of quality of news media reporting on issues related to accountability and corruption

Indicators Related to Audit Agencies as IAs

- existence of a clear auditing mandate enshrined in legislation for the supreme audit institution (SAI)
- role of the SAI included in the national constitution
- protection of the SAI's independence by way of legislation or strong tradition
- direct reporting relationship by the head of the SAI to the legislature without political interference
- SAI power to determine which audits will be done and how they will be done
- SAI freedom to determine how audit findings will be reported
- SAI power of unrestricted access to information it needs to do its audit work
- adequate level of funding for SAI (for example, for office space, staff, communications facilities, investigation and monitoring activities)

- adequate level of administrative capacity in SAI (for example, number and level of staff, equipment and materials, internal management structures and practices)
- percentage of government budget (or of government programs) audited in a financial year
- percentage or number of cases of breaches of laws, regulations, procedures, etc., being investigated fully, fairly, and transparently through to enforcement
- SAI reports easily available to members of the public or the news media

Indicators Related to "Audit-Like" Agencies as IAs

- independent inspector general's office that regularly monitors public contracting and procurement practices
- independent ethics office that monitors and implements a formal public sector code of ethics
- independent anticorruption agency to detect breaches of laws and regulations related to public sector corruption
- audit-like agencies with an adequate level of funding (for example, for office space, staff, communications facilities, investigation and monitoring activities)
- audit-like agencies with an adequate level of administrative capacity (for example, number and level of staff, equipment and materials, internal management structures and practices)
- percentage or number of cases of breaches of laws, regulations, procedures, etc., being investigated fully, fairly, and transparently through to enforcement

Indicators Related to the Judiciary as an IA

- number of criminal cases involving political, economic, and institutional elites
- wide availability of written rules, regulations, and procedures for carrying out functions of the courts
- percentage of appointments to the bench, or promotions, based on merit criteria
- degree of security of tenure within the judicial sector
- degree of independence of the judiciary from the legislature and the executive branch
- extent to which judicial rulings are reliably enforced

- judicial salary as a percentage of what comparable professionals earn in the private sector
- presence of an internal disciplinary office in judicial sector

Indicators Related to the Legislature as an IA

- index of effectiveness of legislative oversight of the executive branch
- index of legislative committee oversight of executive activities
- index of quality of legislative processes
- presence of an active public accounts committee and/or finance committee (or similar body) that focuses on oversight of public financial management
- number of staff per legislator or per committee
- adequate process for legislative review of the budget
- level of confidence among legislators that the legislature has the capacity to perform its function and act as an independent body
- level of confidence among citizens that the legislature acts as a check against the executive branch
- legislature rules permitting equitable participation by opposition parties
- opposition members given resources (office, staff, and so forth) comparable with those of ruling party

General Indicators

- code of conduct on ethical behavior for politicians and public servants that is adequate, well known, and well enforced
- public perceptions of corruption in the delivery or provision of selected government services
- private sector perceptions of public sector corruption
- percentage of citizens who show confidence in government
- percentage of citizens who think government is addressing their priorities

Index